# Economic Liberalization in Developing Countries

*Edited by*
Armeane M. Choksi and
Demetris Papageorgiou

Basil Blackwell

© The International Bank for Reconstruction and Development/The World Bank

First published 1986

Basil Blackwell Ltd
108 Cowley Road, Oxford OX4 1JF, UK

Basil Blackwell Inc.
432 Park Avenue South, Suite 1503,
New York, NY 10016, USA

*British Library Cataloguing in Publication Data*
Economic liberalization in developing countries.
1. Developing countries—Commercial policy
I. Choksi, Armeane M.    II. Papageorgiou, Demetris
382'3'091724        HF1413

ISBN 0–631–15023–4

*Library of Congress Cataloging in Publication Data*
Economic liberalization in developing countries.

Includes index.
1. Developing countries—Economic policy—Congresses.
2. Developing countries—Commercial policy—Congresses.
3. Monetary policy—Developing countries—Congresses.
4. Economic stabilization—Developing countries—Congresses.
5. Chile—Economic policy—Congresses.
I. Choksi, Armeane M., 1944–    II. Papageorgiou, Demetris.
HC59.7.E3116 1986        338.9'009172'4        86–6153
ISBN 0–631–15023–4.

Typeset in 10/11pt Bembo by Photo·graphics
Honiton, Devon.
Printed in Great Britain by The Camelot Press, Southampton

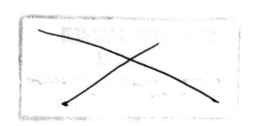

Economic Liberalization in
Developing Countries

# Contents

# Contributors

The chapters for this volume were originally given as papers presented to 'Economic Liberalization: Adjustments During the Transition Period', Washington, DC, 1983.

*Liaquat Ahamed* Country Policy Department, World Bank
*Bela Balassa* Department of Political Economy, Johns Hopkins University, and consultant, World Bank
*Trent Bertrand* Country Policy Department, World Bank
*Armeane M. Choksi* Country Policy Department, World Bank
*Rudiger Dornbusch* Department of Economics, Massachusetts Institute of Technology
*Sebastian Edwards* Department of Economics, University of California at Los Angeles, National Bureau of Economic Research, and consultant, World Bank
*James Hanson* Industry Department, World Bank
*Arnold C. Harberger* Department of Economics, University of Chicago, and consultant, World Bank
*Anne O. Krueger* Vice President, Economics and Research Staff, World Bank
*Katherine Krumm* Country Policy Department, World Bank
*Deepak Lal* Department of Economics, University of London, and consultant, World Bank
*Ronald I. McKinnon* Department of Economics, Stanford University
*Michael Michaely* Department of Economics, Hebrew University, and consultant, World Bank
*Michael Mussa* Graduate School of Business, University of Chicago, and consultant, World Bank
*Demetris Papageorgiou,* Country Policy Department, World Bank
*Simon Rottenberg,* Department of Economics, University of Massachusetts, and consultant, World Bank
*Marcelo Selowsky* Research Adviser, Operational Policy Staff, World Bank
*Frank Veneroso* private consultant
*Sweder van Wijnbergen* Development Research Department, World Bank

# PART I

## Introduction

# 1

# Economic Liberalization: What Have We Learned?

*Armeane M. Choksi and Demetris Papageorgiou*

The oil crises and interest rate shocks, and eventually the debt problems in Latin America and Africa, have put increasing pressure on policy-makers to re-evaluate past approaches to managing economic growth. In particular, the merits of development strategies based on inward-looking trade regimes, extensive and complicated systems of government controls on goods and factor markets, and restrictions of capital movements across international borders are now being reconsidered. Although countries may not yet be ready to embrace the notion of uncontrolled markets, economic liberalism is clearly in resurgence. The recent reforms in China, the attempts towards a decontrol of India's economy, and Indonesia's recent reduction in tariff rates all point in the same direction: namely, the increasing willingness of governments of developing countries to accept the market's verdict on resource allocation and to integrate their economies in the international trading system. This is not to say that all governments are now embarked on the road to complete economic liberalism, but simply to underscore that the "planning and control" mentality and approach to economic development is clearly giving ground to the acceptance of market forces.

To the extent that these policy re-evaluations are translated into action, policy-makers face complex problems regarding the management of the transition. As each country's initial conditions are distinctly different, the desirable transition path to follow will depend on the specific institutions and economic situation of the individual countries. Nevertheless, several general issues concerning intertemporal efficiency may arise:

1 Should countries willing to undertake such policy reforms implement them all in one stage, or should they adopt a gradualist approach? Gradualism in policy reforms may lower the adjustment costs of the transition relative to the one-stage approach, but the benefits would also be delayed, and the net present value of gradualism may not necessarily be higher than that of the one-stage approach. Political considerations, however, may dictate a gradualist route.

2 If gradualism is adopted, should there be uniform or discriminatory treatment of sectors? If uniform, what are the choices among alternative uniform approaches? If non-uniform, what should be the nature of and the reasons for discrimination between activities?
3 What is the proper sequence for implementing trade policy reforms in the presence of administrative controls and quantitative restrictions? Should there be a separate stage consisting of the replacement of quantitative restrictions by tariffs? What are the efficiency and distributive effects of alternative sequences? Are there particular patterns of tariff reductions that have adverse overall welfare effects?
4 In the presence of other controls and regulations, such as on factor markets and nontraded sectors, what are the implications for the way one might approach policy reforms?
5 If both the capital and current account are controlled and regulated, which should be opened first and which second? Is any one ordering superior to another?

While these are some of the key questions of economic efficiency that arise in the process of economic liberalization, policy reforms often follow time-paths that are perceived to be politically sustainable, even though there may be more efficient alternative paths. It has been argued, for example, that, for policy reforms to be sustainable, the costs that they impose on some key social groups cannot be excessive as these groups may prevail on the government to abort the reforms. At the same time, to be politically acceptable, the reforms should show immediate gains for other groups so that a constituency or coalition of winners can be quickly formed in support of such reforms. Therefore, important questions of political economy relevant to liberalization may arise. For example, which are the likely groups to win by the changes in the policy environment? How long is it expected to take for them to realize those gains? Which are the likely losers, what is the size of their losses, and how fast would the losses be realized? What is the role of other policies, such as adjustment assistance, in compensating for these losses?

This volume discusses many of these issues. The chapters should be of interest to both policy-makers and academics. This introductory chapter, in the form of a review, provides a survey of the issues of transition and the views expressed by the authors in this volume.

Krueger (chapter 2) presents a broad review of issues of policy reforms which lead to an open, deregulated economy. She defines liberalization broadly as any policy which reduces the restrictiveness of controls. It may be the complete removal, or the replacement of a more restrictive set of controls with less restrictive ones, such as those of international trade. She starts her discussion with a description of an illiberal economy, its salient features of controls, and the underlying reasons leading to the imposition of such controls.

What, then, are the basic elements of an illiberal economy? How do economies reach a stage of controls and regulations which makes inevitable

a difficult transition to a liberal one? Krueger suggests that there seems to be a logic that is not yet clearly understood that leads to the escalation of controls and regulations. One motivating factor for the introduction of regulation, which has been observed with regularity, is as a response to some real or perceived crisis. This normally induces the private sector to attempt to circumvent it, which in turn motivates the regulators to modify, intensify, or introduce new interventions. Furthermore, experience of countries with extensive controls and regulations indicates that non-economic objectives, as well, play an important role in the emergence of controls and regulations. The economic policies in India, China, Tanzania, Turkey, and some Latin American countries of low food prices for urban residents, extensive welfare programs, trade restrictions on manufactured imports, regulations on interest rates, and investment licensing are examples of interventions designed to meet such non-economic objectives.

Krueger then unravels the strong relation that exists between macro-economic policies on the one hand, such as fiscal, monetary, and domestic credit, and controls and regulations on individual markets on the other. For example, inflation, associated with expansionary fiscal and monetary policies, often leads governments to impose direct controls on prices and markets. A fixed nominal exchange rate, controls on the prices of goods and services produced by public sector enterprises, controls on the prices and investments of the private sector, indexation of wages, and regulations of the nominal interest rates are all examples of the interventions imposed by the state as it attempts to contain the inflationary pressures or offset some of its effects. Few governments, in the face of high rates of inflation, have adopted exchange rate policies that would minimize the adverse effects of inflation on the balance of payments. The political and economic factors that lead to inflation usually lead to balance of payments crises.

Krueger outlines which policy reforms, when undertaken individually, are likely to be welfare-improving even in the presence of other controls and regulations. This is an important issue, as experience suggests that governments do not embark on a wholesale liberalization of their economies. She considers several liberalization reforms in five separate markets — agriculture, finance, labor, the exchange rate, and traded goods — and concludes that there is a large number of partial reforms which could improve welfare.

Krueger then discusses the issue on which little systematic work has been done: the appropriate timing and sequencing of reforms. She mentions that some economists have concluded that in some cases the instantaneous dismantling of all controls may, in fact, be non-optimal. As an example, she refers to the difficulties that may be encountered when capital account transactions are opened as the current account is liberalized. Krueger suggests that a possible optimal dismantling of balance of payments controls might start with the liberalization of the current account transactions followed by the decontrol of agriculture prices and the domestic labor and capital markets, leaving the capital account transactions for last. There are others who have different views. This is an empirical issue; no theory has

been systematically tested against the facts to provide any presumption on the ordering of liberalization, the length of the delay, or whether the capital account should be liberalized gradually or instantaneously with the other markets.

Michaely's chapter, on "The Timing and Sequencing of a Trade Liberalization Policy," addresses one of the specific questions raised by Krueger. This is a topic of particular importance to those who wish to advise on or implement efficient and sustainable trade liberalization policies. As Michaely points out, while comprehensive studies on liberalization cycles have been undertaken, the specific problems of phasing and sequencing trade policy reforms have not been adequately addressed, particularly in the empirical literature.

Michaely argues that the proposition that liberalized free conduct of international transactions is superior to a regime of controls and protection is a "comparative statics" statement, which yields no guidance for the design of policy transition. Starting from a regime of protection, a country may be able to choose many different paths toward free trade. Some of these paths will be superior to others, but one must necessarily be optimal for the country in question. Consequently, the relevant question is, What are the determinants of the timing, phasing, and sequencing of successful and sustainable liberalization paths? He discusses three of them extensively: (a) the speed of implementation policies, in particular the advantages and disadvantages of a one-stage versus a multi-stage implementation; (b) the attributes of the various stages of policy implementation; and (c) the relationship between import liberalization and other policies on the one hand, and the general sequencing of implementing policy reforms on the other.

In particular, the issue of the speed by which trade liberalization policies are implemented should be of great interest to policy-makers. Assuming that the post-liberalization, neutral trade regime is superior to the current distorted one, a shift from one state to another should be made as soon as possible. But, would the costs of the adjustment process, however defined, be larger if policy changes were swift and sudden than if they were more gradual? Furthermore, is the credibility assigned by individual economic agents to the policy change related to its implementation speed? It may be argued that radical measures of liberalization would seem to be more credible than minor ones. Consequently, a single-stage policy may be expected to yield a stronger response in reallocating resources than a multi-stage policy. In a world free of rigidities, Michaely suggests that this reasoning would be justified; a single-stage reform would be superior to a multi-stage one. However, in a world in which rigidities exist, other considerations ought to be brought into play.

The most important of these considerations is the sector-specific nature of capital goods and human capital. Michaely suggests that, immediately following the introduction of trade policy reforms, it is inevitable that some resources, i.e., sector-specific physical and human capital, would be unemployed and would not be absorbed by the expanding sector. These

unemployed resources would be greater the less time has elapsed since the policy change, the speedier the implementation of policies has been, the larger the changes in relative prices implied by the reforms are, and the less convincing these policies have been.

Another consideration is that trade reforms tend to change the distribution of income. Many agents in the country will consider this an undesirable shift. An immediate and large change in trade policies would lead to a relatively large and sudden impact on income distribution, whereas a gradual change would have less of an initial impact. A priori, it cannot be known whether the resulting income distribution will be viewed as superior or inferior to the initial one. Based on these, Michaely concludes that a gradual multi-stage implementation of the liberalization policy may be superior to a once-and-for-all change.

In concluding on the speed of the process of liberalization, Michaely suggests that the process should be faster the fewer rigidities there are in the labor market, and the less sector-specific is the physical and human capital, the more flexible and adaptable are the responses of entrepreneurs, the shorter is the life-span of the physical capital in the contracting activities, and the higher are the elasticities of substitution in production among various activities. Clearly, economic and institutional attributes would differ from case to case and from country to country. Consequently, he suggests that there is no a priori, clear-cut rule-of-thumb on the relationship between the desired speed of implementing a liberalization policy and the level of development of the economy undertaking it.

Michaely then discusses two important questions about the various attributes of the stages of the implementation process. The first concerns shifts in the form of protection, such as from quantitative restrictions (QRs) to tariffs. One approach would be to start the process of trade liberalization by shifting from QRs to protection with tariffs without greatly affecting the price level of protection. An alternative approach would be to dispense with this stage and start lowering protection gradually by relaxing the QRs themselves along with tariffs. The advantages of shifting from QRs to the price mechanism of tariffs would be stability in and knowledge of the protection level for each protected activity, both of which are absent under QRs. This shift would make the levels of protection not only stable but also known, and this would greatly facilitate the preannouncement of future levels of protection. Multi-stage implementation of liberalization would be very difficult, if not impossible, to achieve with a system of QRs.

The second important attribute of the stages of a trade liberalization policy would be the choice between non-uniform and uniform treatment of different activities. A major advantage of a uniform treatment is its simplicity and its association with fairness, which could facilitate the implementation process.[1] A differential treatment of activities suggests a

---

[1] Fairness only in the sense that no activity is singled out in the policy reforms for special treatment, but not in the sense of uniformity of effects.

large measure of discretion. This in turn may entail friction, political difficulties, and uncertainty regarding the future course of a liberalization policy. In addition, a uniform treatment, in some cases, would be more likely to lead to a lower variance of protection along the liberalization path, and this is clearly an advantage. Counteracting these is the argument that each sector or activity would respond differently to changes which must be taken into consideration. If the contraction of an industry is likely to result in a larger unemployment than the contraction of other industries, there may be justification for introducing a more gradual process in the removal of protection from this industry than in the liberalization of the others. But this would require a knowledge about differential reactions in various industries, which in most cases would be impossible to determine.

In adopting a uniform set of rules for tariff reduction, Michaely highlights three alternative approaches. One is an equally proportional, across-the-board reduction of protection of all activities. The second is the reduction of protection rates by equal amounts, and the third alternative is "the concertina method." In the latter approach, all protection rates which at the initial stage are above a certain ceiling are reduced to that particular ceiling, with no changes in other rates; at the next stage all rates are brought down to a lower ceiling; and this process is continued until the trade regime is liberalized. Evaluating on a priori grounds the pros and cons of these alternative methods, Michaely concludes that in most cases employment considerations seem to have been the prime reasons for adopting discriminatory, non-uniform paths of liberalization. He suggests that activities whose contractions are expected to generate a relatively large unemployment of human and physical capital could be potential candidates for a slower process of liberalization than the rest of the economy. He speculates that the activities that have been singled out for favorable treatment would be relatively more intensive in human capital and labor — the more so, the higher the sector-specificity of the human capital they employ.

Michaely then discusses the relationship between trade liberalization and (a) exchange rate and export promotion policies; (b) income maintenance policies; (c) capital market policies; and (d) other restrictive policies. In each case, he underlines the favorable effects on welfare of policy reforms, and points out that the nature of such reforms and the manner by which the other reforms should appear in the sequencing of implementation of the policy.[2]

In chapter 4, the emphasis again is not on the merits of a free trade regime, but rather on the dynamic properties of an optimal path of trade liberalization. Specifically, Mussa presents an analysis of the speed of

---

[2] The issues highlighted in Michaely's chapter are currently under empirical investigation in 19 developing countries in a World Bank research project, "The Timing and Sequencing of a Trade Liberalization Policy" (ref. 673–31), under the direction of D. Papageorgiou, M. Michaely, and A. Choksi.

implementing free trade policies under various assumptions of the economy: its technology, income redistribution, and two specific functional forms relating the rate of unemployment arising from the reduction of protection to the rate by which resources are absorbed outside the previously protected sectors. His analysis is carried out with a two-sector, two-factor model — one for the protected (import-competing) sector and the other for the taxed (export) sector, and labor and capital. The model assumes that the technology imbedded in the economy allows labor to move frictionlessly between sectors but not the capital stock, which can only do so by using up labor services to transform itself from old to new capital for the expanding sector. The model also allows for new capital out of current output. Mussa investigates conditions under which a gradual transition in commercial policies can be analytically justified. He considers two broad regimes, one in which no divergences exist between social and private values either because of public policies or market imperfections, and one in which five such distortions are incorporated in the analysis.

Under the regime of no distortions, the analysis gives a clear answer as to the optimal speed of trade liberalization. Instantaneous implementation of free trade is analytically superior to any other alternative because, under the assumptions made, the economic agents will adjust to the desired long-run conditions at a minimum social cost. A slowing down of the implementation of free trade will delay the signals for private incentives to relocate resources outside the previously protected sector, and therefore will delay output expansion.

When distortions are assumed this conclusion does not necessarily hold. Mussa considers five possible causes of a wedge between social and private valuations: tax systems, capital market imperfection, systematic errors in expectations on the part of private agents, monopolies and monopsonies, and price rigidities. In their presence, no *general* case in favor of gradualism in the implementation of trade policy emerges. For example, if distortions cause private agents to adjust too quickly to the long-run conditions, such as systematic errors in expectations, gradualism in implementing trade reforms may be appropriate. Gradualism slows down the adjustment process itself and therefore reduces the loss of output. Other distortions, however, have the opposite effect: they slow down the transition to the free trade situation. For example, this could be the case with income taxes, which may dampen the privately perceived benefits to reallocate resources away from the protected sector. In such instances, Mussa's analysis suggests that, to keep the adjustment process on an optimal path, the initial step of trade liberalization should go beyond the removal of protection and should actually impose *net subsidies* on the previously disprotected sector.

In considering the relation between trade liberalization and income distribution, Mussa recognizes that a case for gradualism can be analytically defended. The issue is the trade-off between limiting the loss of income and wealth of the factors affected and the forgone social output arising from inefficient policies of protection. The nature of the trade-off depends, among others, on the degree to which factors of production are specific

to their industries. Depending on the degree of specificity, immediate implementation of free trade will lead to a corresponding unemployment of resources, while a gradual implementation of free trade, just gradual enough to prevent *new capital*, both human and non-human, from being invested in the previously protected industries, will tend to minimize the levels of unemployment of resources.

Finally, Mussa analyzes the interaction between the rate of unemployed resources and the dynamic properties of trade liberalization. He postulates a reduced-form relationship of the rate of unemployment in the protected sector to the rate of employment in the other sector. Therefore, in his analysis the dominant economic consideration is the balance between the marginal social cost of unemployed resources in the previously protected sector to the marginal social benefits gained by having them employed elsewhere. The optimal path of commercial policy that would satisfy this marginal condition depends crucially on the particular form this relationship takes. Two specific relationships are considered, both of which suggest that a gradual phasing out of policies of protection is a preferred path.

In chapter 5, Rottenberg takes up the issue of adjustment compensation to factors of production which realize absolute or relative losses following the implementation of public policies. Such compensations have been recommended and defended on grounds of both efficiency and equity. The efficiency argument rests on the assumption that socially "efficient" policy changes can be guaranteed to improve the community's welfare only if losers are compensated for the monetary losses the policy change imposes on them. One specific argument on efficiency that has been advanced suggests that such compensation will permit resources to move to their most highly valued uses by securing the consent to a policy change that would otherwise be resisted by the losers. The equity argument supposes that losses produced by policy change ought to be reimbursed because changes in policy imply a breach of contract. In addition to the issues of fairness which it raises, this argument also involves dimensions of political economy. Rottenberg examines the effects of compensation on efficiency and equity on the basis of economic analysis, and then squares its prediction against the evidence of several cases in which adjustment compensation policies have been adopted. Specifically, he addresses adjustment compensation policies that have been designed to mitigate losses suffered because of policy change.

Rottenberg's conclusions suggest that, however reasonable and attractive any compensation policy appears on the surface, its defense may be derived from questionable premises. For example, compensation may secure only rhetorical consent to policy change; it cannot, and often has not, assured real consent. If compensation payments are provided from governmental revenues, some forms of revenue-raising *may* distort prices that in themselves generate inefficiencies. Moreover, such payments may be sub-optimal in the sense that they divert Treasury's funds to uses which are perhaps socially less valuable than other uses, as for example road construction, education, health, etc. In addition, compensation policies imply a *moral*

*hazard*; economic agents are given incentives to alter behavior in ways that will produce compensatory payments for them. On equity grounds, it does not seem warranted to distinguish between losses from policy change and losses from other causes, natural or man-made. But more important, it is reasonable to assume that market transactions discount the possibility of adverse changes in policy, in which case compensation payments are not warranted. After examining a number of cases of compensation policy, Rottenberg concludes that such policies more often than not serve neither the purpose of efficiency nor the goal of equity.

Harberger's chapter 6 analyzes the relationship between large capital inflows and macroeconomic policies in developing countries and its consequence on economic growth. In recent years, substantial swings in international capital flows have been observed in several middle-income developing countries concurrently with the implementation of stabilization policies, trade liberalization policies, policies designed to open the international capital accounts, and policies aimed at deregulating the domestic financial markets. Harberger attempts to explain the experience of three Latin American countries — Argentina, Chile, and Uruguay — with large capital inflows at the time they were stabilizing and liberalizing their economies. He first addresses a welfare question: Are there any "externalities" in developing countries' foreign borrowing, and, if so, what are the characteristics of such externalities, and the nature and objective of corrective public policy? The second question he examines is the macroeconomic implications of substantial or "excessive" foreign debt on the domestic price level, GDP growth, employment, savings, wages, etc.

The externality identified is the "country risk," that is, the risk which foreign lenders attach to the country's overall economic performance as reflected usually in the balance of payments situation. This risk is unrelated to the specific attributes of the project financed by the foreign funds. Harberger concludes that it is the "country risk" that gives rise to the divergence between the marginal and average social cost of foreign borrowing, which, in turn, explains the presence of a rising supply curve of foreign funds to developing countries. He therefore argues that, similar to the treatment of other externalities, a tax should be assessed on foreign transactions to force economic agents to internalize the "external" cost of foreign borrowing. He discusses some of the available options and concludes that a tax on foreign borrowing equal to the difference between the interest rate which countries are charged on their international borrowing and the London Interbank Offer Rate (LIBOR) is best suited for the job. Furthermore, such a tax has the advantage of varying according to the country's economic strength or weakness as perceived by the international capital market, which is normally indicated by the country's premium over LIBOR, and it is independent of the course of inflation in the borrowing country.

Postulating his preference for smooth economic growth for most of the economic aggregates, Harberger then analyzes the effects of large switches in capital inflows and outflows on the "smoothness" of such growth.

Following his simulation model, he traces the ripple effects of capital movements to economic growth and concludes that stretching the inflow of capital over time has considerable merit. He therefore suggests that a reasonable policy to implement would be, on the margin, to tax short-term capital inflows more heavily than long-term ones while maintaining the overall consistency of this tax with the objectives established from the analysis of externalities.

Edwards, in chapter 7, highlights four major issues of economic liberalization: (a) the issue of the welfare effects of partial liberalization attempts; (b) the issue of the determinants of the appropriate speed of liberalization; (c) the issue of the relationship between liberalization and stabilization policies; and (d) the issue of the order by which markets should be liberalized. He concludes that, in the absence of externalities or other policy distortions, markets should be liberalized instantaneously. If externalities are present, however, gradual liberalization may be called for. He also finds that the relation between stabilization and liberalization policies is crucial in determining the success or failure of trade reforms. He finds, however, less agreement from theory and evidence as to the appropriate order for the liberalization of current and capital accounts of the balance of payments. This topic has recently attracted considerable attention from academics and policy-makers.

Edwards develops a trade model of three goods and two factors to analyze formally the effects of current and capital accounts liberalization on production and income distribution. He analyzes the differential effects of alternative orderings of liberalizing these two accounts. To the extent that real costs are realized by resources moving in and out of uses, there is an argument for synchronizing the effects of opening both accounts to avoid resources moving first in and then out (or vice versa) of particular sectors. If, as is suggested by many, the capital account adjusts faster than the current account, then synchronizing the economic effects of opening both would require opening the current account first. Edwards's own analysis, however, does not yield strong results regarding the appropriate order for liberalizing the current and capital accounts of the balance of payments. But on empirical evidence, and on a variety of a priori analytical considerations, he suggests that a prudent strategy would be to liberalize the current account first. He finds that the strongest empirical case for this ordering is the relation between capital inflows and the real exchange rate. He cites the examples of Korea in 1964, Argentina in 1978, and Chile in 1980, from which he infers that the capital account should have been opened more slowly than the trade account so that the maturity of the increased stock of foreign debt that followed the liberalization would have spread through time, thus reducing the degree of real appreciation of the exchange rate.

Several of the issues discussed in these chapters are then examined in the context of Chile's recent history of economic liberalization. In particular, Chile's trade liberalization has generated much debate. Some have argued that economic liberalism has failed in practice, while others have maintained

that the study of the Chilean experience in the 1970s highlights the problems associated with the transition process rather than with economic liberalization per se.

The discussion centers on some key facts concerning the Chilean economy in the past decade. It emphasizes the fluctuations of economic aggregates such as unemployment, money supply, exchange rates, and real rates of interests. It provides a useful background to understanding and interpreting the roots of Chile's serious economic crisis in 1982–3. Chapters 8–10 present the Chilean stabilization process of the 1970s and some of its most important policies, such as monetary policies, foreign exchange policies, labor laws, credit, and banking policies, and the divestiture of public enterprises. They also examine, in some detail, Chile's economic performance since 1974. Furthermore, they provide discussion on the relation between the liberalization of the domestic financial markets and the capital account, and the Chilean economy's extremely high interest rates and low domestic saving ratios of that period. They point to the sources of growth between 1975 and 1980, and to sources of the recession in 1982–3, including the January 1983 agreement with the IMF; and they highlight the detrimental role that inconsistent policies have played in Chile.

# PART II

---

# General Issues in Economic Liberalization

# 2

# Problems of Liberalization

*Anne O. Krueger*

The experience of the past three decades has convinced almost all analysts that systems of direct controls and attempts to "thwart the market" are inefficient, if not ineffective, instruments for achieving virtually any objective.[1] The enormous success of Europe and Japan in expanding output and raising living standards was clearly related to the sustained liberalization of trade and capital flows. For the developing countries, progress has differed markedly between countries, and a major explanatory factor has been significant differences in economic policies. The highly successful developing countries have generally had liberalized trade and payments regimes, which in turn have been feasible only with relatively liberal domestic economic policies.

Despite the clear evidence on the subject, a large number of developing countries remain caught in a stifling web of controls over economic activity. In many cases there is general agreement that the controls no longer serve, even if they once did, the purposes for which they were imposed. Many countries have had periods in which efforts were made to alter the regime and reduce or eliminate reliance on direct controls on one or more aspects of economic activity. Those efforts have sometimes met with failure, and have made others reluctant to attempt the removal of controls. The question to which this chapter is addressed is why that should be so: What are the problems of liberalization? Why, given the evidence that the benefits of liberalization are so great, is it so difficult to accomplish? Why are politicians (and often the entire community of informed citizens) so reluctant, if not downright unwilling, to liberalize their economies? A simple answer might, of course, be that politicians are misinformed and, for one reason or another, are oblivious to the benefits attainable by liberalization. While there are undoubtedly instances where that is so (or where vested political interests have enough stake in the existing system to ensure that its maintenance is rational from the viewpoint of those in power), such

[1] Reprinted with permission. From *World Economic Growth*, ©1984, Institute for Contemporary Studies (ICS Press), San Franciso.

circumstances are disregarded here. instead, the focus is upon the difficulties that arise in the process of attempting to liberalize the system, and upon reasons — both political and economic — why a prime minister, even if convinced of the long-term benefits of liberalization, might be reluctant to attempt it, or, if attempting it, might fail to achieve his objectives.

At the outset, it is necessary to define what is meant by "liberalization." A narrow definition would be that a market is liberalized if there are no quantitative restrictions attempting to control either buyers or sellers, from which it would follow that liberalization is the act of removing quantitative controls. The difficulty with this definition is that there are a number of economic policies which can have the effect of reducing the restrictiveness of given quantitative controls, such as releasing more foreign exchange to permit imports under a licensing regime. Since a more "restrictive" set of controls is presumably one in which market participants would pay more to carry out the transactions that are not permitted, more liberalization, to be consistent, must imply a greater reduction in the scarcity value attached to restrictions. Hence, liberalization is, for purposes of this chapter, defined as any policy action which reduces the restrictiveness of controls – either their complete removal, or the replacement of a more restrictive set of controls with a less restrictive one. Under this definition, it should be noted, an action such as devaluation, given an import-licensing regime, liberalizes that regime.

A second initial question has to do with the range of markets to be subjected to analysis. There are direct controls in almost every country — rent controls in New York City, the underpricing of electrical and telephone services in many developing countries, and the pricing of urban transport almost universally, to name just a few. While their removal can result in difficulties of the sort discussed here, it proves convenient to focus on a narrower set of markets, but a set that is nevertheless interrelated and frequently subject to controls in developing countries. That set of markets includes the foreign exchange market (both for current and capital account transactions), the financial market, the labor market, and the market for agricultural commodities. In important ways, controls on those four markets have interrelated in ways that have had important macroeconomic effects, and have been a focal point of many liberalization efforts.[2]

As a starting point for analysis, it proves convenient to sketch the conditions that prevail, or have prevailed, in many developing countries in which direct controls have been used. Thereafter, attention focuses in turn on the macroeconomic and microeconomic issues of liberalization that have arisen about which our understanding seems satisfactory. This then sets the stage for a consideration of issues of timing and ssquencing of

---

[2] In the 1970s, the energy market was subject to controls very similar to those relating to agriculture in many countries. Most of the analysis of agriculture that follows applies also to energy, but it is not discussed separately, largely in order to focus the discussion.

liberalization efforts, about which most unresolved questions seem to revolve. A final section then summarizes the analysis and provides some conjectures as to factors increasing the likelihood of successful liberalization attempts.

## I  THE PROTOTYPE ILLIBERAL ECONOMY

In ways that are not well understood, there seems to be a logic to the evolution of direct controls on prices and quantities over time. Once intervention has occurred, e.g. in the foreign exchange market, the responses by private agents to the initial intervention often elicit modifications, and usually intensifications, of the control system. To illustrate, an initial move toward import licensing generally reduces incentives to export, evokes cries of "unfair" from many who attempt to persuade the authorities that the system should be altered to take into account their particular circumstances, and provides incentives to evade the regime via smuggling, under- or over-invoicing, or engaging in black market transactions. All of these responses tend to induce the authorities to restrict imports further, to modify and usually complicate the allocation rules for those imports, and also to increase surveillance. Those actions in turn are likely to evoke a further response from agents responding to the altered incentives. As the profitability of evading or avoiding regulations increases, the discrepancy between private and social profitability widens with mounting consequences over time.

Because of these "dynamic" tendencies, the typical economy in which liberalization is contemplated and would yield high returns is not one in which a single market is regulated: rather, it is usually an economy in which a variety of markets are subject to controls of varying degrees of severity and enforcement. Often, those controls are accompanied by macroeconomic difficulties that may or may not stem from the same underlying factors.

Because multiple markets are subject to intervention, the very concept of "liberalization" can mean different things in different contexts; and an attempt to sort out liberalization problems conceptually must start with an identification of the types of controls initially in effect and a recognition of the interaction between them. As a starting point for analysis, it is useful to consider the interaction between macroeconomic imbalances and intervention in individual markets.

### Inflation and Controls

Economists have long recognized that a perfectly anticipated inflation might have relatively low economic costs, largely because markets would adjust to inflationary expectations so that the real interest rate and other relative prices would not differ significantly from those that would obtain in the absence of inflation. In reality, however, price increases, and altered

inflation rates, usually result from an effort on the part of the government to obtain control over resources without offsetting tax increases. Sometimes this effort to obtain resources is part of planned increases in public investment programs, although sometimes it is the immediate counterpart to direct controls (as, for example, when food prices to consumers are maintained at below-market levels through rationing while farmers are paid at higher prices).

Either way, once inflation starts, the usual response of governments is to attempt direct controls to offset some of its apparent effects. Maintaining a fixed nominal exchange rate, with reluctant adjustments that lag significantly behind inflation, is one of the most frequent responses. In many cases, governments have kept the prices of public sector services, including utilities, transport, and outputs of public enterprises, constant in an effort to "control inflation." In the presence of an underlying inflationary process, of course, the budget deficit induced by financial losses of those activities tends to intensify inflationary pressures further, while simultaneously increasing the degree of distortion in the economy arising from regulated prices. In some instances, governments have attempted to impose price controls over private sector economic activity. There have also been efforts to index wages and, even more frequently to regulate nominal interest rates.

These markets — especially foreign exchange, credit, and labor — play key roles in the allocation of resources throughout the economy. When they are controlled costs can be very high, and their liberalization is essential for markedly improved economic performance. Usually, however, liberalization measures are combined with policies aimed at least in part at reducing the rate of inflation, rather than at freeing the individual markets while permitting inflationary pressures to continue. Thus, it proves impossible to analyze direct controls and efforts to eliminate them without taking into account the macroeconomic setting in which those efforts are undertaken. While some countries have experienced inflation without direct controls, and a few countries (most notably India) have resorted to direct controls in the absence of inflation, the majority of direct controls either have been imposed in an effort to reduce inflation rates or have intensified in their restrictiveness because of domestic inflation (as with a fixed nominal exchange rate).

Hence, there are strong and important interactions between the macroeconomic processes — the government budget and the determination of the money supply and domestic credit — and control conditions in individual markets. Moreover, when the nominal rate of interest and/or the exchange rate is fixed, reduction in the rate of inflation automatically permits some degree of liberalization, in the sense that the relevant price deviates less from the level that would obtain with prices that appropriately reflect opportunity cost than it would at a higher inflation rate.

### Balance of Payments Difficulties

In principle, a country experiencing internal inflation could live within its budget constraint either by permitting its exchange rate to flat (although

there are interesting questions as to why domestic residents should continue to hold domestic money) or by strictly rationing available foreign exchange by one system or another. The latter technique would of course entail the distortion costs associated with disparities between the domestic marginal rate of transformation in production and the marginal rate of transformation through trade. However, either system would permit the continuation of domestic inflationary policies without necessarily triggering balance of payments difficulties.

In practice, however, few governments that have experienced inflation have fully adopted either policy. Indeed, the same political and economic factors that lead to domestic inflation usually lead to balance of payments deficits. Even when exchange controls and import licensing systems are in place, the nominal exchange rate is adjusted too little and too late, and excess demand for goods is satisfied partially by imports financed by running down reserves or borrowing from abroad.

Often, the build-up of debt permits the continuation of trade and payments imbalances, and hence of expansionary macroeconomic policies, for a period of time. However, as debt and debt service obligations increase while foreign exchange earnings stagnate or decline, lenders are increasingly reluctant to extend additional credit. Debt servicing difficulties, or the inability to borrow sufficiently to finance existing import orders, are frequently the condition that triggers policy changes.

Serious debt servicing obligations in themselves confound any process of adjustment. In part this is because they must be met; in part it is because the level of expenditure must be cut by at least the amount to which borrowing was previously excessive. However, difficulties are intensified largely because foreign debt has political connotations that make the perceived "foreign intervention" troublesome, and the "debt crisis" atmosphere is probably not conducive to systematic preparation of a liberalization plan and its political acceptance.

While a few genuine liberalizations have taken place where existing foreign debt or an inability to sustain previous borrowing levels was neither a trigger nor a serious problem (e.g. Korea in the early 1960s), these have been the exception rather than the rule. And, as international financial markets have become increasingly integrated in recent years, debt servicing difficulties have, if anything, assumed increasing importance as both an impetus to policy reform and an additional problem to be resolved if those reforms are to be successful.

This complication is especially important in countries where there has earlier been substantial reliance on quantitative restrictions to restrain import levels; for in those cases a necessary condition for liberalization is that the domestic price of importables must be permitted to fall relative to the domestic price of exportables. When imports have been so restrained, both imports and exports are below the levels and shares of GNP that would prevail in the absence of the distortion. What is required, therefore, is an expansion of both imports and exports. The least inflationary means of achieving this would be to combine an increase in the nominal exchange rate with simultaneous import liberalization. This would bring down the

domestic price of importables while raising that of exportables, which in turn would minimize the inflationary consequences of liberalization. However, when import levels have been sustained by borrowing, and further credit is not possible, it becomes necessary to curtail imports. Such further curtailment is consistent with liberalization only if either the level of economic activity declines to shift import demand downward, or the nominal exchange rate is adjusted upward by a substantially larger amount than would be the case with an increased import flow.

The former choice — domestic recession — is politically painful and economically wasteful. (Economic activity would have to shift downward by the amount by which imports must decline *times* the inverse of the marginal propensity to import.) Especially if there are lags prior to an export response to increased incentives, the size of the required shift may be significantly greater than would be consistent with liberalization in the long run. The latter alternative — a larger devaluation — could in principle permit the removal of import-licensing mechanisms and the simultaneous adjustment of the demand and supply of foreign exchange. However, the larger size of the required devaluation would in itself give rise to a larger once-and-for-all jump in the price level, which in turn would contribute to the momentum of inflation and would reduce the likelihood that the desired degree of real devaluation could be achieved.

While the observant skeptic may wonder whether a floating exchange rate might attain the desired result, it must be noted that the solution would be consistent with liberalization only if the financial markets were also simultaneously liberalized and the rate of interest permitted to be market-determined. For, with controlled (and usually negative real) interest rates, full liberalization of the exchange rate regime for both current and capital account and a floating exchange rate would surely result in capital outflows, and in a rapid depreciation of the currency (in excess of the rate of inflation).

And, while full liberalization is clearly desirable, few governments (and perhaps even few of their economist advisers) are willing to take the complete plunge of full liberalization of financial and exchange markets simultaneously. Indeed, there is not sufficient experience with the "cold shower" approach to liberalization to provide confidence that its short-term costs can be contained within reasonable bounds. Indeed, if there were legitimate doubts in the early 1970s about the feasibility and desirability of complete instantaneous liberalization, the experience of Argentina, Chile, and Uruguay have further provided support for the skeptics. Whether those experiences should be so interpreted is a topic deferred until later in this chapter. At this juncture the important point is that, in the context of an initial debt servicing crisis, attention is usually focused on the foreign exchange market, and the unpleasant choice in the absence of additional lending from abroad lies between greater inflationary pressures to restore equilibrium, or domestic unemployment and deflation. Obviously, this highlights one of the important contributions that international lending can make to a country when its leaders are genuinely committed to a full liberalization: it can permit higher levels of imports than would otherwise

be feasible to bring about a quick adjustment of relative prices. Not only does this reduce the economic and political strains associated with liberalization; it also reduces uncertainty of businesses as to the likelihood that liberalization will persist.

## Microeconomic Aspects of Liberalization

As already seen, the same reluctance to maintain government expenditures in line with receipts, which generates inflationary pressures, also often results in government controls that, superficially at least, are intended to reduce the observed inflationary consequences. In many instances those controls themselves introduce further macroeconomic distortions into the economy (as, for example, when price controls on the output of public enterprises further fuel the government deficit), but they also distort important markets in the economy.

Inflationary pressures are not the only reason why there are important sectoral distortions, however. Important markets are controlled for other motives: unwillingness to pass on increased energy prices; desires to "keep food prices down"; maintenance of below-market-clearing rates of interest to "encourage capital formation in key sectors" or for other reasons; investment licensing to "guide new investments into socially desirable channels"; and raising the real wage in the controlled part of the economy above its level elsewhere to "protect the worker."

These controls not only have significant economic costs in themselves, but they also interact with other distortions. High labor costs combine with import restrictions to encourage the development of very capital-intensive import-competing activities. Exchange rate overvaluation discourages the production of agricultural exports, and domestic controls on food prices further depress agricultural incomes, which in turn further stimulate outmigration to the cities. Moreover, some controls (such as domestic marketing boards for agricultural commodities) delink domestic prices from international ones, thereby insulating the market in question from any automatic impact in the event of an exchange rate change or other policy shift.

There are interesting and important questions about the payoff from various types of liberalization in the presence of controlled markets elsewhere in the economy to which economists do not as yet have satisfactory answers. What is clear is that the same liberalization measures may have very different impacts depending on the circumstances in other markets in the economy in question, and that an analysis, one market at a time, of the effects of liberalization may yield misleading results.

## II  DIFFICULTIES OF LIBERALIZATION

As the preceding discussion showed, a major difficulty of liberalization is that it is usually undertaken from an exceedingly difficult situation, and often in a crisis atmosphere. Moreover, the fact that the prevailing dis-

tortions have induced uneconomic activities or techniques of production implies that a successful liberalization must be one which penalizes some of those who had earlier responded appropriately to the then-existing incentive structure.

These difficulties are in and of themselves serious enough. In practice, they are often confounded by the simultaneous effort to restore some degree of macroeconomic equilibrium and so liberalize, to a greater or lesser degree, some key markets. Thus, efforts to bring the government budget under control and to reduce the rate of inflation are often inter-twined with policies designed to liberalize imports, to restore producers' incentives in agriculture and energy, and to eliminate price controls and licensing mechanisms.

In most developed countries, inflationary pressures have usually been permitted to be passed through into price increases, and hence few direct controls have accompanied the inflationary process. As a consequence, anti-inflationary policies have generally been undertaken under circumstances in which distortions in key markets are generally substantially smaller than those in some developing countries. Nonetheless, efforts to reduce inflationary pressures have been at best partially successful and have required fairly determined political resolve for considerable intervals of time.

In developing countries in which inflation has been a substantial problem and direct controls have been an initial policy response, anti-inflationary programs are even more complex and fraught with difficulty than in developed countries because of the existence of so many controlled markets. A major difficulty with many liberalization efforts, and especially those focused upon the trade sector of the economy, has been that the liber-alization program has been based on the premise that an anti-inflationary program, simultaneously embarked upon, would succeed.[3]

It seems clear that, in practice, more efforts to liberalize the trade sectors of developing countries have foundered upon the failure of the accompanying anti-inflationary program than on any other single factor. Space limitations preclude a full analysis of the difficulties of combining an anti-inflation program with efforts to liberalize other key markets. Only two fairly obvious points need to be made. First, there are ways in which the dependence of trade liberalization on curbing inflation can be at least reduced. Most notably, a crawling peg, rather than a higher fixed nominal exchange rate, can assure some degree of independence of the two reform efforts. Second, anti-inflationary programs which have built into them safeguards to assure that governments will not resort to direct controls to contain price increases are likely to be, on net, more liberalizing than ones which aim at the lowest recorded rate of price increase over the short term.

---

[3] See Cline and Weintraub (1981), for a series of analyses of these issues in individual countries. See also the paper by Krueger in that volume for further analysis of the interrelationship between inflation and liberalization.

For example, removal of controls on prices of essential government services will in the long run more effectively reduce the inflation rate than will the setting of an initially realistic nominal price, which will again quickly erode unless inflation is contained. Paradoxically, anti-inflationary programs whose policy instruments will succeed only if the inflation rate declines are less likely to bring down the rate of inflation than are programs which will liberalize markets regardless of whether or not the anti-inflationary policies succeed.

With those comments as background, the difficult questions surrounding inflation control, and for that matter whether there can be sustained liberalization against the background of rising inflation rates, are set aside, and the focus is on the liberalization of markets. In this section, two general questions are addressed: (a) What reforms, undertaken individually, are likely to be welfare-improving even in the presence of other controlled markets? (b) Which are the more important markets to liberalize, starting from a situation with multiple controls and distortions? Each of the important markets is then considered, and the most frequently encountered problems of liberalization in each market are discussed in turn. The difficult questions surrounding the timing and sequencing of reforms are deferred to section III.

## Welfare-improving Liberalizations of Individual Markets

The generalized theory of the second-best tells us that, whenever there are non-negligible links between markets, it is in general impossible to ascertain the direction in which welfare will change with a small reduction in the magnitude of a distortion in a single market. Yet, in most countries in which liberalization efforts are contemplated, total liberalization is generally infeasible, and reforms, if undertaken at all, will be undertaken in some markets before they are undertaken in others.

The question arises, therefore, as to when a particular market can be freed in reasonable confidence that the net effect will be welfare-improving. Here, I ignore considerations such as the degree of rent-seeking and the greater incentive effects of competition that may result from liberalization, which tend to the presumption that freeing up any market may yield welfare benefits. Moreover, the analysis must of necessity be empirical rather than theoretical. As such, it must be recognized that situations could arise which deviate from the usual case sufficiently for the presumptions set forth here to be invalid.

Each of the major markets subject to controls will now be considered in turn. Consider first agriculture. The available evidence seems to suggest that producers in agriculture base their production decisions on relative prices within that sector. As such, anything which frees up agricultural prices and brings them more closely into line with relative prices available on the international market is likely to be welfare-improving. For countries that are in any event exporters of food crops, anything which moves relative prices of agricultural commodities closer to their international levels

is probably, on net, potentially welfare-improving. (I ignore here the import short-run welfare losses of low-income persons paying higher prices for food on the grounds that superior measures can be found to yield the same real income transfer.) Thus, freeing producer prices in agriculture to permit them to rise will improve welfare even if the exchange rate is overvalued: the relative prices of alternative agricultural crops will reflect their opportunity cost in the international market vis-à-vis each other, while the price of agricultural commodities relative to other goods and services will move in the appropriate direction.

A more difficult question arises in countries in which comparative advantage lies in export crops. Under efficient resource allocation, these countries would import food. In that circumstance, decontrolling domestic producer prices under import licensing may raise food prices relative to export crops. In the presence of an overvalued nominal exchange rate, resources may be further pulled from export crops to food, with possible negative welfare implications. Hence, there is probably some question as to whether liberalization of domestic prices of agricultural commodities is necessarily welfare-improving unless it is accompanied by moves toward a more realistic exchange rate.

Likewise, it would appear that welfare could always be improved by liberalizing the financial market and permitting the real interest rate to become positive. Since exchange rate overvaluation and artificially low nominal interest rates tend to work in the same direction, and to encourage the introduction of overly capital-intensive activities relative to efficient resource allocation, there is a presumption that moving either the exchange rate or the interest rate in an appropriate direction is likely to improve welfare.

Similar considerations would appear to apply to the labor market: even in the presence of exchange rate overvaluation, the move to a freer market should be welfare-improving. Indeed, to the extent that there is exchange rate overvaluation, reduction in the real wage will increase the profitability of activities in which a labor-abundant country has a comparative advantage.

Finally, there is the exchange rate and the market for traded goods. A first question is whether the move from a licensing system to a uniform tariff, holding the total level of imports constant, is welfare-improving. In theory, anything could happen: resources previously allocated to exportables could be pulled into import-competing activities previously subject to less-than-average protection, possibly resulting in a further loss in welfare. In practice, it seems likely that, provided exporters are permitted to purchase their intermediate goods and raw materials at international prices,[4] a uniform rate of tariff is likely to be potentially welfare-superior

---

[4] This qualification is made because most licensing systems implicitly or otherwise permit imports of intermediate goods and raw materials at lower-than-average rates of duty. To increase duties on these goods without permitting exporters to purchase at international prices would lower effective protection rates, presumably already negative, to them.

to import licensing and associated dispersion of implicit tariff rates.

There is also a question of the welfare effect of raising the nominal exchange rate in the presence of other controls in the system. Although one can imagine a number of circumstances (such as domestic price controls) which might result in a smaller impact of the exchange rate change than would take place with no other distortions in the system, it is difficult to imagine a situation in which increasing the nominal exchange rate was not welfare-improving. On one hand, the move necessarily reduces the bias of the trade regime toward import substitution. This follows because, with import licensing, the domestic price of exportables will increase. With the quantity of imports unaltered or increasing, the relative price of exportables must increase. As already seen, this will move agricultural relative prices in the appropriate direction, and simultaneously will partially offset any distortion in factor markets arising from lower-than-average duties on imported capital equipment.

A third question with respect to the exchange rate is whether it is welfare-improving to liberalize capital flows in the presence of a highly restrictive set of controls on domestic financial flows. While there are some types of partial liberalization that may be welfare-improving in the presence of distorted domestic capital markets (e.g., easing the restrictions on the inflow of private capital), it seems reasonably clear that total liberalization of capital flows is infeasible in the presence of a controlled domestic interest rate: capital outflow would immediately result. An additional aspect of this question pertains to the liberalization of capital flows in the presence of a highly restrictive regime with respect to current account transactions. This is a difficult and important question, and one on which analysis to date has not shed very much light. There is no strong presumption: one could legitimately argue that, since exchanges of assets are exchanges of the capitalized values of income streams, income streams generated by distorted prices are probably the inappropriate ones at which to trade. It would then follow that capital account liberalization should not be undertaken unless both current account and domestic financial transactions are already liberalized. Whether further analysis can shed additional light on this important question remains to be seen.

It would appear, therefore, that, with the possible exception of a liberalization of agricultural prices in the context of overvaluation of a country with comparative advantage in tree crops, and a move to liberalize capital account transactions in the presence of domestic financial controls or current account controls, there is a presumption that liberalization of any of the other markets typically subject to controls is likely to be welfare-improving.

## Which Are the Most Important Markets to Liberalize?

Whereas there are some theoretical presumptions that permit inferences about the direction of welfare change resulting from the liberalization of individual markets, it is much more difficult to provide a solid a priori basis for inferring the order of magnitude of costs associated with controls in

different markets. Circumstances vary both with the nature of the controls in place and with the structure of the domestic economy. It might be, for example, that two countries had controls in both labor and capital markets, but that country A had relatively small intervention in the labor market but high negative real rates of interest, while country B's labor legislation significantly raised the real cost of labor but its nominal interest rate was only slightly below that which would prevail in the absence of regulation. In some countries controls may be relatively light in some markets and much more stringent in others, so that the welfare ranking would differ for that reason. Differences in economic structure may also matter. For example, it is probably a reasonable conjecture that controls on producer prices in agriculture are more detrimental to welfare in some poor African countries than are overvalued nominal exchange rates (although the combination of the two is certainly more harmful than either one alone would be). The same set of distortions in Korea would very likely be ranked in the opposite order in terms of their welfare effects: given the level of development of the economy and the diminished relative importance of the agricultural sector, exchange rate overvaluation might clearly be more costly.

All that can be done, therefore, is to venture some tentative hypotheses about circumstances under which different controls might be more or less detrimental. Starting with the foreign trade market, it is likely that controls are more costly the smaller the size of the domestic market, and the higher the per capita income of the country (because a larger fraction of economic activity is affected by the relative price of tradables with economic growth). Certainly, for the countries now considered middle-income, it would appear that controls over foreign trade and overvalued exchange rates have been a major, if not the biggest single, source of distortion.

By much the same reasoning, controls over producer prices in agriculture have probably been more costly the lower the country's per capita income (because of the higher share of GNP originating in agriculture), the more the country's comparative advantage within agriculture lies in export crops, and the greater its overall comparative advantage in agriculture.

This leaves the labor and financial markets. Here, there is less evidence on which to base a judgment. There can be little doubt that subsidization of capital goods (either explicit or implicit) can become increasingly costly over time, as the Korean and Israeli experiences have amply demonstrated. It is a reasonable conjecture that the distortion is probably the major source of difficulty in both of those economies. The interesting questions, however, center more on the interaction between labor and capital market distortions on one hand, and trade and exchange liberalization on the other.

In particular, a question of some importance is the extent to which the benefits of liberalization of the trade regime can be realized in the presence of highly restrictive wage legislation or controlled financial and capital markets. It is of some interest that the highly successful Far Eastern exporters had relatively free labor markets as well as liberalized trade regimes, while regulation of financial markets and interest rates persisted.

There is no instance that I know of, however, where a country's trade liberalization has been highly successful in the context of highly restrictive (and enforced) regulations surrounding the labor market.

## Problems of Liberalizing Individual Markets

It now seems fitting to examine the issues associated with liberalization in each of the key markets that affect overall resource allocation — the foreign exchange market, the labor market, the financial (and implicitly capital) market, and sectoral markets (most notably, the agricultural market).

Turning first to foreign exchange, three issues are of particular importance. One, the interrelationship between anti-inflationary programs and the liberalization of the trade regime, has already been discussed. It bears repeating that more efforts at liberalizing the trade regime have foundered because a new, nominal exchange rate was pegged and inflation did not abate than for all other reasons combined. The second issue pertains to the elimination of quantitative restrictions, while the third relates to the difficulties surrounding the transition process.

Obviously, if it were possible to move to a completely open trade regime, questions concerning the dismantling of quantitative restrictions would arise only in connection with the pace of the program, a subject deferred to section III below. In most instances, however, the range of policy choices acceptable to politicians does not include an immediate move to free trade, but may include alterations of the existing machinery of controls. In some instances quantitative restrictions have lost most, if not all, of their force through administrative devices including the transference of items to a liberalized list for which licensing is not required, or the abolition of licensing requirements altogether. (These actions were taken by Turkey in the devaluations of 1970 and the liberalization of 1980–1, respectively.) In other instances, administrative changes have significantly reduced the restrictiveness of the regime. These can include such measures as reducing the number of approvals required for a license, changing the import regulations from a negative list (all items not enumerated may not be imported) to a positive list (all items not specifically listed may be imported), or simply granting licenses more readily to all comers. Finally, in a few instances a country has dismantled quantitative restrictions, with the intent of liberalizing but maintaining the degree of protection afforded to domestic producers. Two such cases were Israel and the Philippines.[5]

This latter attempt, while seemingly the most rational from an economist's viewpoint, is apparently the most difficult. While once-and-for-all administrative changes may have very different effects on the degree to which protection is reduced in different industries, experience suggests that

[5] See Baldwin (1975, chapter 3) and Michaely (1975, chapter 2) for a description of these efforts.

the reduction in protection afforded through quantitative restrictions in that way is feasible. By contrast, laborious efforts to replace quantitative restrictions with tariffs provide ample time for political pressures to be brought to bear; efforts of tribunals to find "fair" criteria for determining protection levels and then to apply them seem inevitably destined to slow down the entire process, if not to render it entirely ineffective.

One other troublesome aspect of import liberalization should be noted. In some countries, raw material and intermediate good imports have been liberalized first, on the plausible theory that all producers will better be able to compete when confronted with international prices for their inputs. While this argument is impeccable as far as producers of exportables are concerned, it is flawed for import-competing producers: if protection on inputs is reduced or removed before protection on outputs, effective protection to domestic producers in fact increases in the process of liberalization. This consideration brings clearly into focus the distinction between moving toward free trade and liberalizing the trade regime.

When it comes to the labor market, much less is known, and systematic study of liberalizations and how they have come about is urgently needed. Inpressionistically, most successful liberalizations appear to have come about not by the removal or reduction in existing wage levels, but rather by a failure to adjust wage levels fully with future inflation. Carvalho and Haddad (1981), for example, have demonstrated how the Brazilian minimum wage gradually became ineffective as ever higher percentages of the labor force were paid wage rates in excess of the minimum.

Financial market liberalization has been the focal point of considerable analysis,[6] although most of it was undertaken under the assumption that capital was relatively immobile internationally, which may have been an acceptable assumption in the 1960s. With the greater willingness of developed countries' private financial institutions to lend to developing countries in the 1970s, a host of new issues has arisen, and there seem to be a large number of poorly understood problems. In the 1960s some countries, notably Brazil and Korea, seem to have been able partly to liberalize their financial markets without great difficulty. In more recent years, however, several efforts at financial liberalization have witnessed financial difficulties of major magnitude: Argentina, Chile, and Turkey appear to be recent examples. Whether difficulties arose because of liberalization in the financial sector and the resulting competition between banks, or whether instead there was interaction between the liberalization of financial markets and that of the foreign exchange market is a question requiring further analysis.

Turning finally to sectoral markets, the issues appear to be more political than economic. Whereas there are questions about the speed of response of the trade sector, the response of the banking sector to deregulation, and

---

[6] See McKinnon (1973) for an analysis of the importance of developing financial markets.

so on, there are fewer questions regarding economic behavior when sectoral markets are concerned. Instead the difficulties become increasingly political, as income-distributional questions come to the fore. Resistance to reforms of pricing of food, urban transport, energy, and other publicly provided goods and services is encountered largely because of consumer, rather than producer, interests.

## III  TIMING AND SEQUENCING REFORMS

The discussion up to this point has focused largely upon what is known about liberalization and its problems. There remain two major issues, on which much less is known, but which may be important if the probability of successful transition to a more liberalized economy is to be increased. These relate to the appropriate sequencing and timing of reforms.

The issue can best be posed by positing a set of initial conditions and then raising a series of interrelated questions. Assume an economy subject to exchange control, import licensing, a negative real interest rate with credit rationing, indexed real wages with resulting open unemployment, and suppression of producer prices in agriculture. Assume further that the objective is to remove all of these distortions to the system, with a minimum present value of the expected costs of the transition. A first question is whether total and simultaneous removal of all controls is cost-minimizing. Unless the answer to that question is positive, questions then arise as to the speed at which controls should be dismantled (the timing issue) and the chronological order in which individual markets should be decontrolled.[7] A final question is whether, if a single distortion will remain in the system (e.g., domestic inflation, owing to a large government budget deficit), total and simultaneous removal of all other distortions is optimal.

The issues of sequencing and timing arise only if one believes that simultaneous and immediate removal of all controls is neither optimal nor feasible. There are some grounds for believing that the rapid removal of all controls may be the least painful way of proceeding: new signals in place will prevent resource misallocation in response to altered signals before the transition is complete; instantaneous adjustment may prevent political opposition to the move from diluting it; and, since there is considerable evidence that uncertainty about the likelihood that policy initiatives can be sustained delays response to altered policy signals, an immediate trans-

---

[7] There is another reason why instantaneous abandonment of the entire control regime might be infeasible: when liberalization starts from a situation in which there is a large government deficit, it inherently requires time to reduce government spending and raise taxes. In that circumstance, one might question whether total decontrol of all other markets should precede macroeconomic stabilization. I have nowhere seen an analysis of this circumstance, and thus subsume it under other reasons for objecting to instantaneous decontrol.

formation of the economic environment may reduce uncertainty. If these considerations are overriding, the issues of timing and sequencing to not arise except in a second-best context.

There are those, however, who believe that total and instantaneous dismantling of all controls may be non-optimal. The difficulties associated with opening up capital account transactions before the current account has been liberalized have already been discussed. A plausible argument can be made that optimal dismantling of controls might start with current account transactions, agricultural pricing, and the domestic labor and capital markets, leaving capital account transactions initially subject to controls. These controls would be removed (gradually? suddenly?) in a second stage of the liberalization, once domestic resources had responded to altered policy signals.

Assuming that one could demonstrate that capital account liberalization should be delayed. I know of no theory, or set of conditions, to provide any presumption as to the length of delay, nor, for that matter, whether the capital account liberalization should then be gradual or instantaneous.

While the capital account would appear to be the best candidate for delayed liberalization, others have argued for gradual liberalization of current account transactions or of domestic financial markets. The basis for the argument is largely judgmental, however, and it is difficult to present a systematic case. Clearly, further analysis of the liberalization efforts of the 1970s, especially in cases where domestic and international capital markets were important, is called for.

## IV  SUMMARY AND CONCLUSIONS

The major problem with liberalization, as with so many other economic policy problems, is that politicians, government officials, and the informed public can readily infer those interests which are likely to be damaged in the short run by any liberalization effort; they cannot so readily see the economic activities that were harmed, and hence did not prosper, because of regulations. Moreover, even some of those who would in the long run benefit by liberalization (as, for example, the Korean businessmen who became exporters in the 1960s but were entrepreneurs in import substitution industries in the 1950s) perceive the short-run harm that it would cause to their interests, and fail to recognize the new opportunities that would arise in the longer run.

That difficulty is political, and it pervades discussions of almost all changes in economic policy. When considering liberalizations in developing countries, the political resistance to liberalization is intensified by the enormous magnitude of the changes called for. It is almost unthinkable to citizens who have lived with exchange control, poor-quality domestic products, and domestic inflation that their country's economy could behave far differently under a liberalized regime.

Add to that the genuine difficulties of transition — the necessary dislocations, the period of uncertainty that is likely to obtain until new signals have been maintained for a while, and the macroeconomic difficulties that in themselves present overriding problems — and it is small wonder that liberalizations are difficult to undertake and carry out. While it is clear that further research can increase understanding of ways in which the cost of transition can be reduced, it also seems likely that it will take determined leadership in individual countries for successful liberalization efforts to be undertaken.

## REFERENCES

Baldwin, Robert E. (1975), *Foreign Trade Regimes and Economic Development: The Philippines*. New York: Columbia University Press.

Carvalho, Jose and Haddad, Claudio (1981), "Foreign Trade Strategies and Employment in Brazil," in Anne O. Krueger, Hal B. Lary, Terry Monson, and Narongchai Akrasanee (eds.), *Trade and Employment in Developing Countries*. I. *Individual Studies*. Chicago: Chicago University Press.

Cline, William R. and Weintraub, Sidney (eds.) (1981), *Economic Stabilization in Developing Countries*. Washington, DC: Brookings Institution.

McKinnon, Ronald (1973), *Money and Capital in Economic Development*. Washington, DC: Brookings Institution.

Michaely, Michael (1975), *Foreign Trade Regimes and Economic Development: Israel*. New York: Columbia University Press.

# Comment 1

*Sebastian Edwards*

Anne Krueger has presented a very interesting and stimulating discourse on the problems of economic liberalization. She covers much ground and draws extensively on her wide knowledge of the subject. She also raises a series of important questions, some of which, as she points out, remain unanswered.

Because Krueger addresses such a broad range of issues, I have divided my comments into four areas, covering what I believe to be the most important aspects of economic liberalization: (a) the problems relating to the welfare effects of partial liberalization reforms; (b) the appropriate speed of liberalization; (c) the relationship between liberalization and stabilization programs; and (d) the order or sequencing of liberalization.

What can be said about welfare effects when distortions existing in the economy are to be reduced only partially, rather than fully? We know from the theorem of the second-best that, in general, there is not much we can tell about the welfare effects of partial reforms. Depending on the characteristics of the economy and the cross-elasticities, almost anything can happen: welfare can increase, welfare can be reduced, and so on. However, this is not a satisfactory answer if we are interested in policy questions and in pursuing general economic reforms. We must investigate further to see if we can establish some rules of thumb that will indicate whether partial liberalization will improve welfare. Krueger attempts to do this by considering a stylized economy with four markets: the foreign exchange and current accounts of the balance of payments; the domestic financial markets; the labor market; and the agricultural market. With two possible exceptions — the liberalization of agricultural prices with an overvalued currency, and the liberalization of the capital account in the presence of trade and domestic financial distortions — she concludes that liberalization of any individual market on its own is going to improve welfare.

While I am sympathetic to this idea, it should be recognized that this is an extremely difficult subject, and Krueger's treatment of it is somewhat loose. I believe that it would not be difficult to construct examples which would give results exactly opposite to those she presents. Given the complexity of the subject, more time should be devoted to better understanding the welfare effects of partial liberalization.

New research on this subject should focus on a question raised but not answered by Krueger, that is, on the public perception and credibility of liberalization reforms. The welfare effects will differ radically depending on the order of liberalization; economic agents' confidence that full liberalization will occur; and public skepticism regarding implementation of proposed reforms (as in the recent experience in Argentina).

The second part of my discussion addresses the speed of liberalization: if all markets are not to be liberalized instantaneously, how fast should they be liberalized? This question is tackled in section III above, where, after reviewing some considerations provided in the literature, Krueger takes a position in favor of rapid liberalization. To reach this conclusion, she relies on the credibility issue. The discussion in the literature regarding the speed of liberalization has been fairly extensive, although not very organized. Most of the discussion has dealt with the liberalization of trade, but the analysis can easily be extended to the liberalization of any market.

The arguments as to how fast a liberalization should proceeed can be classified into two broad categories. The first refers to pure welfare arguments, and the second refers to arguments related to the political economy of protection. Regarding pure welfare aspects, the critical questions are, are there externalities in the economy, and are there adjustment costs? We know from free trade theory that, in the absence of externalities and adjustment costs, equiproportional reduction of all distortions is welfare-improving. So, in order to maximize the present value of welfare gains, liberalization should be very fast or instantaneous.

However, once externalities are introduced, the question becomes less clear. For example, consider a factor-specific model with minimum wages, where the reduction of tariffs (if rapid) will result in a reduction of employment, output, and welfare. In that case, as the second-best policy, if one cannot act on the primary distortions, there might be an argument for liberalizing slowly.

The second set of arguments on the appropriate speed of liberalization refers to the political economy of protection. This literature has used two types of arguments. The first deals with the feasibility of reform. A number of authors, starting with Little, Scitovsky, and Scott, have pointed out that a very important consideration is that the reform should proceed through to its end; in order for that to happen, it is argued, we should not offend too many people. As long as people are offended, they will lobby against the reform. One way of not offending people, thus making reform feasible, is to proceed slowly.

The second type of argument regarding the political economy of protection deals with the question of credibility. If the reform goes slowly, people may not believe that it will go through to its end; if this is the case, they will not make necessary adjustments. This was the case in Argentina, where firms borrowed from abroad in order to remain operating at a (temporary) loss. As it turned out, tariffs were not in fact reduced, and the foreign borrowing was a good investment.

The third issue refers to the relationship between liberalization and stabilization. Krueger devotes much space to this issue, pointing out that

most liberalization attempts have occurred at the same time as a stabilization effort was underway. As she notes, this introduces some difficulties in the empirical evaluation of the effects of a liberalization reform. If both liberalization and stabilization are undertaken simultaneously, how can the effects of one reform be separated from those of the other? How do we attribute "certain percentage points of unemployment to the reduction of tariffs in Chile," for example, or to the stabilization effort of 1975? Those are important questions, but it is very difficult to find an empirical answer to them.

I believe that this is one of the major weaknesses of the analysis which can be explained by Krueger's use of a very broad definition of liberalization. The main problem with this definition is that it does not allow us to distinguish between different intensities of reform. A liberalization-with-stabilization attempt of the type that the International Monetary Fund (IMF) would typically try to persuade governments to follow (where, basically, quantity restrictions are dismantled) is very different from a major effort of the kind Chile went through in 1970s, where tariffs were dramatically reduced to a uniform 10 percent level. These are completely different things; they should be considered as different policies, and be analyzed in a different way. While one might agree that it is desirable to liberalize a little bit while a major stabilization effort is underway, it is not necessarily true that a major liberalization should be undertaken at the same time as a drastic anti-inflationary attempt. It is important, then, to clarify the degrees of liberalization we are talking about. We are not always talking about the same thing. We are talking about different degrees, and different experiences.

Also, regarding the relationship between liberalization and stabilization, there are a number of points that deserve more attention and research. One of the most important points, which has been noted by Krueger, is the role of exchange rate policies during the liberalization process. She has advocated a "crawling peg" and the manipulation of the exchange rate in order to solve the problem that arises with a balance of payments crisis, and when there is a serious foreign debt problem. I would like to see more rigorous analysis in this area, especially dealing with two things. First, with regard to the difference between nominal and real devaluation, we know that our policy tool is the nominal exchange rate, and we have to examine very closely the conditions under which a nominal devaluation can be transformed into a real devaluation. Second, we have to consider the role of intermediate and tradable inputs and how it might affect the successful manipulation of the nominal exchange rate. Also, I think that the use of the exchange rate as a stabilization tool, as used by the Southern Cone countries — the preannounced exchange rate — deserves more attention. There has been work on the subject, but I believe that, as a profession, we should devote more effort to fully understanding this kind of policy.

The fourth and last part of my discussion deals with the order of liberalization, and here I will be very brief, since the topic is covered at

length in chapter 7 below. Here, the question is: If you cannot liberalize all markets simultaneously, which markets should be liberalized first? In this area there are some very clear rules; for example, one should not liberalize the capital accounts of the balance of payments before liberalizing the domestic capital market — otherwise, a huge outflow of capital will take place.

We know less about the desirable order of liberalization between the current and capital accounts. In general, and as is pointed out in chapter 7, I am in agreement with Krueger's proposition that the current account should be opened first, and the capital account should wait until the effects of the liberalization of the current account have taken place.

# Comment 2

*Marcelo Selowsky*

Anne Krueger tries first to identify a pattern or logic in the evolution of controls leading to the "prototype illiberal economy." Second, she discusses reforms in a second-best world and identifies specific problems in the phasing and sequencing of these reforms. I have two major comments related to these topics.

## HOW DO WE END UP IN THE ILLIBERAL ECONOMY? SOME EXTENSIONS

To a large extent, Krueger explains controls as a response to macro-economic crisis situations; that is, they result from efforts to repress the effect of expansionary policies or inflationary finance on key market and political prices (foreign exchange, credit, food prices, etc.), particularly when external borrowing is no longer available. In other words, they result from attempts, either by the government of the economy, to live "beyond their means."

I believe that this is only part of the story, and that the "illiberal economy" is not only the product of macroeconomic crisis — to which controls are a response: one could also conceive of these controls as rational interventions that have carefully evolved over time, and whose motivation must be better understood for a better identification of alternative liberalization policies in the future.

We observe long histories of controls which have smoothly evolved over time and have not been the product of short-term situations.[1] They seem to have been the result of a careful evaluation of how to achieve non-economic objectives under a variety of fiscal and administrative constraints. A large part of these controls and distortions can be explained by the attempt to achieve these objectives at a minimum fiscal cost. Low urban food prices can be achieved by low procurement prices to farmers, tax on

---

[1] Examples are India, Sri Lanka, Greece, and most Central American countries, particularly before the oil price shocks.

food exports, or subsidized food imports, all of them transferring the burden to farm producers. The optimal instrument — a generalized consumption subsidy — is substantially more expensive and cumbersome from an administrative point of view. We can observe even more subtle types of government behavior. Governments many times offset these disincentives on the output side of agriculture by subsidizing inputs, particularly credit and imported inputs. Why such a roundabout and distortive mechanism of compensation? Administratively, it is easier to intervene in the trade flows; in other words, it is easier to subsidize inputs through the central bank or customs than it is to implement a generalized food consumption subsidy.

Distortive interventions in the labor market can be explained likewise; social security systems funded by a tax on the use of labor are an inefficient way of raising labor's welfare. A better alternative — for them to be funded from the central budget — is clearly more expensive from a fiscal point of view.

The rationale for trade restrictions, particularly on manufacturing imports, has also evolved independently of crisis situations in the balance of payments. These restrictions have been used to promote highly visible urban employment quickly. The cost of the policy, induced by a lower equilibrium exchange rate to be faced by exports and import-competing agriculture, is felt in the long run and is spread across a less vocal, less organized, less politically relevant rural sector.

In summary, the "illiberal" economy is not solely the product of short-term macroeconomic crisis, where controls are the instruments of "containment." These controls can also be looked upon as a rational system of interventions toward which governments have evolved given their objectives and constraints. One could even view the illiberal economy as a state characterized by an "equilibrium" level of controls, a system no government is willing to disturb to the extent it will involve a negative political payoff. If we believe that political acceptability is the major constraint for economic liberalization, a better understanding of the factors leading to the illiberal economy is fundamental. It would allow us to identify transition steps — and the possible role of the Bank — that minimize those short-term costs of concern to politicans, even if we sub-optimize the total present value of benefits of reform.

## MACROECONOMIC STABILIZATION AND ECONOMIC LIBERALIZATION

In my view, these concepts should be more clearly distinguished. By stablilization we usually have in mind a program of expenditure control of the fiscal budget (when the source of the problem is inflationary finance) or of a country's aggregate demand (when it is financed by unsustainable levels of external borrowing). Both are related to the budget constraint of the government or to the intertemporal budget constraint of the country.

By liberalization, we mean removal of controls generating discrepancies between economic signals and the opportunity cost of resources. The problem is more one of correcting relative prices than a problem of controlling aggregate expenditure.

The need to distinguish these concepts arises from the fact that (a) empirically these two phenomena do not always appear together; (b) even if they do, it is not obvious that both programs should be carried out simultaneously; and (c) from an analytical point of view, their objectives and welfare issues are so different and difficult that one might like to consider them separately.

According to Krueger, economic liberalization is usually undertaken in a crisis atmosphere or accompanied by simultaneous efforts to restore macroeconomic equilibrium. At first, this appears as a positive statement. Nevertheless, other statements seem to imply that both programs *should* be carried out simultaneously. Even more, some statements imply that multilateral lending should support countries experiencing a debt-servicing crisis if their leaders decide to go for a "full liberalization" effort. This is not obvious. It is clear that macro-adjustment must take place prior to liberalization; but should they take place simultaneously?

In my view, a full liberalization effort should wait for a more "normal" year, when the economy has already achieved a minimum amount of internal and/or external balance. It should wait until (a) a lower inflation rate has been achieved — when the original problem was inflationary finance; and (b) adjustments are made in the exchange rate and aggregate demand compatible with more sustainable levels of external borrowing, given the present structure of trade restrictions. To add the short-term costs associated with factor reallocation to the costs associated with a stabilization effort does not seem an optimal welfare solution; i.e., it concentrates all costs in a short period of time.

# PART III

## Issues in Trade Liberalization

# 3

# The Timing and Sequencing of a Trade Liberalization Policy

*Michael Michaely*

## I SUBJECT MATTER

Liberalization policy is often contemplated as a measure of primary importance, and is expected to improve the allocation of an economy's resources,
lead to greater efficiency, expand the economy's output, and accelerate its
growth. The manner in which such policy is introduced — the desirable
*path* of policy implementation — should be an integral element in the
consideration of such a policy. Yet, while comprehensive studies of liberalization periods as a whole are available, the problem of *phasing* and
*sequencing* such a trade policy has not usually been addressed, either in the
empirical investigations or in the analytical literature of liberalization policy.

This chapter intends to define the issue of trade policy sequencing: to
identify its major components in a fashion which would make them subject
to further study, and in particular to formulate them in a manner which
could provide an analytical framework for empirical research.

Liberalization policy is defined as actions leading to the contraction of
effective protective rates, i.e., to the lowering of the levels of such rates,
and the reduction of their variance. In an environment where policies are
biased in favor of import substitution, the introduction of policies providing incentives for the production of exportables will constitute an act
of liberalization, since they reduce the variance of protection across sectors
and move the economy toward a neutral trade regime. A complete liberalization would mean the elimination of virtually all protection and a near-
zero variance in the system. The term "liberalization policy" will be
reserved here for actions concerned with protection generated by *commercial*
policy (i.e., that policy which involved the economy's international trade):
it will not refer to regulatory policies (such as price controls or general
subsidies to output), in which transactions with the outside world are not
singled out. The existence of such policies is, however, relevant to

liberalization policy, and will thus have to be observed in a complete study of the issue.

The target of a liberalization policy is assumed to be the eventual achievement of free trade. Note that this does not preclude the existence of *some* discriminatory treatment of industries — for reasons of terms-of-trade effects, exceptionally large (positive or negative) externalities, or obvious effects on income distribution. The desirability of a liberalization policy will not, in itself, be part of the subject matter of this chapter. The presumption that free conduct of international trade should be preferred to a regime of protection is based on principles of economic theory, and is amply supported by empirical evidence. It has been repeatedly demonstrated, in both time-series studies of individual economies and in comparative country studies, that the opening of economies to free trade leads to higher income levels and higher rates of economic growth. It will thus be taken for granted here that a liberalization policy is desirable. ✓

The proposition that liberalized, free conduct of international transactions is superior to a regime of controls and protection is a "comparative statics" statement, but it yields no guidance for the design of policy implementation. Starting from a regime of protection, many paths may lead toward a liberalized regime, but some of these paths are inferior to others. The cumulative result of some paths might even be negative. Of all potential paths, one must be optimal. While no situations are identical, some crucial elements determining this path may be expected to be common to a sufficiently large number of countries, over long stages of development, so as to be able to indicate general principles concerning attributes of the optimal path.

Consequently, the fundamemtal question to be addressed in this chapter is, What are the principal determinants of the timing, phasing, and sequencing of successful and sustainable liberalization attempts ?

## II  THE GENERAL ISSUE

The optimal sequence of implementing a liberalization policy is that which maximizes the present value of the net addition to the economy. Several criteria follow: (a) costs and benefits during the transition period should be considered, along with net benefits expected when the process of implementation is complete; (b) the sooner the final situation is reached, the higher the benefit; on the other hand, net costs and benefits at the early stages of the process are particularly important, as compared with the net benefits in the long run; (c) the evaluation of each stage should encompass net costs and benefits and effects on the future course of development. Often a policy leading to large net benefits in one stage may lower benefits afterwards, or vice versa. Developments at various stages are necessarily parts of a complex process, in which both economic and political elements play important roles. A full exploration of this process will not be attempted here.

The long-run, steady-state benefits of liberalization are well known and will be restated here only briefly. The conduct of free trade, qualified by considerations such as those mentioned before, and abstracting from the impact of domestic distortions, leads to a maximum degree of allocational efficiency in the economy, to specialization along the lines of the economy's comparative advantage, and to an optimal use of the economy's resources. Technical efficiency probably also increases with liberalization in those activities which would exist with or without protection, by virtue of competition of world markets with local production. In addition, liberalization relieves two specific and crucial scarcities. One is the shortage of foreign exchange: the opening of the economy, boosting its export activities (whether by removal of protection from import substitution or by granting equal protection to exports), leads to an increase of foreign exchange proceeds, and hence to an increase in importing capacity. The economy can thus sustain more imports of intermediate inputs and capital goods, which are often necessary ingredients in the expansion of production and acceleration of the economy's growth. The other scarcity exists where protection is granted not by tariffs or other price mechanisms, but by quantitative restrictions (QRs) of imports. On one hand, a protection scheme of this nature leads to the forced idleness of resources owing to the unavailability of complementary import components. On the other hand, it may also lead to social waste arising from the stockpiling of such imports in anticipation of later shortages. A further waste involved in the QR system is the loss of income incurred by "rent-seeking" activities. This waste could be removed not only by a liberalization in the general sense, but also by merely changing the form of protection from QRs to regulation by the price mechanism.

Aside from production gains from liberalization, sight should not be lost of the consumption gains: the equalization of domestic with international relative prices of the country's traded goods would change consumption patterns, increasing further the community's welfare.

In the short run, however — i.e. during the transition period — both costs and benefits may be expected. The benefits are those just specified, increasing gradually with time; the nature of the costs will be described below.

This chapter will attempt to indicate those factors which determine the achievement of maximum benefits and minimum costs during the transition process. Another major issue which is closely related, yet separate, is the survivability, or sustainability, of a liberalization policy, that is, its uninterrupted implementation and long-term persistence. Higher eventual and transitional benefits, and lower transitional costs, will obviously increase the likelihood of sustainability. Thus, cost and benefit factors will help to evaluate the survivability of a policy pattern. Other factors indicating the degree of survivability may be identified more directly. Political as well as purely economic elements affect the determination of a survivable path.

The question of sequencing of a liberalization policy consists of three components:

1 How fast should the process of implementation of liberalization be? In
  particular, is a once-and-for-all, one-stage liberalization superior or
  inferior to a multi-stage policy?
2 What could be the attributes of stages of implementation?
3 What should be the relationships between liberalization of imports and
  other economic policies in the determination of the general order of
  policies?

In all these issues, income distribution, as well as efficiency considerations, would be involved. Political considerations as well as economic
effects will have to be evaluated. These issues will be further specified
here, along with a brief discussion of the problems involved.


## III  SPEED OF IMPLEMENTATION

Granting that a post-liberalization situation is superior to the initial position,
it would seem that a swift liberalization — leading to the immediate
realization of the benefits yielded by the new superior situation — would
be desirable. This consideration would call for a single-stage policy of
liberalization, implemented entirely at once. In addition, the response to a
policy change is strongly dependent on the credibility assigned to it by
individual economic agents, that is, on the degree to which they believe
that the policy measure will be a lasting one. Presumably, a radical measure
of liberalization would seem more credible than a minor one, even if the
latter is presented as only the beginning of a series of future changes. The
single-stage policy, seen as a stronger signal, may be expected to evoke a
stronger response than a multi-stage implementation. Were the policy
considered in a world free of rigidities, and in which all capital were
malleable, this reasoning would be justified; in the real world, however,
other considerations must be added.

Production is likely to decline in an activity from which protection is
removed (partially or totally), but such decline is *not* inevitable. If the
degree of protection removal is small, and the impact of liberalization on
income expansion and growth is both substantial and imminent, the positive expansionary effect may outweigh the negative substitution effect.
However, if the degree of protection removal from an activity is large, a
positive outcome would not be probable; the activity will contract, and
fewer resources will be employed. These resources are physical capital
(including natural resources) and labor (including both "raw labor" and
human capital). Were it possible immediately to channel these resources to
an expanding activity, no waste would be involved. But capital goods are
to some extent specific, and the contraction of the sector would simply
leave them unemployed. This also applies to the human capital element in
labor, which is largely sector-specific. If "raw labor" were transferred fully
to the expanding sectors, the unemployment of capital would still not
invalidate the conclusion that, in the aggregate, the reallocation of resources

must be beneficial: unemployment of capital indicates that it could not yield any rent since its marginal product (given the new set of prices) is zero or negative, in which case its unemployment is superior to its employment in the contracting activity. For two reasons, however, the transfer of raw labor will be hindered. One reason is that at the wage rate expected at the expanding sector — the value of the marginal product of raw labor (plus the non-specific element of human capital) in that occupation — labor would refuse to work, even though this wage rate represents a higher value than that assigned, at the margin, to leisure. The other reason, which has a time element attached to it, is the absence of complementary factors: employment of the available labor in the expanding sector requires the expansion of other factors (e.g., specific physical capital, managerial capacity) which are not immediately available. The longer the time horizon, the smaller the impact of this factor on the creation of unemployment. The extent to which this is an important consideration would be, inter alia, a function of the industrial structure of the activities concerned. In general, this frictional unemployment would be less severe the more the adjustment is carried out *within* firms, rather than by the elimination of some firms and the creation of others. Obviously, it would also depend on the degree of specificity of capital: the more a new production pattern could be carried out in existing plants, the less unemployment should be expected. By way of generalization, the more resources are called to move among widely different activities (e.g., between urban and rural sectors), the greater the significance of the frictional elements. To some degree, though, it is inevitable that some resources will be unemployed, rather than transferred immediately to an expanding industry; this would be more severe the shorter the time lapse since the policy change.

Aside from the loss of production, unemployment would naturally tend to change income distribution in a manner likely to be considered undesirable. Furthermore, unemployment of labor is likely to be regarded by the unemployed and by society at large as a situation whose cost exceeds the loss of income. For all these reasons, the minimization of unemployment must be a crucial political factor in determining liberalization policy.

Of course, other factors also affect income distribution. As has just been noted, the change in relative prices resulting from a liberalization policy leads to the reduction of quasi-rents enjoyed by owners of physical and human capital in the contracting industries — potentially to the point of complete elimination of such rents — and, on the other hand, to increases of rent enjoyed by capital owners in the expanding activities. If the change in relative prices is large and sudden, these changes in rents will be very large, causing a large measure of income redistribution. At the other extreme, a gradual and *preannounced* change in prices would lead to only minor losses and gains of rent by owners of existing capital. In the contracting sector capital would depreciate slowly; in the expanding sector it would be built gradually, with only very slight changes in the rate of rent. Labor would start moving as soon as the new signals were announced.

An immediate and large change would thus lead to a relatively large impact on income distribution, whereas a gradual change would minimize it. A priori, it cannot be known in a general way whether the income distribution existing at the starting position is superior or inferior to the one that would be established with a large and immediate change in relative prices. It is known, however, that the status quo generally enjoys a particular esteem in the eyes of the public and of policy-makers; policy-induced changes are often considered "unfair" and to be avoided. To the extent that this is the case, it contra-indicates an immediate and large change in relative prices.

Thus, it is generally presumed that a gradual, multi-stage implementation of a liberalization policy is superior to a once-and-for-all, immediate, act involving a large change. The discussion above indicates some guidance as to the *speed* of a multi-stage process of implementation. In general, the process should be shorter, *ceteris paribus*, when there are few rigidities in the labor market, less specific physical and human capital resources, flexible and adaptable responses by entrepreneurs, and a short life-span of physical capital (and, of lesser relevance, of human capital) in the contracting activities. The process of implementation should thus be faster the higher the elasticities of substitution in production among various activities, and the faster the reaction of potential movers to the expanding sectors.

These attributes would obviously differ from case to case. It is difficult to say a priori, by way of generalization, how the level of development of an economy may be expected to affect this set of factors. On one hand, the element of "raw", unskilled labor is generally larger, in relation to physical and human capital, in less developed economies. This by itself should lead to faster responses to relative price changes, and thus to a lower level of unemployment following such changes, in less developed economies. On the other hand, entrepreneurs are presumably less flexible and adaptable in less developed economies. Similarly, general infrastructure foundations which facilitate mobility are more scarce in these economies. Therefore, no clear-cut rule may be offered on the relationship between the desired speed of implementation of liberalization and the development of the economy in question.

Another consideration which could presumably lead either way is that of *political* feasibility of alternative paths. The one-stage policy, leading to greater unemployment and larger changes in income distribution, may be expected to generate more resistance, and thus be less feasible politically. On the other hand, it may be presumed that a multi-stage process would require a repetitive political struggle which is avoided in the one-stage alternative. The political feasibility of the undertaking and implementation of a one-stage process vs. a *completed* multi-stage process cannot be answered a priori, in general; actual experiences may shed some light on this issue.

## IV ATTRIBUTES OF STAGES OF IMPLEMENTATION

What should policy-makers and policy advisors infer on a priori grounds about the nature of the stages of liberalization? Much of what characterizes the desirable attributes of these stages is implied in the preceding discussion. Yet, a few specific questions may be posed.

The first concerns shifts between *forms* of protection. Government interference in imports often takes the form of quantitative restrictions, rather than (or in addition to) tariffs. Indeed, the term "liberalization" is very often understood to be a shift from a QR system to protection through tariffs, rather than the lowering of protection involved in a tariff system. Assuming that a country is in this starting position, the first question would be, Is it desirable to begin a process of liberalization by shifting from QRs to protection through tariffs, without affecting the levels of protection, or would this stage be better dispensed with, performing the gradual lowering of protection by a gradual relaxation of the quantitative restrictions?

Shifting protection to the price mechanism has a few major advantages. First, it may contribute to the removal of the unintended (and, most probably, unknown) discrimination which is inevitably embodied in a system of QRs. Thus, an apparently shift in the *mechanisms* involves a change in the nature of protection, lowering (perhaps considerably) its variance. This in itself may make it a desirable first step toward liberalization.

No less important is the fact that, by making levels of protection known, this shift greatly facilitates the preannouncement of *future* levels of protection. A multi-stage implementation of liberalization makes sense only if the correct signals are given in advance: the future course of the process should be known from its start. This would be difficult, if not impossible, to achieve with a system of QRs; neither the government nor private economic agents can be expected to possess the knowledge required to transform a future (preannounced) level and structure of QRs into levels of prices and protection. Hence, the signals must be transmitted directly by announcing *prices*; this, in turn, requires an initial transfer to protection through prices.

The main argument against this initial stage might be the *time* involved in the process of transferring one system to another: an unduly long time, during which no other liberalization steps are undertaken, may offset the advantages. Another possible argument which could work either way is the impact of the shift in mechanism on income distribution. The quota profits enjoyed by the holders of import licenses under QRs (unless these licenses are auctioned in the market) would be transferred to recipients of the government expenditures or to other taxpayers. This may be regarded as "fair" (if one views the unearned quota profits bestowed by the government as "unfair"), and may thus increase the desirability of the change;

but if deviations from the status quo are viewed as "unfair", so would this shift be judged. Likewise, such shift in income distribution may diminish the political feasibility of implementation of this stage of the process, and consequently, of liberalization as a whole.

An important attribute of stages of the process would be the establishment, or the absence, of a uniform treatment of activities. One of the major advantages of a uniform treatment is its simplicity, and its association with "fairness", which would facilitate the implementation of the process. A differential treatment of activities inevitably implies a large measure of discretion. This introduces an element of friction, political difficulties, and uncertainty about the future course. All these would be avoided by a once-and-for-all introduction of a uniform set of rules to guide the future course of the process. In addition, a uniform treatment would be more likely to lead to a lower variance of protection rates along the liberalization path, which is an obvious advantage, given that the absence of any variance is the ultimate, preferred situation.

Against these, the differential responses of various industries must be weighed. If the contraction of one activity is likely to result in significantly larger unemployment than the contraction of others, it may be logical to introduce stages so that the removal of protection from that activity would be made more gradual. Obviously, this would require knowledge or judgment about differential reactions in various activities — both those which contract and those which are the potential new employers of released factors.

A "uniform" path of liberalization is defined as a policy code in which no specific activity is mentioned. This does not, however, rule out an *unequal* treatment of different activities possessing different relevant attributes. In a "uniform treatment", the dominant such attribute would be the initial level of protection on the eve of liberalization, when some variance (usually very large) exists among protection levels. At least three alternative uniform paths may be followed. One is an *equiproportional* ("across-the-board") reduction of protection of various activities. This path has the advantage of leading to an increased convergence of protection rates, and a gradual reduction of the variance in the protection system. A second possible rule is the reduction of protection rates by equally large *absolute* doses. This has the deficiency of potentially leading, at least in the initial stages, to *increased* variance in the system of protection rates. On the other hand, it may have the advantage of making the transitory impact on employment less severe by avoiding large reductions of relative prices in the highly protected activities. The slower the responsiveness of expanding activities, and the stronger the reduction of total employment yielded by changes in prices, the more obvious is the advantage of such a path.

---

[1] Corden (1974). Similar rules are indicated in the general literature of optimal tax reforms: see, for instance, Hatta (1977). For an analysis of "across-the-board" tariff reductions, see Bruno (1972).

The third alternative is what has been described in a different context as the "concertina method."[1] This works as follows: in the initial stage of the policy, all protection rates above a certain ceiling are lowered to that ceiling, with no changes in other rates; in the next stage, all rates are brought down to a lower ceiling; and so on. This rule would not only consistently lower the variance in the protection system, but would also have the advantage of reaping the highest possible net benefit from any change in the production and consumption patterns. The transitory damage from unemployment is a function — assuming all activities to be equally prone to such damage — of the *size* of change in production. The production and consumption gains, on the other hand, are functions of both the sizes of changes in production and consumption and the *protection levels* of the contracting activities.

This may be easily demonstrated in a partial equilibrium context with the aid of figure 3.1, which employs the so-called "triangles method." $S$ is the domestic supply curve and $D$ is the (compensated) demand curve for an importable good. $P_w$ is the world (i.e., free trade) price of the good; and $t_1$, $t_2$, $t_3$ are alternative tariff levels. To simplify the presentation, the distances $AH$, $HG$, and $GF$ are all given as equal. A tariff reduction from the level $t_3$ to $t_2$ would create a production welfare gain of the area $ECGF$, and a consumption gain of $NMSR$. A further reduction, to level $t_1$, would

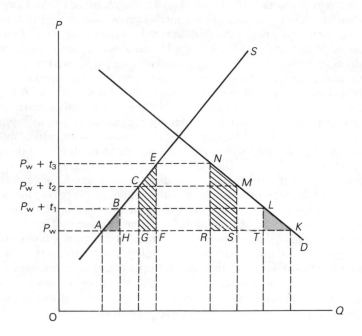

FIGURE 3.1

lead to the combined gain of *CBHG* and *MLTS*. A still further reduction, to zero (the elimination of the tariff), would create a gain of *BAH* and *LKT*. These gains decline with each further step of tariff reduction, while the effect on the size of production is equal (by construction) at each stage. Hence, *ceteris paribus*, the highest net benefits should be expected from the contraction of activities (and the expansion of consumption) where protection levels are highest. On a priori grounds, this policy pattern would seem to be superior to all others, as long as differential responses of various activities are ignored, and a uniform policy path is followed.

Following the preceding discussion, employment considerations appear to be a primary motivation for the adoption of a discriminatory, non-uniform path of liberalization. This may involve several elements. In general, activities whose contraction would result in a relatively large unemployment of labor should be candidates for a slower, more prolonged process of liberalization. These may be activities which are relatively labor-intensive; even more so, activities intensive in human capital; and more particularly so, the more specific that human capital is to the activity on hand.

It is worthwhile noting some forms of discrimination which, though common, should be avoided. First, a large measure of liberalization of intermediate goods, leaving finished goods highly protected, is harmful to the process of liberalization as a whole. It increases effective protection in activities which produce the finished good, thus leading to their expansion, while on efficiency grounds their contraction would most often be called for. The increased protection thus granted to many activities (while protection of other local activities is *not* lowered, since most often imported intermediate goods have no domestic counterparts) makes such a discrimination popular — hence easy to implement — but makes the goal of eventual complete liberalization even more difficult to achieve. A legitimate argument for the removal (or relaxation) of quantitative restrictions on imports of intermediate inputs is that their existence leads to highly inefficient processes of production. But the removal of QRs should be accompanied by the imposition of tariffs as long as the final-goods activities are protected.

Similar arguments apply to the liberalization of imports of capital goods, in advance of the liberalization of activities which produce consumer goods. Moreover, such discrimination not only grants higher effective protection to many activities; it also confers a larger measure of protection the higher the capital-goods intensity of the activity, thus giving particular encouragement to industries which employ *small* amounts of labor. If unemployment of labor is the major impediment to a process of liberalization, such a policy would then make the implementation of liberalization more difficult, more liable to lead to a net loss to the economy, and less likely to be carried through to a final stage of full liberalization.

## IV  IMPORT LIBERALIZATION AND OTHER POLICIES IN THE SEQUENCE

This section will be devoted to observations about the relationships between the sequencing of import liberalization and the implementation of other policies. A preliminary consideration, which is not concerned strictly with the sequencing of *policies*, is that of the initial circumstances which make the success of liberalization policy more or less likely. Neither inflation nor unemployment is conducive to a successful liberalization. Inflation, *unaccompanied* by accommodating exchange rate changes, is bound to lead to a balance-of-payments deterioration, making the maintenance of a free market for imports a more difficult undertaking. A state of high unemployment would again make free imports, with their associated transitory unemployment, more difficult to defend and sustain. For similar reasons, an initial situation of a severe balance of payments deficit (owing to inflation, unfavorable movements of the country's terms of trade, bad crops, or any other reason) would make the introduction of liberalization policy more difficult, and its future survivability less likely. Thus it would seem that a liberalization policy is most likely to succeed if introduced under what may be roughly described as domestic and external equilibrium.

Closely associated with this is the nature of macroeconomic policies pursued alongside the liberalization policy. Very often — perhaps on most occasions — liberalization would be considered not in the context of an initial equilibrium, but rather in economies suffering from inflation, perhaps in combination with acute balance of payments difficulties. In these circumstances, a liberalization policy would stand a chance of success only if it were undertaken in conjunction with a stabilization policy and with an appropriate exchange rate policy — policies which would have to be undertaken for their own sake, regardless of the adoption of a liberalization policy.

The following brief discussion will deal with four policy spheres: (a) exchange rate and export promotion policies; (b) income maintenance policies; (c) capital market policies; and (d) other restrictive policies. In the first two we assume that some policies are called for because of the liberalization; and, indicating their nature, we ask how such policies should appear in the sequencing of implementation of the policy. In the third case we assume that restrictive policies have been followed in the markets concerned and that, as part of a general relaxation of interference, liberalization in those markets accompanies a policy of import liberalization.

### Exchange Rate Policy and Export Promotion

For clarity, we may assume that the starting position before liberalization is that of a balance of payments "equilibrium" in a very narrow sense; that is, given all the price and quantity restrictions on imports and at the

existing exchange rate, the "basic" payments account is balanced. Import liberalization, increasing the size of imports, must thus be accompanied by an effective exchange rate devaluation. The latter may take a great variety of forms, from a uniform, formal devaluation to a discriminatory system of export promotion policies.

In this process, some import-competing activities decline, whereas others — primarily export, and presumably also some other import-competing sectors — expand. This involves not only a shift of sales of existing production between the home and the foreign markets, but also a structural change entailing a shift of productive resources. As emphasized earlier, it may be presumed that, in this process, contracting activities respond more quickly than potentially expanding activities. Insofar as the foreign transactions are concerned, it may thus be expected that, in a general way, similar price reductions in the liberalized sectors and price increases in the other (mainly export) activities would lead to an import surplus.

Several alternative solutions may be considered. One is to have a relatively (relative, that is to the extent of liberalization) large price increase in the export sector in the initial stages. This would increase the extent of responsiveness, and of export expansion, after a while, but it would still not relieve the balance of payments problem in the initial stage. A corollary drawback is the fact that such a large price increase must involve, particularly in the initial stage, the creation of a large rent element in the encouraged (export) sector — the consequences of which were mentioned above.

Another response might be the securing of foreign aid to bridge the initial gap between exports and imports. Aside from the feasibility of such policy, it should be noted that, even if the foreign exchange gap is closed in this way, the problem of initial disparities between expansion and contraction of activities, with the consequent effect on employment, would not be solved by the availability of additional foreign exchange.

A third response — an extreme version of the first alternative — which a priori seems to be superior, is the *advancing* of export promotion (by formal devaluation or through export promotion measures), so that it precedes the first stage of import liberalization;[2] by the time the latter starts, the process of expansion of export activities would already be in progress. The possible drawback of such sequencing is that, if the encouragement of exports is mismatched with the decline of import substitutes (in the opposite direction from the one described before), this sequence might lead to an inflationary pressure rather than to a reallocation

---

[2] This could be done either through export subsidization or through a formal devaluation, compensated on the import side by lowered tariffs. Recall that the introduction of export subsidies, given the existence of import barriers, is considered part of a liberalization policy.

of resources. Also, the danger always exists that a delay in the start of implementation of actual import liberalization might jeopardize the whole process.

### Income Maintenance Policies

The major relevant income maintenance policy is, in the present context, a scheme of unemployment benefits, perhaps augmented by special attention and extra benefits in the case of labor dismissed in the contracting sectors. Compensation for lost rent in these sectors may also be considered, but would seem a priori to be more difficult to handle rationally.

Income maintenance policies would be more important when the gaps between responses of contracting and expanding activities are larger, and the process of implementation of the liberalization policy is swift. By lessening the extent of income contraction incurred by the losing parties, and by partially relieving the burden of unemployment, such policies would make the liberalization policy look more "fair", and would undoubtedly make its implementation more feasible politically. The obvious disadvantage of income maintenance policies is that they tend to hinder the mobility of factors, thus further aggravating the unemployment to which they are responding. Schemes which provide motivation for mobility and absorption in new activities would diminish the extent of this impact.

### Capital Market Liberalization

General theories which may be applied to the interaction of liberalization in the goods market with that of the capital and labor markets provide us with little guidance for policy. We know that the existence of distortions in one market implies that the elimination of distortions in another does not necessarily increase welfare. Thus, if distortional restrictions in the capital (or labor) market are maintained, it cannot be ascertained that import liberalization would be beneficial. However, a simultaneous *complete* liberalization of *all* markets must be beneficial; similarly, in a world with two markets, a complete liberalization in one market would make a liberalization policy in the other necessarily beneficial.

To make these general statements somewhat more specific, it may be observed that restrictions in the capital market could be of a nature that reinforces the distortions arising from import restrictions. Or, to the contrary, one set may tend to offset the other. Thus, rationing of long- and short-term credit, capital grants, concessionary loans, investment licensing, and similar measures of interference in the capital market may be applied to direct capital toward or away from the protected activities. In the first case, removal of restrictions in one market while they remain intact in the other is most likely to be beneficial. In the second case, liberalization in one market may lower the economy's welfare, leading to a greater misallocation of resources than found in the two offsetting schemes.

In a similar way, and for the same reasons, no general statement about the *sequences* of two components of liberalization may be made. Granting that the eventual liberalization of both the goods and the capital markets is beneficial, it cannot be stated whether a first stage, of partial removal of restrictions in the goods market, should best be accompanied by no removal of restrictions in the capital market, by a complete removal, or by a partial removal. Likewise, in line with what has been said so far, it cannot be said in a general way whether either a partial or a complete liberalization in the capital market should precede, accompany, or follow a partial liberalization of goods.

### Relaxation of Other Restrictive Policies

As noted at the outset of this chapter, the "liberalization" with which this project is concerned is that of foreign trade transactions. Other regulatory policies, however, are often practiced. Interference in capital markets forms one component of such policies, but there are various others. Commonly found are price and wage controls as well as a variety of subsidy schemes in the goods and factor markets.

A liberalization policy may be accompanied by relaxation of other policies of intervention. Sometimes these changes may result directly from liberalization, in which case the sequence is obvious. The relaxation of QRs would be followed by the abolition of domestic rationing and price controls of imported goods, rather than the other way around. In other instances, these obvious relationships do not exist. All that can be said, then, is that no *general* preference for the order of policies may be established on a priori grounds. Empirical observations may provide some lessons about the association of such sequencing with the likelihood of success of a policy package.

## V LESSONS FROM AVAILABLE EMPIRICAL STUDIES

Episodes of liberalization have been studied in several research projects over the last 15 years. Some mention may be found in the series of seven country studies (Argentina, Brazil, India, Mexico, Pakistan, the Philippines, and Taiwan) included in the project of *Industry and Trade in Some Developing Countries* (OECD, 1970). However, while protection policies form one of the main topics in this study, information on liberalization episodes in a manner which may illuminate the issues of present concern is scarce.

This is largely true also for a more recent project on *Development Strategies in Semi-Industrial Economics*, directed by Bela Balassa (Balassa, 1982). Six countries (Argentina, Colombia, Israel, Korea, Singapore, and Taiwan) are investigated in this study, which explores effective protection and other forms of intervention that determine the economy's allocation of resources between tradables and non-tradables, and which may discriminate between

export and import substitution. The study thus focuses on the degree of openness of a country's policy scheme, but, again, the issues concerning the design of a successful liberalization policy are not addressed.

Liberalization policies occupy a more central place in the series of country studies included in the NBER project, *Foreign Trade Regimes and Economic Development*, directed by Jagdish N. Bhagwati and Anne O. Krueger (National Bureau of Economic Research, 1974–8). Nine country studies were published in 1975 and 1976: Chile, Colombia, Egypt, Ghana, India, Israel, the Philippines, South Korea, and Turkey. In addition, one of the two synthesis volumes of this project is devoted to this topic (vol. X). Emphasis in these volumes is placed on the relationship between liberalization and stabilization policies, with relatively little attention paid to the issue of sequencing of a liberalization policy. The main findings which are relevant for the design of liberalization policies will be surveyed here briefly.

1. *A shift from QRs to protection by tariffs.* Three country experiences contain episodes of liberalization in which the declared aim of the policy was to leave the level and structure of protection largely unchanged, but to replace QRs by tariffs and similar devices, thus by the (constrained) use of the price mechanism. These are the liberalization episodes in Ghana, 1966–71; in Israel, 1962–7; and in the Philippines, 1960–5. All these episodes are judged "successful" experiences, although in the Philippines, and more sharply in Ghana, the policy was eventually reversed. What appears most striking is that, in all these episodes, a presumed change in only the form of the protection system led in fact to a significant change in level and structure, in the direction of a reduction of protection of the most highly protected activities, greater uniformity of the system, and (as a result) substantial changes in levels and structures of imports.

2. *The role of the foreign exchange rate and of export promotion.* Perhaps the most common element found in country experiences is that the first stage of liberalization fails, and the policy is reversed, when the "real" rate of foreign exchange falls — either because the nominal exchange rate is fixed or because, when it is crawling, it fails to rise to the extent of domestic inflation. In the absence of strong price incentives to exports other than through the exchange rate, exports fall, or at least fail to rise, while imports tend to increase substantially. This is detailed particularly for the liberalization episodes in Chile (1956–8, 1959–61, 1965–70), Colombia (1965–6), and Ghana (1966–71). In Israel, on the other hand, a successful and permanent liberalization of part of the system was achieved in 1952–5, despite a starting position of a complete absence of foreign exchange reserves, owing to a substantial increase in the real exchange rate.

3. *Credibility of signals.* In a number of episodes it appears that liberalization failed, or was reversed, because it did not seem credible. The assumption that future stages would not be undertaken, or even that the first stage would soon be reversed, was prevalent; these types of expectations lead to a particularly large accumulation of imports, and tend of course to become self-fulfilling. Episodes of this nature are discussed particularly in the review of experiences in Chile and Colombia. A gener-

alized conclusion, emphasized in Krueger's synthesis as well as in the discussion of Chile, is that the past history of liberalization episodes in the country is of crucial importance: the more frequent the failures of such experiments, the stronger must be the initial signals (that is, the degree of lowering protection in the economy in the first stage) to be accepted by the public as valid indicators of future policy.

4. *Importance of initial circumstances and external development.* To succeed and proceed beyond the first stage, the initial stage of liberalization has to manifest its positive fruits within a relatively short time. A policy of liberalization is always a radical change of which a general awareness exists. As a result, the public tends to identify developments following liberalization as products of that policy. Consequently, a liberalization undertaken under favorable circumstances — a rising real income, good harvests, or favorable changes in external terms of trade — is more likely to succeed; whereas liberalizations in which such circumstances were unfavorable (India following 1966 was perhaps the best example) were bound for an early reversal.

In sum, while this series of studies contains a considerable amount of evidence and analysis on the relationship between liberalization and stabilization, it provides little empirical guidance for the issue of sequencing of liberalization. For the most part, the evidence available in this source would tend to support the following propositions: (a) the first stage of a liberalization must be accompanied by an appropriate exchange rate policy; (b) it should be undertaken when external developments are favorable; (c) a shift from QRs to protection by tariffs, even when intended to lead only to a change in the form of protection, in fact tends to lower and rationalize protection. On the other hand, it is a time-consuming process.

Another project related to the present study is that of *Trade and Employment in Developing Countries*, directed by Anne O. Krueger (National Bureau of Economic Research (1981–3) and covering 12 countries (Argentina, Brazil, Chile, Colombia, Hong Kong, Indonesia, Ivory Coast, Korea, Pakistan, Thailand, Tunisia, and Uruguay) as well as specialized topics. This study is concerned primarily with the long-term issue of the effect of a more "neutral" commercial policy on employment, through the shift in demand from import-substituting to export activities. As such, its focus is entirely different from the issue of appropriate sequencing of liberalization policies.

A recent study which partly addresses the concerns of the sequencing of liberalization policies is that of Nelson (1983), which explores the political process in the implementation of liberalization and stabilization policies. The study's conclusions are based on the recent experiences of five countries (Ghana, Jamaica, Kenya, Sri Lanka, and Zambia). Among others, the country studies identify the interactions of policies with the political machinery.

Finally, it may be mentioned that recent literature provides at least three instances of somewhat detailed discussion of the "transition period", and the prescription of programs for the sequencing of liberalization policies. In all these instances, the proposals are presumed to rely on the authors'

observations of the world experience; they are not based on references to actual episodes. One discussion is by Little, Scitovsky, and Scott (OECD, 1970, volume VI). (Although it is a synthesis of seven country studies, the proposal finds partial support only in reference to the experience of Taiwan.) Another is by Bela Balassa (1977, Essay 1). The third is found in a document by Keesing (1979).

All of these authors agree that liberalization policy should be carried out in stages. Little et al. propose a first stage which is a purely nominal shift in the form of protection, incorporating an exchange rate change: QRs would be removed, and the exchange rate would be devalued to the level which is regarded as an (eventual) equilibrium in the absence of price measures of intervention (tariffs, subsidies, or export taxes). Concurrently, tariffs should be adjusted and export taxes imposed (or raised), so that local prices of all importables and exportables should remain unchanged at this stage from their initial levels. From then on, tariffs and export taxes should be gradually lowered, until they are completely eliminated (save for instances such as optimal export taxes when terms-of-trade effects are present). This process should be accompanied by an increase in indirect taxation and subsidies for labor.

Balassa's first stage is roughly similar, except that no explicit mention is made of a shift from a QR system. He recommends a first stage of a "compensated devaluation," but the compensation should not be quite "full"; that is, it should not be a compensation by tariffs and export taxes which leaves prices entirely unchanged. The occasion should be used to favor exports to some extent, by lowering the prices of protected importables while increasing the prices of exportables. From then on, tariffs and export taxes should be reduced in annual installments, with all of the sequences being preannounced. In cases of an initially very high level (diversity) of protection, a subdivision is recommended: preannounced reductions should be made over a period of (some) five years, by the end of which tariffs are only partly eliminated. At that stage the system should be re-examined, and a new, final stage of preannounced changes should be introduced.

While the initial stage recommended by Little et al. is neutral, and Balassa's first stage is export-biased, Keesing's program would be concerned only with exports. In his first stage, protection of importables is left unchanged. But exports are to be promoted by any and all measures, from devaluation unaccompanied by export taxes (except on primary, traditional exports) to retention quotas, direct subsidies to output, credit on concessionary terms, etc. Keesing realizes that these are distorting measures, introducing discriminatory protection of exportables. These distortions would then be removed at a later stage, along with the distortional protection of importables. The details of this later stage, which would come only long after the first, are not specified. In effect, Keesing's transition period does not refer to what would be generally regarded as "liberalization", but to the introduction of a discriminatory protection system for exports, equivalent to the system existing for imports and intended to offset the past bias against exports arising from the latter.

REFERENCES

Balassa, Bela and associates (1971), *The Structure of Protection in Developing Countries.* Baltimore: Johns Hopkins Press for the International Bank for Reconstruction and Development and the Inter American Development Bank.

Balassa, Bela (1977), *Policy Reform in Developing Countries.* Oxford: Pergamon Press.

Balassa, Bela and associates (1982), *Development Strategies in Semi-Industrial Economies.* Baltimore: Johns Hopkins Press for the World Bank.

Bhagwati, Jagdish N. (1971), "The Generalized Theory of Distortions and Welfare," in Bhagwati et al. (eds), *Trade, Balance of Payments and Growth.* Amsterdam: North-Holland.

Bruno, Michael (1972), "Market Distortions and Gradual Reform," *Review of Economic Studies*, 39, 373–83.

Corden, W. M. (1974), *Trade Policy and Economic Welfare.* Oxford: Clarendon Press.

Hatta, Tatsuo (1977), "Market Distortions and Gradual Reforms," *Review of Economic Studies*, 9, 373–83.

Johnson, Harry G. (1965), "Optimal Trade Intervention in the Presence of Domestic Distortions," in Richard E. Caves et al., *Trade, Growth and the Balance of Payments.* Amsterdam: North-Holland.

Keesing, Donald B. (1979), "Trade Policy for Developing Countries," World Bank Staff Working Paper no. 353.

Lancaster, K. and Libsey, R. G. (1956), "The General Theory of Second Best," *Review of Economic Studies*, 24, 11–32.

Magee, S. P. (1973), "Factor Market Distortions, Production and Trade: A Survey," *Oxford Economic Papers*, 25, 1–43.

National Bureau of Economic Research (1974–8), *Foreign Trade Regimes and Economic Development*, 11 volumes. I, *Turkey*, by Anne O. Krueger (1974); II, *Ghana*, by J. Clark Leith (1974); III, *Israel*, by Michael Michaely (1975); IV, *Egypt*, by Bent Hansen and Karim Nashashibi (1975); V, *The Philippines*, by Robert Baldwin (1975); VI, *India*, by Jagdish N. Bhagwati and T. N. Srinivasan (1975); VII, *South Korea*, by C. R. Frank, Kwang Suk Kim, and L. E. Westphal (1975); VIII, *Chile*, by Jere R. Behrman (1976); IX, *Colombia*, by Carlos F. Diaz-Alejandro (1976); X, *Liberalization Attempts and Consequences*, by Anne O. Krueger (1978); XI, *Anatomy and Consequences of Exchange Control Regimes*, by Jagdish N. Bhagwati (1978). New York: Columbia University Press (vols I–XI) for NBER; Cambridge, Mass.: Ballinger (vols X–XI) for NBER.

National Bureau of Economic Research (1981–3), *Trade and Employment in Developing Countries*, 3 volumes. I, *Individual Studies* (1981); II, *Factor Supply and Substitution*, ed. Anne O. Krueger (1982); III, *Synthesis and Conclusions*, by Anne O. Krueger (1983). Chicago: University of Chicago Press for NBER.

Nelson, Joan M. (1983), "The Political Economy of Stabilization in Small, Low-income Trade-dependent Nations." Unpublished manuscript, Overseas Development Council.

OECD (1970), *Industry and Trade in Some Developing Countries*, 6 volumes. I, *Brazil*, by Joel Bergsman; II, *India*, by Jagdish N. Bhagwati and Padma Desai; III, *The Philippines and Taiwan*, by Hsing Mo-Huan, John H. Power and Gerardo P. Sicat; IV, *Mexico*, by Timothy King; V, *Pakistan*, by S. R. Lewis; VI, *A*

*Comparative Study*, by Ian Little, Tibor Scitovsky, and Maurice Scott. London: Oxford University Press for OECD.

Tyler, William G. (1976), *Manufactured Export Expansion and Industrialization in Brazil*. Tübingen: J. C. B. Mohr.

# Comment 1

## Bela Balassa

Michael Michaely defines liberalization policy as "actions leading to the contraction of effective protection rates," further adding that "the term 'liberalization policy' will be reserved here to actions concerned with protection generated by *commercial* policy." He explicitly excludes from his purview price controls and general subsidies to output, which, however, bear on effective protection rates; other policies are introduced largely as an afterthought; and, apart from the case of "economies suffering from inflation, perhaps in combination with acute balance of payments difficulties," no consideration is given to the need to reduce distortions outside the strictly defined trade area for the sake of the success of the trade liberalization effort.

The basic assumption underlying this approach is that protection-induced distortions among traded goods dominate in the developing countries, and hence liberalization policy should be concerned with removing these distortions. Further assumptions underlying the approach include full capacity utilization, the prevalence of inter-industry specialization, and the predominance of allocative gains from trade liberalization. I will consider the implications of removing these assumptions in the following.

A review of policy reforms undertaken by developing countries fails to show that import liberalization would have played a central role in these reforms — although Israel might have been an exception. Rather, exchange rate reform has had central place, mostly involving the devaluation of the exchange rate, the elimination of multiple rates, and the adoption of a crawling peg system. This fact points to the importance of distortions between traded and non-traded goods in the developing countries, distortions which need to be corrected in the framework of a liberalization program.

Exchange rate changes have in general been accompanied by policy measures in other areas, including price liberalization and the liberalization of capital and labor markets, in developing countries engaged in reform efforts. The practical experience of these countries indicates the need to proceed on a wide front in removing distortions in product and factor markets. Thus, one may object to the "compartmentalization" of measures in concentrating on the liberalization of trade to the neglect of other areas.

This is desirable not so much for the essentially negative second-best considerations referred to by Michaely, since in the developing countries reducing distortions in a single area will rarely be welfare-reducing, but for positive reasons as the measures taken in different areas will reinforce each other.

In particular, the full exploitation of the benefits of trade liberalization requires liberalizing domestic capital markets and vice versa. For one thing, the liberalization of domestic capital markets permits orienting new investments into export sectors that receive more favorable treatment as trade is liberalized. For another thing, the liberalization of trade is a precondition for the efficient use of financial resources upon the freeing of domestic capital markets.

A further question concerns the survivability of the reform effort. According to Michaely, "the minimization of the level of unemployment should . . . be of major importance" in this regard. He also claims that "for two reasons, the transfer of raw labor must be hindered. One reason is that at the wage rate expected at the expanding sector . . . labor would refuse to work . . . . The other reason, which has a time element attached to it, is the absence of complementary factors: employment of the available labor in the expanding sector requires the expansion of other factors — specific physical capital managerial capacity, and the like — which are not immediately available."

It is difficult to accept the proposition that the transfer of labor should be hindered even if the stated assumptions are fulfilled. But, in real-life situations in the developing countries, neither of the two assumptions is likely to hold. For one thing, there is no presumption that wages would be lower in expanding export activities than in contracting import-substituting activities. In fact, increases in profits in export activities as the bias against exports is reduced will permit paying higher wages. For another thing, industries in the developing countries are generally characterized by *excess capacity*, although Israel may again be an exception. This is explained by the fact that, given the limited size of markets in the developing countries, building ahead of demand is a rational action on the part of the firm.

The full capacity assumption also underlines Michaely's recommendation against undertaking export promotion in advance of import liberalization. In his view, "this sequence might lead to an inflationary pressure rather than to reallocation of resources." But Michaely also assumes that "contracting activities respond more quickly than potentially expanding activities." This means that changing incentives simultaneously for import-substituting and for export activities would result in increases in unemployment and in the deterioration of the balance of payments. To avoid such an eventuality, it would be desirable to start with export promotion, which will lead to increased exports in a situation of excess capacity, and to follow it with import liberalization.

This conclusion is strengthened in the case of an initial balance of payments deficit that is often observed in the developing countries. One

may then undertake a compensated devaluation, i.e., a devaluation accompanied by commensurate reductions in import protection, so that incentives to exports are increased while import prices remain unchanged. Alternatively, incentives to exports may be granted directly in the form of export subsidies in, for instance, the francophone African countries that cannot modify their exchange rates (Balassa, 1982).

Such a sequencing of policy reform in the trade field has been observed in most developing countries that have undertaken important reforms. Examples are Korea in the mid-1960s, Chile in the mid-1970s, and Turkey in the early 1980s. The experience of these countries shows the potential for export expansion from available capacity. In Turkey, for example, manufactured exports more than doubled in response to the incentives provided in 1981, a year of world recession.

The practical success of this sequencing may be explained by the possibilities for increasing capacity use in the developing countries. This will not permit avoiding the creation of unemployment that Michaely considers to be the principal bane of trade liberalization, but a compensated devaluation will lead to increased employment under conditions existing in these countries. Policy-makers in developing countries, then, may forgo providing the unemployment benefits and other forms of compensation Michaely recommends; nor would this be practicable, given the budgetary constraints under which developing countries operate. Thus, one cannot subscribe to the view that "the major relevant income maintenance policy is, in the present context, a scheme of unemployment benefits, perhaps augmented by special attention and extra benefits in the case of labour dismissed in the contracting sectors from which protection is removed."

At any rate, experience indicates that labor is not the principal obstacle to trade liberalization in the developing countries as Michaely seems to believe. Apart from the fact that — with appropriate sequencing — one can minimize unemployment, for better or for worse, labor is rarely an effective pressure group in developing countries, the major exception again being Israel. Thus, in developing countries where stabilization efforts have led to unemployment and a decline in real wages, this has not hindered the liberalization of trade.

Rather than labor, business interests have constituted the main obstacle to trade liberalization in the developing countries. In this connection, I recall discussions with Argentine businessmen one-and-a-half decades ago, when suggestions for export-promotion-cum-tariff reductions met with strong resistance. The opposition may be explained by the desire to avoid a decline of profits in import-substituting activities.

There is no cause for despair, however. While, under Michaely's assumptions of inter-industry specialization and predominantly allocative gains from trade liberalization, there would indeed be "a structural change — involving a shift of productive resources," and "in an activity from which protection is removed partially or totally, production is likely to decline," these assumptions may not reflect reality. For one thing, intra-industry specialization has considerable importance in the developing countries; for

another thing, improvements in $X$-inefficiencies are an important source of gains from trade liberalization in these countries.

Nearly two decades ago, I explained the absence of a decline in any of the industries of the member countries of the European Common Market following tariff reductions on intra-EEC trade by the prevalence of intra-industry specialization, under which adjustment involves changes in the product composition of individual industries rather than resource shifts between industries (Balassa, 1966). More recently, I have shown that intra-industry specialization has assumed increased importance in the developing countries, in particular in the newly industrializing country group (Balassa, 1983).

Also, as Bergsman (1970) first noted, improvements in $X$-inefficiencies represent a possible response to trade liberalization under conditions existing in the developing countries, where the limited size of national markets does not encourage competition. International comparisons indicate, in fact, that there is considerable scope of improvements in $X$-inefficiencies in these countries.

The described considerations have been recognized in the World Bank's structural adjustment programs for countries, such as the Philippines, whose industries are provided with financial resources to help them adjust to free trade. The adjustment may involve rationalizing operations, reducing product variety, and changing product composition, in particular by shifting to exports.

In the presence of intra-industry specialization and improvements in $X$-inefficiencies, then, the difficulties of adjustment will be less than Michaely assumes. Nevertheless, there is a learning process in regard to the adjustment process that needs to be taken into account in the phasing of reform measures. This, in turn, leads to the choice among alternative modes of trade liberalization.

The choice is not between immediate and gradual liberalization, as Michaely suggests, since "a single-stage policy of liberalization implementing it fully at once" hardly presents a practicable alternative for the developing countries. In fact, under circumstances existing in these countries, it would be unrealistic even to propose implementing a program that would lead to optimal policies within a period for which the reform measures can be determined — and announced — in advance. At the same time, it is of particular importance to announce the reform measures in advance, so as to give firms time for adjustment.

My own experience is that an action program of four to five years is sufficiently long to make major progress in reforming incentives and, at the same time, is sufficiently short for the decisions to implement the measures to be considered credible. At the end of this period, a second action program may be prepared that can conceivably lead to the adoption of optimal policies. The learning process that occurs during the first reform period may permit minimizing opposition to such a course of action.

A related question is the phasing of tariff reductions. Michaely considers three alternatives, including equiproportional tariff reductions, reductions

in protection rates by equally large absolute doses, and reducing above-ceiling protection rates to a ceiling that is lowered over time. There is a fourth alternative that is superior to these three, I believe. It involves tariff reductions on all products at differing rates, with higher tariffs being reduced more than lower ones. This alternative, used in the Tokyo Round of Multilateral Negotiations, has the advantage of including from the outset all activities in trade liberalization, and avoiding the possibility that only the water in the tariff is eliminated at the initial stages.

A further question relates to the elimination of quantitative import restrictions. Michaely suggests transforming quotas into equivalent tariffs. This will not be desirable, however, as once tariffs are raised it may be difficult to lower them again. A more appropriate procedure would be to liberalize quantitative import restrictions over time, setting as a target the elimination of these restrictions at the end of the first period of adjustment. Such phasing would permit firms to prepare for the elimination of quantitative restrictions without raising tariffs in the process.

In conclusion, emphasis should be given to the need for output-increasing policies in developing countries with unused capacity. Experience indicates that such policies can lead to rapid increases in exports, which, in turn, facilitate the task of import liberalization. At the same time, trade policies cannot be considered in isolation but should be integrated into an overall reform of development policies.

## REFERENCES

Balassa, Bela (1966), "Tariff Reductions and Trade in Manufacturing among the Industrial Countries," *American Economic Review*, LVI (56), 466–73.

Balassa, Bela (1982), "Structural Adjustment Policies in Developing Economies," *World Development*, January 10, 23–38.

Balassa, Bela (1983), "Industrial Prospects and Policies in Developing Countries," pp. 257–78, in *Reflections on a Troubled World Economy. Essays in Honor of Herbert Glersch*. London: Trade Policy Research Centre.

Bergsman, Joel (1970), *Brazil's Industrialization and Trade Policies*. London: Oxford University Press.

# Comment 2

## Armeane M. Choksi

Michaely offers us a useful and interesting approach to a taxonomy of issues which are fundamental to the problem being discussed. Much of his statement is based on a priori notions, but it does outline the major considerations that should be brought to the fore.

I would like to focus on three particular points, some of which Michaely has touched on above. One is the political dimensions of trade liberalization; the second is the relationship with other policies, which we have already discussed briefly; and the third refers to the credibility of policy change.

On the political side, it is often asked if our policies are so good, why are governments reluctant to pursue them? Clearly, governments must be maximizing an objective function that is very different from the one assumed in the analysis. I would hypothesize that this objective function would be constituted by some considerations of growth, some notion of what is a fairer income distribution, and some notion of their own welfare.

These three may not be equally weighted, and one does not know, in fact, how they are weighted — probably differently in different countries. I want to focus on the latter two considerations. One aspect of the fair income distribution concept is really identifying the winners and losers of policy change. The governments may genuinely misjudge the winners and losers, and this may explain their reticence in undertaking trade policy reform.

Another aspect may be that they simply place a very different weight on the winners and losers from what is implicitly assumed in conventional analysis. This presents us with the imperative of correctly identifying the winners and losers, particularly when we undertake our policy recommendations in various countries through Structural Adjustment Losses (SALs) or policy dialogue with countries; but, more importantly, we need to devise appropriate mechanisms for compensation, if they exist.

The second area, the one of the governments' own welfare, is the more interesting one, in my opinion. First, governments are understandably concerned with their own survivability. This may suggest that their own discount rate — contrary to the thrust of much traditional project evaluation literature — may well be much higher than the social discount rate. Consequently, the costs, which governments often fear, will manifest

themselves earlier than the benefits, and will be weighted much more than the benefits. Thus, you may have a situation where governments would not undertake a policy change if they felt their survivability was at stake — a government which is in power for only four to five years would clearly be leery of undertaking radical policy reforms. Examples abound in this area in various countries.

A second dimension of the same problem is the benefits and rents that would accrue to the bureaucrats in power. They themselves may suffer significant losses in income by eliminating a variety of trade restrictions; for example, in licensing, one can look to the domestic policy environment and find what Krueger has referred to previously as "rent-seeking activities."

How else can one explain regimes such as India, which essentially has had the same trade regime for over 35 years, until very recently. Some liberalization has been undertaken, but it is very little at the present moment; we will have to wait and see what happens there. My question is, is there really no feedback group in this sort of system? The policies of governments in power in India tend to be the same. Is there no feedback mechanism by which one learns from one's own historical experience, or from the experience of other countries? I leave it to the Fabian Socialists to use political ideology as a major motivating force behind the actions of the governments.

The second point I wish to address is the relationship with other policies. In many ways, I suspect that the success of trade liberalization will crucially hinge upon the nature of the related policies. In particular, as the case of Latin America has demonstrated, the effects of liberalization may well be negated by other policies — for example, stabilization measures, or exchange rate regimes in the presence of fixed real wages. If both stabilization and liberalization measures are needed, then they may, in fact, affect the sequence of the liberalization steps that could be undertaken. For example, one particular sequence may suggest itself under a stable economic environment, and an entirely different sequence may suggest itself if a stabilization program has been put in place.

Finally, one last point, which is on the credibility of policy change. Clearly, insufficient work has been done on the trade policy side, though much more has been done on the macro-policy environment. The real question that arises is, how are expectations of economic agents formed? To what extent have past policy measures actually been implemented, not just in trade, but also in other domestic policies? If, for example, a government has undertaken a series of domestic policy measures, then has retreated on them, and then announces a trade liberalization — would we expect the economic agents' behavior to be independent of government reversals on other policies?

Most of us would agree that the behavior of economic agents will depend quite crucially on past actions of the government, and most of our current analyses assumes complete credibility in government actions. This is not so in reality. Thus, the government has undertaken a variety of trade

liberalization measures; and there is already an attitude of "let's wait and see what happens" among various economic actors in the game. We have had a certain policy regime there for a long time, and knowing the political philosophy of the government, it may, in fact, retreat before very long. Consequently, the agents' behavior will be modified accordingly, and the announced liberalization measures may not have their intended impact.

# 4

# The Adjustment Process and the Timing of Trade Liberalization

*Michael Mussa*

## INTRODUCTION AND SUMMARY

This study is concerned with the appropriate time-path of commercial policy for a country that has already determined that a more liberal trade policy is in its long-run best interest. In contrast to the question of a country's best static trade policy, which has been extensively discussed in the economic literature, the subject of the present study has received scant attention.[1] However, unless one believes that most countries have already achieved their optimum trade policies, or that the best time-path of policy is always and unquestionably to move immediately to the best long-run policy, then the question of the appropriate time-path of commercial policy should be regarded as an interesting and important issue.

The approach that will be adopted in examining this issue is to assume that a country with a high level of protection granted to domestic industries that produce goods competing with imports has decided, for whatever reasons, that a more liberal commercial policy, with a much lower level of protection for import-competing domestic industries, is in its long-run best interest. To keep matters as simple as possible, it will usually be assumed that this country is sufficiently small that it has no influence on the world prices of the goods it trades, and that there are no distortions or externalities that make any policy other than complete free trade the optimal long-run policy for this country. The issue for policy-makers in this country is how to alter commercial policy over time in order to move in an optimal manner from a policy that grants substantial protection to import-competing industries to a policy of free trade.

---

[1] Among the papers that do examine the appropriate timing of trade liberalization or closely related issues are Lapan (1976), Leamer (1980), Mussa (1978, 1982b), Neary (1982), and Martin and Selowsky (1982).

This statement of the issue under study is not meant to suggest that the problem with respect to the optimal path of commercial policy is always how to move optimally to free trade. As is well known, there are circumstances in which a country's best long-run commercial policy is not free trade—especially when its economy is infected by distortions that have some relationship to international trade and that are beyond the scope of government policy. Rather, the suggestion is that, by considering a simple and well defined question, in the context of a well specified analytical structure, some principles will emerge that will have relevance in more general situations. Moreover, while the specific issue under study is the optimal path for commercial policy leading from protectionism to free trade, the principles that emerge in the examination of this issue will presumably have some relevance for related issues concerning domestic policies dealing with taxes, subsidies, price controls and other government interventions into the economic system. No attempt will be made here, however, to draw any conclusions for this broader range of issues from the present analysis.

To limit further the range of the present investigation, it will consider only the optimal path of commercial policy in a program of trade liberalization, and not the appropriate paths of other policies that would normally be used in conjunction with, and in support of, commercial policy in a sensible and comprehensive program of trade liberalization. Among the policies that will not be considered here are the monetary, fiscal, and exchange rate policies that would have to be pursued in conjunction with a more liberal commercial policy in order to ensure an adequate level of aggregate demand and to prevent, as far as possible, an increase in the general level of unemployment. Also not considered are policies of "adjustment assistance" that might be used to facilitate the movement of resources out of previously protected industries or to compensate the owners of these resources for income lost owing to the removal of protection. Further, the only commercial policy that will be considered explicitly is a tariff applied to imported products. No consideration will be given to the question of how to move from a complicated system of tariffs, quotas, export taxes and subsidies, content requirements, multiple exchange rates, and other policy interventions to a more uniform and liberal system of commercial policy.

Having described the limitations of this study, it is now appropriate to summarize the specific issues it does investigate and the results of this investigation. First, the study considers the effect of adjustment costs incurred in moving resources out of previously protected industries and into other activities on the appropriate time-path of trade liberalization. In the absence of such costs, the economy could adjust immediately to the new long-run equilibrium position consistent with its optimal long-run commercial policy. The question is, when instantaneous adjustment is not possible because of costs incurred in moving resources, is there a case for moving more gradually from a policy of protectionism to a liberal trade policy? The answer, in general, is no. Specifically, when private economic

agents who control the disposition of productive resources have rational expectations which allow them correctly to calculate the values of locating these resources in alternative activities, and when there are no distortions of the adjustment process that cause these agents to see private adjustment costs that differ from social adjustment costs, then the adjustment process subsequent to an immediate change of commercial policy to its long-run optimum will be socially efficient. By implication, a slowing down of the implementation of the policy of trade liberalization, which would reduce the privately perceived incentive to relocate resources outside of previously protected industries, would result in a less socially desirable adjustment path for the economy.

Second, when there are distortions affecting the adjustment process, the strong presumption in favor of an immediate move to the best long-run commercial policy as the best time-path of policy disappears. Unfortunately, for the variety of distortions that might reasonably be thought to affect the adjustment process, there is no general indication of how the time-path of commercial policy should deviate from the policy of an immediate move to the best long-run commercial policy. For some distortions, such as that which arises when economic agents hold static expectations concerning the incomes that will be earned by factors located in different activities, adjustment occurs too rapidly following an immediate move to the best long-run commercial policy. In these cases, there is an argument for gradualism in reducing the level of protection in order to slow the adjustment process. For other distortions, such as that created by taxes on factor incomes which affect the privately perceived benefits of factor movements, adjustment occurs too slowly following an immediate move to the best long-run commercial policy. In these cases it is desirable for the level of protection initially to be reduced to below its long-run optimal level (imports or exports should be subsidized if free trade is the best long-run policy) in order to increase the speed with which resources are moved out of the previously protected industries. Thus, no general case for gradualism emerges from consideration of the implications of distortions that might affect the adjustment process.

Third, a general case for gradualism in trade liberalization can be based on a desire to limit the income and wealth losses sustained by owners of resources initially employed in protected industries. For reasons that will be discussed, limitation of such losses may be a valid and important objective of policy-makers even if the owners of these resources are not among the poorer members of society (and even if their losses do not correspond to any social loss). Under reasonable assumptions about the structure of the economic system, it can be shown that a more gradual policy of trade liberalization moderates the income and wealth losses sustained by owners of resources initially employed in protected industries, though at some cost in terms of the efficiency of the economy's adjustment path. The issue for policy-makers concerned with limiting the losses of these resource owners is to make the appropriate trade-off between limiting those losses and ensuring reasonable efficiency of the adjustment process.

Among the factors influencing the nature of this trade-off are the degree to which resources employed in protected industries are specific to those industries. When adjustment must occur primarily through depreciation and attrition, little may be gained in terms of the efficiency of the adjustment process by pushing trade liberalization more rapidly than the rate required to prevent new capital from being invested and new workers from training for jobs in those industries.

Fourth and finally, the appropriate time-path of commercial policy in a program of trade liberalization may be influenced by the possibility that resources employed in protected industries may become unemployed as a result of reductions in the level of protection. Because of the difficulty in specifying a satisfactory and acceptable model of why resources become unemployed, the analysis of this issue in the present study is based on an assumed reduced-form relationship which relates the rate at which resources are moved out of protected industries to the amount of unemployment experienced by those continuing to seek employment in these industries. If one accepts this presumption as valid, the optimal path of commercial policy is that which balances the marginal social cost of increased unemployment of resources in protected industries (which results in a loss of output) against the marginal social benefit of stimulating more rapid movement of resources out of these industries. The time-path of the level of protection that maintains this balance depends critically on the shape of the reduced-form relationship between the rate of movement of resources and the level of unemployment. With a proportional relationship, it turns out that the optimal long-run commercial policy is not free trade, because when the economy gets sufficiently close to its free trade equilibrium, the marginal social benefit of moving additional resources out of protected industries becomes very small and ultimately smaller than the social cost of output lost because of unemployment of these resources. Along the path of convergence to this optimal long-run commercial policy, however, the level of protection exhibits peculiar "overshooting" behavior. Specifically, in the optimal program of trade liberalization, the level of protection is initially reduced to below its long-run optimal level (and perhaps to below zero) and is subsequently raised back to this optimal long-run level. This peculiarity disappears when the reduced-form relationship between the rate of resource reallocation and the level of unemployment is not proportional, but the rate of resource reallocation relative to the level of unemployment becomes large at low levels of unemployment. It is argued that this is reasonable if decisions about the industries of employment for newly produced capital and workers entering the labor force are strongly influenced by relatively small differences in expected earnings between industries. If this argument is generally correct, then the time-path of commercial policy that trades off appropriately the marginal social cost of increased unemployment against the marginal social benefit of more rapid adjustment will be a path along which the level of protection is gradually reduced to its long-run optimal level.

# I ADJUSTMENT COSTS AND THE TIMING OF TRADE LIBERALIZATION

If productive resources could move instantaneously and without cost among alternative uses, and product and factor prices could adjust immediately to clear markets, there would be no interesting issue concerning the optimal timing for a policy of trade liberalization. In that case the best policy would be to move immediately to the optimal long-run commercial policy.

In real world economies, of course, productive resources cannot be moved instantaneously among alternative uses, and movement of many resources is a costly activity in terms of direct or opportunity costs. Therefore, the adjustment to any sudden change in economic conditions will be spread out over time. Moreover, during the period of adjustment following a sudden trade liberalization, the value of final output produced in the economy will be reduced to the extent that costs are incurred in the adjustment process. Because these costs tend to be higher the more rapidly adjustment takes place, the system should not adjust too rapidly to changes in economic conditions. To some, this might suggest slowing the process of trade liberalization in order to limit the costs that the economy incurs during the adjustment.

The main purpose of this section is to demonstrate that this intuitively plausible notion is not, in general, correct. Even though costs rise with the pace of adjustment, it is not generally desirable to slow the pace of liberalization in order to limit the costs of adjusting to a new commercial policy regime. Provided that the economic agents who control the allocation of resources perceive private costs and benefits from resource movements which correspond to true social costs and benefits, they will make the socially correct decisions concerning the pace of adjustment. Therefore, the case for gradualism in implementing a policy of trade liberalization depends on the social efficiency of private decisions on resource movement (Section II), on income redistribution effects of sudden liberalization (Section III), or on unemployment effects of liberalization (Section IV).

## A Two-sector Economy with Adjustment Costs

To develop the main proposition concerning the influence of adjustment costs on the appropriate timing of trade liberalization, it suffices to consider a relatively simple model of a two-sector economy. It is assumed that the output of the protected sector, $X$, and the output of the rest of the economy, $Z$, are produced in accord with standard, neoclassical, constant-returns-to-scale production functions, using two inputs, labor and capital:

$$X = F(L_X, K_X) \tag{1}$$
$$Z = G(L_Z, K_Z). \tag{2}$$

Labor is assumed to be freely and instantaneously mobile between $X$ and $Z$, but capital (which presumably includes human capital) is assumed to be specific, at least at a moment of time, to the industry where it is located. This is intended as a convenient simplifying assumption, not as a description of a real-world economy.

An essential element of the present model is the specification of the technology of the adjustment process for the redistribution of existing capital and for the construction and allocation of new capital. For analytical simplicity, it is convenient to assume that these two adjustment activities are being pursued separately and that each utilizes only labor in its production process. Formally, it is assumed that the amounts of labor used in capital movement, $L_M$, and in investment in new capital, $L_I$, are determined by

$$L_M = \psi(|M|) \qquad \psi(0) = 0, \psi' > 0, \psi'' > 0 \tag{3}$$

$$L_I = \phi(|I|), \qquad \phi(0) = 0, \phi' > 0, \phi'' > 0 \tag{4}$$

where $M$ is the rate of movement of old capital out of $Z$ and into $X$, and $I$ is the rate of production of new capital, which may be allocated to either industry to replace depreciating old capital or to add to the industry's capital stock. Taking account of movement of old capital, allocation of new capital, and depreciation of old capital, the rules governing the rates of change of the capital stocks in the two industries are given by

$$\dot{K}_X = M + I_X - \delta K_X \tag{5}$$

$$\dot{K}_Z = -M + I_Z - \delta K_Z \tag{6}$$

where $I_X \geqq 0$ and $I_Z \geqq 0$ are the amounts of new capital allocated to $X$ and $Z$, respectively, subject to the constraint

$$I_X + I_Z = I \tag{7}$$

and where $\delta$ is the depreciation rate of capital, which is assumed to be the same for both industries.

Aside from the assumption that capital movement and investment in new capital use only labor as a factor of production, this specification captures key elements of the processes governing adjustments of physical and human capital in actual economies. Many types of existing plant and equipment can be transferred to alternative uses, but usually at some cost for restructuring, remodeling, retooling, or relocation. In addition, physical capital may be transferred to alternative uses by allowing existing plant and equipment to depreciate and by relocating the new capital that corresponds to such depreciation. Similarly, it is possible to retrain and relocate workers who have already acquired substantial human capital specific to a particular industry. It is also possible to achieve reallocation of human capital by attrition and by training new workers in skills required for other industries.

Given the specification of the technologies for producing the final outputs $X$ and $Z$ and of the adjustment process, we may address the question of the optimal timing of trade liberalization by considering the policy that would be adopted by a social planner whose objective is to maximize the welfare of a representative consumer in the economy. Assuming for simplicity that the economy is small and takes the world relative price of $X$ in terms of $Z$, denoted by $P$, and that the world rate of interest, $r$, is given, the objective of this social planner may be stated as the maximization of the present discounted value of the economy's final output, $V$, as defined by

$$V = \int_0^\infty [P\,F(L_X, K_X) + G(L_Z, K_Z)] \exp(-rt)\, dt \tag{8}$$

subject to the technology of the adjustment process specified in (3)–(7), and subject to the overall employment constraint,

$$L_X + L_Z + L_M + L_I = \bar{L} \tag{9}$$

where $\bar{L}$ is the fixed supply of freely mobile labor.[2] The initial condition for this dynamic optimization problem is determined by the initial amounts of capital located in the $X$ and $Z$ industries, $K_X(0)$ and $K_Z(0)$. Since the initial state of the economy is assumed to be the long-run equilibrium position for the economy before trade liberalization when the $X$ industry was protected by an import tariff, it is correct to assume that $K_X(0)$ exceeds the equilibrium size of the capital stock in $X$ that is appropriate under free trade, $K_X^*$, and that $K_Z(0)$ is less than the equilibrium size of the capital stock in $Z$ that is appropriate under free trade, $K_Z^*$.[3]

Without going into formal details of the analysis of the planner's optimization problem (which are discussed in the appendix to this chapter), it is possible to explain the economic principles governing the planner's behavior. The world market price of $X$ in terms of $Z$, $P$, tells the planner the correct way to value output of $X$ in terms of output of $Z$. In addition, the planner needs to calculate a shadow price for a unit of capital located

[2] Since the optimum policy is to move immediately to free trade, we may disregard the consumption distortion cost of tariffs. We could treat the case where the interest rate is endogenously determined by equilibrium in the domestic credit market (with no international capital mobility); this would complicate the analysis without altering its basic conclusions. If the country faced a rising foreign borrowing cost schedule, the planner would need to tax foreign borrowing at a rate making the privately perceived cost of borrowing correspond to the true social cost. With this tax in place there would be no reason for gradualism.

[3] In the present model, the long-run stock of capital, $K_X + K_Z$, is not fixed. It is possible to show that, if $X$ production is relatively labor-intensive, the long-run stock of capital will rise owing to the removal of protection; whereas it will decline if $X$ production is relatively capital-intensive.

in $X$ (denoted by $\mu_X$), a shadow price for a unit of capital located in $Z$ (denoted by $\mu_Z$), and a shadow wage rate for a unit of mobile labor (denoted by $\omega$). The appropriate shadow price for units of capital located in the two industries are the present discounted values of the value of the marginal product of capital in the respective industries, adjusted for the rate of depreciation of capital:

$$\mu_X(t) = \int_t^\infty P F_L[L_X(s), K_X(s)] \exp\left[-(r + \delta)(s - t)\right] ds \tag{10}$$

$$\mu_Z(t) = \int_t^\infty G_L[L_Z(s), K_Z(s)] \exp\left[-(r+\delta)(s-t)\right] ds. \tag{11}$$

Given the socially correct prices for output of $X$ and for units of capital located in the two industries, the planner sets the shadow wage rate to achieve the socially appropriate distribution of labor among $X$ production, $Z$ production, movement of existing capital, and production of new capital. The correct amount of labor to employ in $X$ is the amount for which the value of the marginal product of labor in $X$, $P F_L(L_X, K_X)$, is equal to the shadow wage rate, $\omega$. Taking account of constant returns to scale in production of $X$, this amount of labor can be expressed as $K_X l_X^d (\omega/P)$, where $l_X^d (\omega/P)$ is the labor demand function of an $X$ producer with one unit of capital. Similarly, the correct amount of labor to employ in $Z$ is determined by the requirement that the value of the marginal product of labor in $Z$, $G_L(L_Z, K_Z)$, equal $\omega$, and this is equal to $K_Z l_Z^d (\omega)$, where $l_Z^d(\omega)$ is the labor demand function of a $Z$ producer with one unit of capital.

The correct amount of labor to employ in moving existing capital is determined by the requirement that the marginal social cost of this activity must equal the marginal social benefit. The marginal social cost of capital movement is equal to the shadow wage rate (which measures the social cost of a unit of labor) multiplied by the amount of labor required for a marginal increment in the rate of capital movement, $\psi'(|M|)$. As shown in figure 4.1, the marginal social cost of capital movement, for a given $\omega_0$, is an increasing function of the rate of capital movement, $|M|$. The marginal benefit of capital movement is equal to the absolute value of the difference between the shadow prices of capital in the two industries, with the sign of the difference determining the direction of capital movement. Thus, as illustrated in Figure 4.1, when $\mu_X = \mu_{X0} < \mu_{Z0} = \mu_Z$ and $\omega = \omega_0$, the appropriate rate of capital movement is $|M|$ and the appropriate direction of capital movement is out of $X$ and into $Z$. Applying this condition more generally, we determine that the appropriate amount of labor to employ in capital movement is given by

$$L_M^d (\omega/|\mu_X - \mu_Z|) = \psi[\psi'^{-1}(\mu_X - \mu_Z/\omega)]. \tag{12}$$

The correct amount of labor to employ in producing new capital is determined by the requirement that the marginal social cost of investment

*Trade Liberalization*

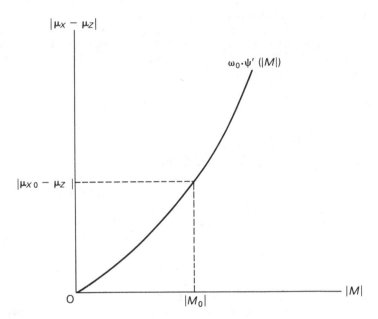

FIGURE 4.1 Determination of the rate of capital movement

in new capital must equal the marginal social benefit. The marginal social cost of new investment is equal to the shadow wage rate multiplied by the amount of labor required for an increment to investment $\phi'(I)$. Since it does not make economic sense to locate any new capital in the industry with a lower shadow value of capital, the marginal benefit of investment in new capital is determined by the shadow price of capital for the industry with the higher shadow price of capital; that is, by $\bar{\mu} = $ maximum of $\mu_X$ and $\mu_Z$. As illustrated in figure 4.2, therefore, the correct amount of investment in new capital is determined by the condition that the marginal cost of such investment equal $\bar{\mu}$. From this condition, we determine that the correct amount of labour to employ in producing new capital is given by

$$L_I^d(\omega/\bar{\mu}) = \phi[\phi'^{-1}(\bar{\mu}/\omega)]. \tag{13}$$

Adding together the amounts of labor allocated to its four different uses, it follows that the total amount of labor allocated by the social planner is given by

$$L^d(\omega, \mu_X, \mu_Z, K_X, K_Z, P) \tag{14}$$

$$= K_X \ell_X^d(\omega/P) + K_Z \ell_Z^d(\omega) + L_M^d(\omega/|\mu_X - \mu_Z|) + L_I^d[\omega/\max(\mu_X, \mu_Z)].$$

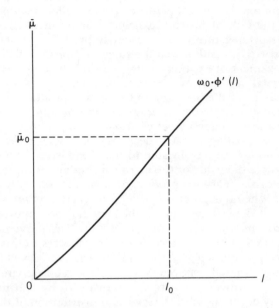

FIGURE 4.2 Determination of the rate of investment in new capital

The constraint that the total amount of labor allocated must equal the available supply, that is, that

$$L^d(\omega, \mu_X, \mu_Z, K_X, K_Z, P) = \bar{L}, \tag{15}$$

determines the appropriate value of the shadow wage rate, given the shadow prices of capital for the two industries, the amounts of capital in the two industries, and the relative output price.

With the determination of the shadow wage rate, every aspect of the planner's optimal behavior at a moment of time is completely determined. Specifically, the allocation of labor among its four uses determines the outputs of $X$ and $Z$, the rate of movement of existing capital between industries, and the rate of production of new capital. The sign of the difference between $\mu_X$ and $\mu_Z$ determines the direction of movement of existing capital and the allocation of all new capital to the industry with the higher shadow price of capital.

Starting from the long-run equilibrium position of the economy when the $X$ industry is protected by a tariff, the path that the economy will traverse under the guidance of the social planner may be described as follows. Since, at the starting point of the economy, the capital stock in $X$ is too large and the capital stock in $Z$ is too small, the initial shadow price for a unit of capital in $X$, $\mu_X(0)$, is less than the initial shadow price

for a unit of capital in $Z$, $\mu_Z(0)$. This implies that, at the starting point along the economy's optimal path, the planner allocates a positive amount of labor to the task of moving existing capital out of $X$ and into $Z$. In addition, the planner directs that all newly produced capital be located in the $Z$ industry. The result is that the stock of capital in $X$ declines through outward movement of existing capital and through depreciation, while the stock of capital in $Z$ grows because of inward movement of existing capital, and because the total amount of newly produced capital allocated to this industry exceeds depreciation of existing capital. As $K_X$ declines and $K_Z$ rises, the differential between $\mu_X$ and $\mu_Z$ narrows and the rate of movement of existing capital declines. All newly produced capital, however, continues to be allocated to the $Z$ industry. Ultimately, a point is reached where the value of the marginal product of capital in $X$ is equal to the value of the marginal product of capital in $Z$, so that $\mu_X$ becomes equal to $\mu_Z$. When this point is reached, the economy will not, in general, have yet reached the long-run equilibrium position appropriate for free trade. Subsequent adjustment does not involve any movement of existing capital out of $X$ and into $Z$, since devoting resources to this activity is not optimal when $\mu_X$ equals $\mu_Z$. Rather, adjustment is achieved by distributing newly produced capital between $X$ and $Z$ in an appropriate manner, with the share of investment going to $X$ gradually rising and the share going to $Z$ gradually declining until the level and distribution of the capital stock reach the long-run equilibrium level and distribution of capital appropriate for free trade.

It should be noted that, for the planner to move the economy along this optimal adjustment path, he must calculate the appropriate time-paths for the shadow prices of units of capital in the two industries. At any given date, these shadow prices depend on the present discounted value of the marginal product of capital in the respective industries. To know what these shadow prices should be, the planner must know the future course of the amounts of labor and capital that will be employed in the two industries. This of course depends on the future course of the shadow prices for units of capital in the two industries. Hence, to move the economy along its optimal adjustment path, the planner must solve a complex dynamic optimization problem in which he concomitantly determines the appropriate paths for the shadow prices of capital in the two industries, for the amounts of labor and capital employed in these industries, and the amounts of labor allocated to movement of existing capital and the production of new capital.

### Optimal Commercial Policy with Private Agents

When decisions about the allocation of resources are made by private economic agents rather than by an omnipotent social planner, government policy influences the adjustment path of the economy only indirectly, by affecting the economic conditions that influence the decisions of these agents. The issue then is how the government should vary the level of

protection over time in order to induce private economic agents to follow a socially optimal adjustment path. If there are no distortions in the economic system other than the pre-existing protection granted to import-competing industries, and if private economic agents have rational expectations about future economic conditions, it can be shown that the optimal policy is to reduce the level of protection immediately to its long-run optimal level and allow private agents to adjust as they see fit. In particular, for the small country described in the preceding subsection, the optimal policy is to cut the import tariff rate immediately to zero and hold it there permanently.

To understand why an immediate move to free trade induces private economic agents to pursue a socially optimal adjustment path, it is useful to consider how such agents, acting exclusively in their own private interest, determine the adjustment path of the economy. Economic agents who own units of capital in the $X$ and $Z$ industries must decide at each moment of time whether they wish to retain their capital in its present industry or pay the cost of moving it to the other industry. They must also decide on the amount of new capital they wish to purchase to replace capital that is depreciating or to add to their stock of capital, and on the industry in which to locate this new capital. To make these decisions, these agents need to calculate the value of a unit of capital located in each of the two industries. Since there are no distortions in the economy, these agents face the same interest rate as the social planner, and income from each unit of capital is equal to the value of the marginal product of capital in the industry where the capital is located, adjusted for the physical depreciation of capital at the rate $\delta$. By the assumption of rationality of expectations, the path that these agents will expect the value of the marginal product of capital to follow in each industry will correspond to the path calculated by the social planner. Hence, the values that private agents will assign to units of capital located in the two industries will correspond to the shadow prices, $\mu_X$ and $\mu_Z$, calculated by the social planner, as defined in equations (10) and (11). Indeed, if there were a market in which economic agents could trade claims to units of capital located in the two industries, $\mu_X$ and $\mu_Z$ would be the market prices of these claims.

Given the values that agents assign to units of capital in the two industries, the benefit that they will realize from moving an existing unit of capital from $X$ to $Z$ must be the difference between $\mu_X$ and $\mu_Z$. This difference determines the price that owners of capital will be willing to pay to move capital out of $X$ and into $Z$. In figure 4.1, this fact is presented by showing a horizontal demand curve for the service of movement of capital at a height equal to $|\mu_{X0} - \mu_{Z0}|$. The supply curve of producers of this service must correspond (under the assumed absence of all distortions) to the marginal cost curve for producing this service, as determined by the wage rate that producers of this service must pay for the labor they employ, multiplied by the amount of labor required to produce a marginal increment in this service. It follows that, if the wage rate paid by producers of this service is the same as the shadow wage rate used by

the social planner, the amount of capital movement determined by private agents will correspond to that determined by the social planner. Obviously, the direction of movement is also the same.

With respect to investment in new capital, it is clear that private agents will direct all such investment into the industry with a higher value of capital, since to do otherwise would imply a loss relative to what they could achieve by making the socially correct decision concerning the distribution of newly produced capital. It follows that the value that private agents will assign to newly produced capital is the value of a unit of capital in the industry where capital has its highest value: that is, the same value $\bar{\mu} = \max (\mu_X, \mu_X)$ used by the social planner to determine the benefit of investment in new capital. The value to capital owners of newly produced capital is the demand price that faces suppliers of such capital, as represented by the horizontal demand curve at height $\bar{\mu}_0$ in figure 4.2. The supply curve for new capital corresponds to the marginal cost curve for its producers, as determined by the wage rate multiplied by the amount of labor required to increase new capital production by a marginal unit. It follows that, if the wage rate facing producers of new capital is the same as the shadow wage rate used by the social planner, then the level and distribution of new capital production determined by private agents will be the same as that determined by the social planner.

The wage rate that faces suppliers of new capital, and of the service of capital movement in the economy controlled by the behavior of private agents, must be the same as the shadow wage rate used by the social planner, because the condition of labor market equilibrium in the privately controlled economy is the same as condition (15) which the planner uses to determine the appropriate value of the shadow wage rate. Specifically, since labor is freely mobile between its four productive uses, it is clear that maximizing behavior by workers who supply a fixed amount of labor, $\bar{L}$, will compel the wage rate to be the same for all demanders of labor. The demand for labor in each of these uses is determined in the privately controlled economy by the same functional relationship that the planner uses to allocate labor to each use. Producers of $X$ and $Z$ each demand labor up to the point where the value of the marginal product of labor in their respective activities (using $|\mu_X - \mu_Z|$ as the price of the service of capital movement and $\bar{\mu} = \max (\mu_X, \mu_Z)$ as the price of new capital) is equal to the market wage rate. Since the sum of these four demand functions yields the aggregate labor demand function defined in (13), and since the supply of labor $\bar{L}$ is the same as for the social planner, it follows that the market equilibrium wage rate implied by the behavior of individual economic agents is the same as the shadow wage rate used by the social planner. This, in turn, guarantees that all aspects of the behavior of the economy are the same, whether controlled by individual economic agents or by the social planner.

If the tariff imposed on imported units of $X$ were not immediately reduced to zero at the start of the process of trade liberalization, the economy would not converge to its appropriate long-run equilibrium

position along the socially optimal adjustment path. This is so because, with a positive tariff remaining on imports of $X$, domestic producers of $X$ will see a price for their output that exceeds its true social value.[4] Consequently, they will employ more labor in producing $X$ than is socially desirable. Moreover, because the market price of domestically produced $X$ is kept artificially high by a tariff, owners of capital in $X$ will see a value of the marginal product of this capital which exceeds the true social value, and will calculate a value for a unit of this capital exceeding its true social value. This will slow the rate at which existing capital is moved out of $X$ and into $Z$. In addition, because the increased use of labor in $X$ comes partly at the expense of labor that should be used in $Z$, the value of the marginal product of capital in $Z$ will be reduced to below its socially appropriate level, resulting in a reduction in the value assigned to a unit of capital located in $Z$. Since the value of a unit of capital in $Z$ is the demand price for new capital that determines the rate of production of new capital, this reduction in the value of a unit of capital in $Z$ implies that adjustment through production of new capital and its location in $Z$ will proceed at less than the socially optimal rate.[5] Thus, any policy of *gradually* reducing the tariff rate to zero, rather than reducing it all at once, results in a suboptimal adjustment path.

Even if the assumptions about the structure of the economy or about the technology of the adjustment process were modified, the basic conclusion of the present discussion would not be modified. In the absence of distortions other than protection, and with the rationality of expectations on the part of private agents, immediate cutting of the level of protection to zero will be the optimal path of commercial policy (for a small country). The reason is that this policy provides private economic agents with the correct price signals upon which to base their individual economic decisions. These are the signals that make the privately perceived costs and benefits of any action correspond to true social costs and benefits and, hence, lead individual economic agents to behave in a way consistent with the maximization of social welfare.

This proposition, of course, is not new in economics. It dates back to Adam Smith's description of the mechanism of the "invisible hand," through which the forces of competition compel individual agents who seek only their own interest simultaneously to serve the social interest. The main point of the present discussion is that the validity of this proposition is not suspended in an economic system where the movement of resources

---

[4] In addition, so long as any tariff remains in effect, there is a consumption distortion loss that results from this tariff.

[5] Even if there is no immediate reduction in the tariff rate but only an announcement of future reductions, the value of a unit of capital in $X$ will fall relative to the value of a unit of capital in $Z$. Thus, the effect of any program of trade liberalization should be to make the value of a unit of capital in $Z$ the effective determinant of the demand price for additions to the capital stock.

among alternative uses is a time-consuming and costly activity and where the agents who control the disposition of these resources must solve dynamic rather than static optimization problems.

## II  DISTORTIONS OF THE ADJUSTMENT PROCESS

A key assumption in demonstrating the desirability of free trade as a country's optimal static commercial policy is that its economy is free of distortions other than those which would be introduced by some other commercial policy. When this assumption is invalid because the country has market power in some of its exports or imports, or because there are externalities associated with producing or consuming these products, or because of other relevant distortions, free trade is not, in general, the best static commercial policy. Similar reasoning suggests that, while an immediate move to a country's best long-run commercial policy may be the best time-path in the absence of distortions affecting the adjustment process, it is not necessarily the best path when such distortions exist. However, in contrast to the theory of static commercial policy, where we have some understanding of the distortions that would justify specific divergences from free trade, we have as yet little understanding of the distortions that would justify gradualism in moving commercial policy to its long-run optimum. Indeed, nothing rules out the possibility that the optimal path in an economy with excessive protection and other distortions would be to reduce the level of protection initially to below its long-run optimal level in order to speed the movement of resources out of previously protected activities.

The purpose of this section is to examine the implications of a variety of distortions that might affect the adjustment process for the optimal path of commercial policy. For simplicity, we will focus on the case of a small country where the optimal long-run commercial policy is free trade, but where imports are initially restricted by a tariff. The analysis is based on the model presented in the preceding section. No attempt will be made, however, rigorously to demonstrate the conclusions of the present analysis. Rather, the discussion will explain the economic rationale for these con-clusions and suggest their application. To limit the range of discussion, we will consider only the implications of distortions of the adjustment process for the optimal path of the tariff rate, and will ignore the importance of other complementary policies that might be used to offset these dis-tortions and obtain a more efficient adjustment path. (Some of these policies are examined in Mussa, 1982b.)

### Distortions Arising from the Tax System

One important cause of distortions in the adjustment process arises from taxes imposed on incomes and products. Consider a general income tax on all factor incomes, or on income from capital. Such a tax distorts the

adjustment process in that it reduces the privately perceived benefit of adjustment to below its true social benefit (i.e., the difference between the present discounted value of the marginal product of capital in the two industries). When income from capital is not taxed, and private capital owners have rational expectations and face the same interest rate as the social planner, the privately perceived benefit of capital movement will correspond to the true social benefit. However, when the income of capital is taxed, private capital owners will see only the present discounted value of the after-tax difference in returns to capital in the two industries as the benefit they will receive from costly investments in moving capital out of the previously protected industry. Accordingly, if the tariff is immediately reduced to zero in the program of trade liberalization, adjustment through the movement of existing capital would proceed at less than the socially optimal rate. Moreover, taxation of income from capital, which reduces the present discounted value of the after-tax return to capital in both industries, reduces the aggregate level of investment in new capital and hence slows the process of adjustment through location of new capital in the $Z$ industry. If the tax on factor incomes or on income from capital cannot be eliminated or offset by an investment tax credit, it is surely not desirable to slow the process of trade liberalization since adjustment is already too slow. If anything, it would be desirable to reduce the tariff rate initially to below its optimal long-run level (i.e., to subsidize imports) in order to stimulate adjustment.

The distortionary effect of product taxes is not as clear as that of income taxes since the effect clearly depends on the particular products being taxed and on their role in the adjustment process. If products used in moving existing capital among industries are heavily taxed, then the privately perceived cost of adjustment through movement of existing capital will exceed the true social cost, and adjustment will occur too slowly. On the other hand, if these products are subsidized, adjustment will occur too rapidly. The case for gradualism would be strengthened if the latter form of distortion were more important than the former.

## Distortions Arising in the Capital Market

Another important source of distortions is the capital market. One such distortion is the divergence between the discount rate used by private capital owners and that used by the social planner. The usual assumption is that the social discount rate is typically lower than the private discount rate. If so, then the privately perceived benefit of moving existing capital or investing in new capital will be below the true social benefit. This means that adjustment in response to an immediate reduction of the tariff rate to zero will proceed at less than the socially optimal rate. To correct this problem it would clearly not be desirable to slow down the process of trade liberalization. If anything, it would be desirable to spur adjustment by initially subsidizing imports and to reduce this subsidy gradually as the economy approaches its long-run equilibrium.

In many countries, capital markets are also distorted because credit is not allocated among firms in an efficient manner through freely functioning credit markets. If existing firms in the protected industry receive allocations of cheap credit they would lose if they shifted their activities to another industry, or if new entrants to expanding industries lack adequate access to credit at interest rates that reflect its social cost, then the process of adjustment subsequent to an immediate move to free trade would be impeded. If this situation cannot be remedied by altering the policies that control the allocation of credit, it might be desirable to increase the incentive for more rapid adjustment by initially subsidizing imports. Such a policy could easily backfire, however, if the financial institutions that have granted credit to the previously protected sector feel compelled to continue to extend, or even expand, credit to these enterprises rather than write off bad loans. In this situation, a more gradual reduction in the level of protection might be desirable to allow credit to be withdrawn from firms in the protected industries and reallocated to firms in expanding industries.

Capital markets would also be distorted if the country as a whole faced a rising supply schedule for foreign loans, but individual enterprises believed that they faced a horizontal supply curve for their own foreign borrowings at an interest rate equal to the average interest rate for the country as a whole. To correct this distortion, the government should tax all foreign borrowing at a rate that makes the private cost of such borrowing correspond to its true social cost. In the absence of such a tax, the private discount rate will be less than the social discount rate, implying that the privately perceived benefit of adjustment exceeds the true social benefit. To retard what would otherwise be an overly rapid adjustment to free trade (and an excessive accumulation of foreign debt), it would be appropriate to reduce the tariff rate gradually to zero, rather than do so all at once.

### Distortions Arising from Errors in Expectations

To determine the benefit of moving capital out of the previously protected industry and investing new capital in the other industry, private capital owners must calculate the values of units of capital located in these two industries. Such calculations are necessarily based on expectations concerning the future paths of the earnings of units of capital located in these industries. If these expectations are wrong, private capital owners will assign incorrect values to units of capital and the adjustment process will be distorted. For example, if capital owners had "static expectations" under which they expected that current returns to capital in each industry would persist indefinitely, then the privately calculated value of moving capital out of $X$ and into $Z$ would exceed the true social value. Adjustment through movement of existing capital would proceed more rapidly than is socially optimal. To correct this problem, it would be appropriate to slow the rate at which the tariff is reduced in order to make the privately

perceived benefit of capital movement correspond more closely to its true social benefit.

There is no reason to believe, however, that capital owners will always expect that current differences between returns to capital will persist into the indefinite future. They might recognize that, as new investment is concentrated in other industries, the differential between the returns to capital in these other industries and in the previously protected industry will diminish. If the rate at which they expect this differential to diminish is greater than the rate at which it would diminish (along the socially optimal path), then private capital owners will calculate too small a benefit from capital movement and adjustment will proceed too slowly. To correct this problem, it would be appropriate to subsidize imports initially in order to stimulate more rapid adjustment.

A specific problem concerning false expectations arises in regard to expectations concerning the future course of the government's commercial policy. The government might reduce the tariff rate to zero and announce its commitment to a continuing policy of free trade, but private agents may not believe that the policy will persist. Unless private agents perceive an offsetting possibility that the government might go beyond a policy of free trade and subsidize imports (or exports), the value that they will assign to moving capital out of the previously protected industry will be less than the social value of such movement. For this reason, adjustment to the new policy of free trade will proceed at less than the socially optimal rate. To correct this problem, the government might wish to subsidize imports initially, which will stimulate rapid adjustment both by its direct effect on the actual returns to capital in the two industries and by its indirect effect of convincing private capital owners of the possibility of such an action in the future.

The difficulty with this solution is that the government might be compelled by political pressures to modify its policy, or might be replaced by another government so inclined. The likelihood that political pressures will lead to a policy reversal may be related to the aggressiveness of the liberalization policy. Thus, a policy of an immediate move to free trade might be thought so unlikely to survive that it would actually restrain adjustment more than a policy of gradual liberalization.[6] On the other hand, a policy of very gradual liberalization might be regarded as such a concession of political weakness and indecision on the part of the government that it would have no credibility with private agents and would stimulate little or no adjustment. A balance must be struck between a

---

[6] If a rapid reversal of a policy of trade liberalization is anticipated, there may be a surge of imports (particularly capital goods and consumer durables) as consumers attempt to take advantage of what they regard as a temporary opportunity to buy these goods at low prices. Such a surge, in turn, makes it more difficult to sustain a policy of liberalization.

policy that is so aggressive that reversal is anticipated, and a policy that is so feeble that it lacks credibility.

### Distortions Arising from Monopoly and Monopsony Behavior

The exercise of monopoly and monopsony power distorts the economic system by creating divergences between the effective price or cost of a product or factor to its purchaser and the marginal cost to its supplier. Exercise of such power should normally result in a slowing of the adjustment process to less than its socially optimal rate. If this problem could not be addressed directly, it might provide an argument for a policy of reducing the level of protection initially to less than its optimal steady-state level in order to induce more rapid adjustment. However, in the absence of specific evidence of the importance of the monopoly and monopsony behavior, this seems like a rather weak reed upon which to base a general argument for an excessively aggressive path of commercial policy.

Another circumstance in which the exercise of market power would impede the adjustment process is if firms, workers, or labor unions in the industries that benefited by liberalization were able to impede the entry of new firms and new capital into these industries. Suppose, for example, that a labor union in the Z industry of the model described is able to prevent entry of any new workers into that industry subsequent to a trade liberalization, and that all workers not in that industry remain fully employed but at wage rates below that of workers in Z. In this case it can be shown that the optimal time-path for commercial policy is to move immediately to free trade. This policy does not result in the same adjustment path as would prevail in the absence of the barrier to the movement of labor into the Z industry. But, taking this barrier as given, it is still the best path for commercial policy.

This conclusion would be altered if the barrier to the movement into the Z industry were not absolute but tended to break down over time at a rate positively related to the wage differential between workers in Z and those employed elsewhere. Maintaining the assumption that labor always remains fully employed, it can be shown that there is a social gain from initially reducing the tariff rate to less than zero in order to speed the movement of labor into the Z industry. This conclusion might be reversed, however, if labor outside the Z industry became unemployed, with the amount of such unemployment depending (as it does in the Harris–Todaro (1970) model) on the differential between the wage rate in Z and in other activities.

### Distortions Arising from Price Rigidities

Failure of prices to adjust immediately (or ever) to market-clearing levels, owing to government controls or rigidities in their operation of price adjustment mechanisms, is another source of distortions that might affect the optimal timing of trade liberalization. Consider specifically the case of a minimum wage fixed by law and not altered by the policy of trade

liberalization. To eliminate the possibility that monetary and exchange rate policy could be used to neutralize the effects of the minimum wage by raising the general price level, suppose that the minimum wage is indexed to the cost of a consumption basket that includes the economy's two final goods, $X$ and $Z$.[7] Further, suppose that the wage rate prior to the removal of protection from the $X$ industry is above the legal minimum; that it would fall to less than the legal minimum as an immediate consequence of the removal of all protection from $X$ if all labor remained employed; but that its long-run equilibrium level under free trade would exceed both the legal minimum and the level prevailing prior to the removal of protection.[8] In these circumstances, it may be desirable to cut the tariff rate immediately only to the level at which the equilibrium wage rate with all labor employed is equal to the legal minimum wage. This will be so if the marginal social cost from the unemployment resulting from a further reduction exceeds the benefit of such a reduction in reducing the consumption distortion cost of the tariff and in speeding the adjustment of the economy. On the other hand, it is possible that the optimal commercial policy would be to reduce the tariff rate initially to below zero. This can happen because a lower tariff rate creates a greater incentive to move capital out of $X$ and into $Z$; and the more rapidly capital moves in this direction, the more rapidly does the wage rate that is consistent with labor market equilibrium with full employment rise above the legal minimum wage.

This analysis can be extended to more realistic descriptions of conditions prevailing in labor markets and more generally in the economy. It might be assumed, for example, that individual workers differ in the amount of labor they can supply in each industry, measured by efficiency units. This introduces the possibility that workers within and outside of an industry could earn different wage rates as an equilibrium phenomenon, and it would allow for the result that a minimum wage would exclude specific workers from employment. (Such a model is analyzed in Mussa, 1982a.) The ambiguity would remain, however, concerning whether it is better to reduce the tariff rate initially by only a fraction of its appropriate long-run adjustment in order to limit unemployment, or to reduce the level of protection initially to below its long-run optimal level in order to stimulate more rapid adjustment.

### Conclusions Concerning the Implications of Distortions

No general presumption appears to emerge that a policy of gradualism in reducing protection is superior to a policy of moving immediately to the long-run optimum policy, or even to an "overshooting" policy. For some

---

[7] See van Wijnbergen (1983) for an interesting analysis of the implications of wage indexing for the effectiveness of commercial policy as a means of stimulating employment.

[8] In the preceding model, if $Z$ production is labor-intensive in long-run equilibrium, then the long-run effect of a reduction in protection of $X$ should be an increase in the wage rate in terms of both final products.

types of distortions, gradualism is the best policy. If these types of distortions are especially important, then gradualism would be justified. For other types of distortions, gradualism is not the best policy, and an "overshooting" policy might be justified.

An explanation for this ambiguity concerning the implications of these distortions may be given in the following terms. The condition that must be satisfied for the economy to be moving along its optimal adjustment path is that the marginal social benefit of more rapid adjustment must equal its marginal social cost. When there are distortions affecting the adjustment process, the path induced by an immediate move to the long-run optimal policy is no longer necessarily optimal because the privately perceived benefits and costs of more rapid adjustment do not necessarily correspond to the true social benefits and costs. There is no strong presumption, however, that the nature of distortions will generally be such that the privately perceived costs and benefits of more rapid adjustment exceed the true social costs and benefits. Hence, there is no general presumption that pace of adjustment subsequent to an immediate move to the long-run optimum policy is too rapid, rather than too slow. Only then would there be a presumption in favor of gradualism in trade liberalization.

Therefore, to build a case for gradualism on the basis of distortions, it is necessary to identify either specific or general distortions where the second-best policy is the gradual adjustment of commercial policy. Obviously no general conclusion can be stated concerning the outcome of case-by-case analyses. With respect to a general class of distortions that might provide a rationale for gradualism, one candidate is the distortions associated with unemployment of resources previously employed in protected sectors of the economy. This issue is examined in section IV. Another candidate is the distortions associated with failures and bankruptcies. Failures and bankruptcies are a normal part of the functioning of the economic system, and do not necessarily imply any distortion of the functioning of the adjustment process. However, if socially valuable capital is destroyed as a consequence, there may be an important distortion of the adjustment process.[9] Gradualism might be justified in this situation as a method for reducing the social losses associated with failures and bankruptcies.

## III  INCOME REDISTRIBUTION AND THE CASE FOR GRADUALISM

A policy of trade liberalization will almost inevitably alter the distribution of income and wealth within society. Consumers will gain from reductions

---

[9] Failures and bankruptcies almost always involve private losses, as individual asset holders are forced to write down the value of their assets. Social losses occur only when socially valuable capital is destroyed as a consequence of a failure or bankruptcy.

in the relative prices of previously restricted imports and their domestic substitutes to the extent that they consume such products; and they will lose from increases in the relative prices of products whose output is stimulated by trade liberalization. On net, consumers should gain from trade liberalization (up to the point of the optimum trade policy) because of the reduction in the consumption distortion loss resulting from excessive protection. But nothing generally guarantees that each individual consumer will gain as a consequence of the changes in relative prices resulting from trade liberalization. Owners of factors of production specific to or used intensively in previously protected industries are likely to suffer substantial declines in income and wealth as a consequence of trade liberalization, while owners of factors of production specific to or used intensively in industries stimulated by trade liberalization should enjoy gains in income and wealth. On net, income and wealth should rise owing to the reduction in the production distortion loss of excessive protection. But rarely, if ever, are the net winners from trade liberalization compelled to compensate net losers; nor is it clear that they ought to be.

Decisions about commercial policy are necessarily political, and politics is concerned at least as much with the distribution of income as it is with economic efficiency. For this reason, an analysis of the appropriate time-path of trade liberalization should consider the effects of alternative paths of commercial policy on income redistribution. For reasons that are intuitively apparent, and will be examined in greater detail in this section, a more gradual policy of trade liberalization should reduce the intensity of the income redistribution effects, but only at the expense of some loss in the efficiency of the adjustment process. The key issue in designing a policy of trade liberalization, therefore, becomes making the appropriate trade-off between reducing the intensity of the income redistribution effects and maintaining the efficiency of the adjustment process.

## The Significance of the Income Redistribution Issue

Before examining the analytical issue of the factors that influence this trade-off between income redistribution and efficiency, it is important to discuss the significance of income redistribution. One reason why the income redistribution effects of trade liberalization might be important is that the poorest members of society are injured (or assisted) as a result of liber-alization. If those industries that are heavily protected prior to liberalization are primarily low-wage industries whose workers would have difficulty finding re-employment if protection were substantially reduced, then losses sustained by these workers would be a serious consequence of liberalization. If such losses could be reduced by a more gradual program of liberalization, this would be a valid and important argument in favor of gradualism even at the expense of some loss in efficiency. In the highly developed countries where some heavily protected industries are low-wage industries, this argument may have practical relevance. In many developing countries, however, the heavily protected industries are not typically the low-wage

industries that employ the poorest members of society. Indeed, in many developing countries the poorest workers are employed in agriculture—an industry that is usuallly disadvantaged by protection granted to manufacturing industries. Of course, protected industries in developing countries usually employ some low-wage workers who might experience difficulty in finding other jobs, and the capital employed in these industries might be owned by the less wealthy in society. However, it would be difficult to build a general case for gradualism in developing countries on the argument that rapid liberalization would typically benefit the richer members of society at the expense of the poorer.

Even if those who suffer reductions in income and wealth are not typically among the poorest in society, income redistribution effects are likely to be important to policy-makers because of their political consequences. Those who are injured as a result of trade liberalization are likely to see liberal trade policies as the cause, and are likely to seek redress of their grievances. In many instances, the political power of these groups is substantial.

Moreover, apart from political necessity or expediency, there may be good reason for governments to pay special attention to those who are injured as a consequence of trade liberalization. In this circumstance, injury is suffered not as a consequence of unforeseen changes in economic conditions that are under no one's control, but rather as the direct result of a deliberate change in government policy. Among those who suffer the most from trade liberalization will be those who have made costly investments in physical and human capital that is relatively specific to the previously protected industries. In many instances, the return that would have been earned on these investments under protection would not have exceeded the normal rate of return on other investments in physical and human capital. Hence, the losses that these individuals suffer as a consequence of liberalization cannot legitimately be regarded as merely a surrender of ill-gotten gains. Rather, they are losses sustained as a consequence of pursuing those investments which previous government policy promoted. For this reason, it might be argued that the government has a responsibility to protect (insofar as it is reasonable) these individuals from inordinately large losses. Moreover, if a government adopts the general attitude that those who are injured as a consequence of policy changes are not entitled to consideration, then it is likely to find that people will be less willing to support government policy. In the case of trade liberalization, the incentive to invest in the industries that ought to expand under a more liberal commercial policy will be blunted if potential investors see the possibility of a later policy reversal and fear that they will receive no consideration for losses they would sustain in the case of such a reversal. Hence, on grounds of promoting more efficient functioning of the economic and political system, it may be desirable to provide some compensation to those injured as a result of trade liberalization.

*The Redistributive Consequences of Alternative Paths of Commercial Policy*

In principle, compensation could be paid to those injured by trade liberalization without altering the most efficient path of commercial policy. In practice, such means of paying compensation have occasionally been used. However, it is difficult to design and implement policies that directly compensate those injured by trade liberalization without distorting economic incentives. The practical means of providing compensation is simply to slow the pace of liberalization.

The theory of international trade generally identifies two considerations relevant in determining the extent to which the income of a particular factor of production is altered as a consequence of changes in commercial policy. If all factors are mobile between industries, then the income of each factor tends to be linked positively to the relative prices of the products of the industries in which it is used relatively intensively. In particular, in a two-product, two-factor economy, the Stopler–Samuelson theorem indicates that a factor's income will rise in terms of both products when the relative price of the product in which it is used intensively rises and, correspondingly, will decline in terms of both products when the relative price of the production in which it is used intensively declines. When all factors are not perfectly and immediately mobile between industries, the incomes of factors that are not immediately mobile tend to be positively linked to the relative prices of the products of the industries where they are presently employed, while the incomes of immediately mobile factors tend not to be so strongly linked to the relative prices of particular products.[10] In particular, in a two-product, three-factor model, where labor is assumed to be perfectly mobile between industries and capital is assumed to be specific to each industry, an increase in the relative price of one industry's product increases the income of capital specific to the other industry in terms of both goods, and reduces the wage in terms of that industry's product while raising it in terms of the other industry's product.[11]

[10] In an economy with many products, and with many factors used to produce each product, some perfectly mobile and some not, virtually any result is possible if one assumes sufficiently weird complementary and substitution relations among factors. While these possibilities may occasionally have practical relevance, they will not be considered in this discussion.

[11] The specific capital model is described in Jones (1971), Mayer (1974), and Mussa (1974). Mussa presents specific formulas that indicate the extent to which each factor's income is affected by a relative price change as a function of parameters describing the production processes. It also indicates how these results generalize to an economy that produces many goods using one specific factor in each industry and one mobile factor common to all industries.

The theory that focuses on the short-run specificity of factors of production to particular industries as the prime determinant of the income redistribution effects of relative price changes is the most relevant theory for understanding the likely redistributive effects of trade liberalization in most economies. In using this theory, however, it should be noted that "labor", which is assumed to be a perfectly mobile factor of production, does not correspond to all labor in actual economies. Much of the labor employed in many industries embodies a substantial amount of human capital that is relatively specific, at least in the short run, to a particular industry. In the discussion that follows, therefore, "capital located in an industry" should be thought of as including not only specific physical plant and equipment, but also human capital sharing the property of short-run specificity.

Using the model of section I, it can be shown that a permanent reduction in the level of protection, as measured by the tariff applied to imports of $X$, implies an immediate reduction of the income of capital located in $X$ relative to the income of capital located in $Z$. Under reasonable additional assumptions it may be shown that the income of capital located in $X$ falls, while that of $Z$ rises absolutely in terms of both goods. The effect of a permanent reduction in the tariff on the values of units of capital located in the two industries, as determined by the present discounted values of their future income streams ($\mu_X$ and $\mu_Z$) is less clear, except that $\mu_X$ must fall relative to $\mu_Z$. This ambiguity arises because the long-run effect of a permanent reduction in the tariff on the income of capital must be the same for both industries, and depends on which industry is relatively capital-intensive. If $X$ is relatively capital-intensive, the long-run level of income of capital will fall in terms of both goods. If $Z$ is relatively capital-intensive, the long-run level of income of capital will fall in terms of both goods. If adjustment to the economy's long-run equilibrium occurs rapidly enough subsequent to a tariff reduction, the long-run effect of the tariff reduction on income of capital in both industries could dominate the short-run differential effect on the income of capital in each industry, with the result that the value of a unit of capital could rise or fall in both industries. It is more likely, however, that the adjustment process works sufficiently slowly that the short-run effects of capital specificity dominate the long-run effects of capital intensity, with the implication that a tariff reduction initially reduces the value of a unit of capital located in $X$ while raising that located in $Z$. This result will be assumed in the following discussion.

It is clear that, if a permanent reduction in the tariff rate reduces the income and wealth of owners of capital initially located in the protected industry, then one way to reduce the losses suffered by these capital owners is to diminish the extent of the reduction in the tariff rate. The disadvantage of this policy is that it leaves the economy with permanent efficiency losses resulting from a tariff exceeding its optimal level. An alternative policy that achieves the same objective is a policy of gradually reducing the level of protection to its long-run optimal level. There are two important reasons

why a gradual reduction in the level of protection diminishes the losses suffered by owners of capital located in the protected industry.

First, by delaying the losses of income implied by future scheduled reductions in the tariff rate, a gradual reduction of the level of protection reduces the magnitude of the initial decline in the present discounted value of the income stream generated by a unit of capital originally located in the protected industry. Second, even a small initial decline in the value of a unit of capital located in $X$ relative to one located elsewhere in the economy (which would be induced by an announced program of very gradual reductions in the tariff rate) induces some capital to move out of the protected industry and discourages new investment from being located in this industry. If the demand curve for the protected industry's product is to any extent downward-sloping or the supply curve of other inputs is upward-sloping, the reduction in the industry's capital stock through outward movement of existing capital and non-replacement of depreciating capital should moderate the decline in the income earned by capital remaining in the protected industry.[12]

Formally, the problem of determining the optimal path of trade liberalization in the light of concerns about the losses suffered by owners of factors in the protected industry can be analyzed in at least two ways. Ignoring for simplicity the consumption distortion loss of protection, the objective of the problem could be stated as the maximization of the present discounted value of the economy's final output, as in section I, but subject to some constraint on the maximum permissible reduction in either income earned by a unit of capital in the protected industry or in the private value of a unit of capital located in that industry. Alternatively, the objective function could be modified by subtracting from the value of output at each date some measure of the political and social cost of losses sustained by owners of capital in the protected industry. In the first approach, the trade-off between efficiency in the adjustment process and limiting the losses suffered by those injured by liberalization is exhibited by considering tighter or looser constraints on the maximum loss of owners of capital located in the protected industry: In the second, the appropriate trade-off is determined endogenously as part of the solution of the maximization problem.

Without going into the details of the formal analysis of either of these formulations of the optimization problem, it is useful to state the following general conclusions that may be derived from such an analysis. First, when the protected industry is labor-intensive, there are circumstances (of limited

---

[12] In the model of section I, the supply curve of the other input, mobile labor, is upward-sloping to the $X$ industry, but the demand curve for the industry's product is horizontal at the world market price multiplied by one plus the tariff rate. In circumstances where domestically produced products are imperfect substitutes for imported products, the demand curve facing the protected domestic industry should be downward-sloping.

practical relevance) in which there is no conflict between the goal of economic efficiency and the desirability of limiting losses sustained by owners of capital located in the protected industries. In these cases, the optimal path is to move immediately to the long-run optimal commercial policy of free trade. Second, when the protected industry is capital-intensive, there are circumstances in which concern for the losses suffered by owners of capital can be sufficiently important that it is not optimal to move all the way to the commercial policy of free trade. This result might be taken as representative of the situation in which some protection is justified on the grounds of raising the incomes of the poorest in society.[13] Third, in the "normal case" where a greater reduction in the tariff rate implies a greater reduction in the income of capital in the protected industry and in the present discounted value of that income, a tighter constraint on the maximum permissible loss of owners of capital in the protected industry or a greater political and social cost assigned to such losses implies a slower optimal rate of reduction of the level of protection. This result provides a valid argument for gradualism in trade liberalization under "normal" circumstances when a government is concerned with limiting the losses sustained by owners of factors of production in the protected sector of the economy.

### Factors Affecting the Trade-off between Efficiency and Redistribution

Economic analysis can contribute to an understanding of the path of trade liberalization that balances appropriately the social and political costs of losses against the efficiency gained by rapid reductions in the level of protection, by indicating the circumstances in which reducing the losses of these factor owners by slow liberalization will or will not have a high cost in terms of the efficiency of the following: (a) the ease with which factors located in protected industries can be moved to activities expanding as a result of trade liberalization; (b) the extent to which factors used in protected industries are specific to those industries and must be worn out (in the case of physical capital), or must retire (in the case of human capital) and be replaced by new factors, in order to be moved to alternative activities; (c) the likely productive life-span of the factors in the previous

---

[13]The analogy here is very weak, reflecting the weakness of the model of section I in dealing with the distribution of income among individuals in society, as opposed to among classes of factors. In this model, all capital earns the same income in long-run equilibrium. Hence, removal of a tariff protecting the capital-intensive industry could reduce the income of capital below some arbitrarily prescribed minimum. It is doubtful, however, that this is at issue in discussing the income of the poorest members of society. To get at that, we would need a model in which different individuals own different amounts of human and physical capital with varying efficiency across industries. Then we might consider how the removal of protection might injure those with small amounts of capital.

category; (d) the geographic distribution of factors used in protected industries relative to the likely geographic distribution of factors that would be employed in industries stimulated by a reduction in protection.

First, consider the circumstances in which factors used in protected industries could move relatively easily to activities that should expand as a consequence of trade liberalization. This would be a likely circumstance if the workers employed in protected industries were largely unskilled, had a high level of general, rather than specific, skills, or had skills that would be transferred to the industries that would expand as a consequence of trade liberalization. This last circumstance would be more likely if levels of protection differed widely within a sector of the economy such as manufacturing rather than between sectors such as manufacturing and agriculture. If some manufacturing industries were heavily protected while others using similar types of labor and capital received negative protection, the factors employed in protected industries could probably move into alternative uses with comparative ease.[14] This would not be likely, however, if all manufacturing industries were heavily protected at the expense of agriculture and mining. With respect to physical capital, movement to alternative uses is likely to be comparatively easy when capital consists largely of office and plant space rather than highly specialized equipment. When circumstances are such that it appears that most factors employed in protected industries could move relatively easily into alternate activities, then income and wealth losses sustained by a rapid reduction in levels of protection should not be enormous, and the efficiency gain from stimulating adjustment should be substantial.

Second, the circumstances in which factors used in protected industries must be allowed to wear out or retire and be replaced by new capital or new workers are essentially the reverse of those described in the preceding paragraph. When these circumstances are descriptive of the factors employed in protected industries, then it is likely that these factors will sustain substantial and prolonged income losses as a consequence of a rapid reduction in the level of protection. Aside from reducing the consumption distortion cost of protection, however, little efficiency may be gained by reducing the level of protection more rapidly than is necessary to discourage new workers from acquiring skills specific to the protected industries or new capital from being invested in the protected industries. In these circumstances, a gradual rate of reduction of the level of protection at near the rate that discourages new factors from moving into the protected industries, may be the best policy.

Third, when labor and capital cannot move easily out of protected industries, the expected productive life-span of these factors may be an

---

[14] The activities that will expand as a result of a reduction in protection will depend to some extent on the factors that are available in the economy and on the prices at which these factors make themselves available.

important guide for the pace of liberalization. If many of the workers with specific skills in protected industries have only relatively short periods remaining in their working lives, they are unlikely to pay the costs and suffer the dislocations associated with moving to other jobs, even if they suffer substantial reductions in income (including reductions arising fron unemployment) as a consequence of a rapid decline in the level of protection. Hence, little efficiency can be gained by a rapid reduction in the level of protection that imposes substantial losses on these workers. In contrast, if most workers in protected industries have many years remaining in their productive lives, the prospect of many years of lower income if they remain in their present jobs (or unemployed, waiting for work in the previously protected industry) may induce them to incur the costs of retraining and relocation in order to find new jobs in expanding industries. In this case, a more rapid reduction in the level of protection serves some purpose in increasing economic efficiency. The same principles apply to physical capital, though policy-makers may be less concerned with losses sustained by capital owners than by workers.

Fourth, the geographic location of protected industries may be an important factor influencing the appropriate pace of trade liberalization. If these industries are located in larger metropolitan centers, where workers employed in them have reasonable prospects for finding employment in other, expanding industries, then the losses they will suffer owing to liberalization should not be too large, and efficiency is likely to be promoted by a relatively rapid pace of liberalization. On the other hand, if the protected industries are dominant employers in smaller centers which are isolated from areas where workers might reasonably expect to find employment in expanding industries, then a rapid pace of liberalization is likely to generate very substantial losses for these workers and for the owners of capital in the protected industries. In this circumstance, it may be appropriate to reduce the level of protection more gradually in order to limit income losses for workers and capital workers in the protected industries and to allow adjustment to take place through attrition and depreciation.

Finally, it should be emphasized that the general state of the economy influences the appropriate pace of trade liberalization. In a rapidly growing, vibrant economy, labor and capital released from protected industries can much more easily be absorbed in other industries than is likely to be the case in a slowly growing or stagnant economy. The implication is that trade liberalization can probably proceed more rapidly and with smaller losses to factors employed in protected industries when liberalization is undertaken in such a growing economy. It should be recognized, however, that in an expanding world economy a policy of trade liberalization (combined with appropriate monetary, fiscal, and exchange rate policies) may have some capacity to transform a stagnant, slowly growing national economy into one with a healthier rate of economic progress.

## IV UNEMPLOYMENT AND THE PATH OF TRADE LIBERALIZATION

It is widely believed that the process of adjustment subsequent to a sudden reduction in the level of protection will involve not only a gradual movement of resources out of previously protected activities and into other activities with a higher product value, but also substantial unemployment of some of these resources, perhaps for an extended period of time. Concern with the social cost and political consequences of such unemployment (especially of labor) is probably an important reason for resistance to the implementation of programs of trade liberalization. Concern with these costs would also seem to provide a rationale for gradual implementation of more liberal trade policies in order to reduce the amount of unemployment they generate, or at least to spread the cost of such unemployment over time.

The purpose of this section is to investigate the influence of unemployment resulting from trade liberalization on the optimal path of liberalization. In this investigation, it is assumed that some amount of unemployment (specifically, of labor) is an inevitable concomitant of any reduction in the level of protection, and that a larger reduction generates both a larger immediate increase in unemployment and a more rapid movement of workers out of the previously protected activity. These assumptions imply that there can be no liberalization without enduring some cost of unemployment, and that more rapid liberalization has both a cost, in the form of higher short-term unemployment, and a benefit, in the form of more rapid adjustment. The problem, therefore, is to choose the path of liberalization that appropriately balances these costs and benefits.

Three important limitations cast some doubt on the validity or generality of the conclusions of this investigation. First, there is no attempt to model or analyze the details of the economic and institutional arrangements that lead to the assumed reduced-form relationship between the level of unemployment of workers in a previously protected industry and the rate at which they move to other industries.[15] Presumably this has something to do with the determination of wage rates, but no mention is made of that process in the discussion that follows. It is certainly possible that conclusions of the subsequent analysis, particularly the conclusions relating to social welfare, might depend in a critical way on the details of the structure underlying the reduced-form relationship between the level of unemployment and the rate of adjustment of the labor force. Second, the only policy tool that is considered in the subsequent analysis is the level

---

[15] This relationship might depend on expectations concerning the future course of economic variables, including the government's commercial policy. Hence, it might not remain stable in the face of policy changes.

of protection, specifically the *ad valorem* tariff rate applied to imports. It is possible that, through the use of other policy tools, such as wage subsidies, retraining programs, or relocation assistance, the government could reduce the unemployment cost of trade liberalization while facilitating the adjustment process. This possibility, however, is not considered. Third, the subsequent analysis focuses on the effects of unemployment in the previously protected industry on the optimal path of commercial policy. It does not consider the effect of the overall unemployment rate on the path of commercial policy. Rather, the implicit assumption underlying the analysis is that an excess supply of labor in the previously protected industry is always matched by an excess demand for labor in the rest of the economy. In many situations this assumption may not be valid, and in others its validity may be contingent on pursuit of appropriate monetary, fiscal, and exchange rate policies, in concert with the policy of trade liberalization.

To clarify further the nature and scope of the present investigation, it is useful to emphasize that the "level of unemployment" that will be referred to in subsequent discussion is always to be interpreted as the level of unemployment in the previously protected industry, in excess of the level of unemployment normally prevailing in that industry, and which is assumed to prevail in the rest of the economy. It is assumed that an increase in the level of unemployment, so defined, increases the rate at which workers move out of the previously protected industry and into other industries. This assumption would probably not be appropriate if the "level of unemployment" were understood to mean the general level of unemployment in the economy as a whole. An increase in the general level of unemployment would presumably have a negative effect, or no effect, on the rate at which workers move out of the previously protected industry, since an increase in the general rate of unemployment (holding the structure of unemployment constant) would presumably decrease workers' perceived probability of finding employment outside that industry. For this reason, it would be desirable to keep the general level of unemployment low during a period of trade liberalization, while simultaneously raising the level of unemployment in the previously protected industry.

## The Social Cost of Unemployment

Before beginning a formal analysis of the influence of unemployment on the optimal path of commercial policy, it is useful to consider briefly the nature of the social cost of unemployment. By definition, an unemployed worker does not produce anything that is included in the standard measure of the value of national output. The social loss from unemployment of this worker, however, may differ from the value of the output he would produce if employed. Discussion of a few specific cases serves to illustrate this point.

First, consider a worker formerly employed at a very high wage in a heavily protected industry who would like to continue to work in his old

job at his old wage, but who is unwilling to accept available work in another job at a much lower wage rate. This worker has suffered an individual economic loss as a result of the removal of protection. There is not, however, any social loss necessarily associated with his unemployment. Certainly, the amount he would have earned in his job is not a valid measure of the social loss from the disappearance of that job, since the value of the output of that job was artificially inflated by the previous grant of protection. Moreover, if this worker chooses to remain unemployed and use his time in non-market activities, rather than accept work at a wage that reflects the social value of the marginal product of his labor, then it might be concluded that there is no social loss from his unemployment. If this worker chooses to remain unemployed only because he receives a subsidy (e.g. unemployment compensation) that is contingent on his unemployment, then the social loss can be measured as the difference between the value of what he would produce when employed (in a new industry) and the value he assigns to non-market uses of his time.

Second, consider a worker who remains unemployed so that he can search more efficiently for a higher paying job. This is a common assumption in search theory models of unemployment. For this worker, unemployment is a productive activity, even though its output (finding a better job) is not included in the usual measure of the value of the economy's output. If there are no externalities in the search process arising from one worker's search interfering with the search of others when there are a fixed number of jobs, then the private benefits of search should correspond to the social benefits (ignoring some complications arising from taxation). In this case, the technology of the adjustment process from moving workers between industries has the same essential properties as the technology of the adjustment process for moving capital in the model presented in section I. The privately perceived cost of adjustment (including the cost of being unemployed) will correspond to the true social cost, and the privately perceived benefit will correspond to the true social benefit. Thus, while there is a social cost of unemployment, this cost is appropriately taken into account by the agents responsible for determining the extent of unemployment—leaving no rationale for government intervention. Of course, if there are distortions affecting either the privately perceived cost or benefit of unemployment, then there is a rationale for government intervention along the lines discussed in section II.

Third, the costs of unemployment are not evenly spread across members of society, but tend to be heavily concentrated on the unemployed and their families. This concentration is diminished somewhat by unemployment compensation, the provision of public services, and social welfare programs. But, even in societies with extensive social welfare programs, there may be legitimate concern that losses that are heavily concentrated on a small part of society have a greater social cost than those that are evenly spread. This would make the social cost of unemployment exceed the value of lost output.

Fourth, in some cases, the heavily protected industries that will be the principal victims of trade liberalization may be geographically concentrated

and may be dominant or very important employers in certain areas. In such cases substantial declines in employment in previously protected industries may have important, concentrated, and negative spillover effects for other enterprises and workers in those areas. Even when macroeconomic and exchange rate policies are successful in maintaining a level of aggregate demand adequate to absorb resources released from previously protected industries, these local economic difficulties are unlikely to be completely overcome. This may add to the social cost of unemployment associated with the removal of protection in these cases.

Fifth, workers who suffer prolonged periods of unemployment also suffer substantial declines in their human capital, at least as measured by the wages they are subsequently able to obtain. To the extent that this phenomenon reflects a loss in the private return to human capital that is socially less valuable, there is no additional social cost of unemployment. However, to the extent that this phenomenon reflects an actual deterioration in general human capital owing to unemployment, the social cost may well exceed the value of the output lost during the actual period of unemployment.

### A Formal Analysis of the Optimal Path of Unemployment

In order to provide a formal basis for analysis of the influence of unemployment in the optimal timing of trade liberalization, it is useful to consider a simple model of the interaction between adjustment to changes in commercial policy and the level of unemployment (especially in industries directly affected by the commercial policy change). Since the model used earlier in this paper to analyze the optimal timing of trade liberalization treats labor as a perfectly mobile factor, it is unsuitable for analyzing the effects and implications of unemployment of labor. Rather than modifying that model, it is easier to use a model with a somewhat simpler basic structure.

Suppose the small economy under investigation has two industries: the $X$ industry, which has previously been granted protection by means of a tariff from imports of similar foreign goods; and the $Z$ industry, which produces every other good in the economy, including goods for export. Each industry uses a single factor of production, labor, and the output of each industry is a concave function of the amount of labor employed in that industry:

$$X = F(L_X)$$
$$Z = G(L_Z).$$

The amount of labor employed in each industry is always less than or equal to the number of workers who seek work in that industry, and the number of workers who seek work in each industry is assumed to be a slowly adjusting variable. The number of workers who seek work in $X$ is denoted by $N$, and the number of workers who seek work in $Z$ is the

total work force, $\bar{N}$, less those who seek work in $X$. Given the world relative price of $X$ in terms of $Z$, denoted by $P$, the demand for labor in the two industries is assumed to depend on the *ad valorem* tariff rate, $\tau$, that is charged on imported units of $X$. Specifically, the demand for labor in $X$, denoted by $L(\tau)$, is assumed to correspond to the equilibrium level of employment in the $X$ industry with free movement of labor when the tariff rate is $\tau$; and the demand for labor in the $Z$ industry is, by the same assumption, given by $\bar{N} - L(\tau)$. When the demand for labor in an industry is greater than the number of workers in that industry (as will typically be the case for the $Z$ industry in subsequent discussion) there is an unsatisfied excess demand for labor in that industry. When the demand for labor in an industry is less than the number of workers in that industry, the excess supply of labor is unemployed. Since this situation will generally apply to labor in the $X$ industry in subsequent discussion, it is convenient to denote the level of unemployment in this industry (and in the economy) by

$$U = N - L(\tau).$$

Unemployment is assumed to provide the incentive, directly or indirectly, for some workers to move out of one industry and into another. Since subsequent analysis will be concerned with unemployment in the $X$ industry, this assumption can conveniently be embodied in the specification that

$$\dot{N} = -\beta U \tag{16}$$

where $\beta > 0$ measures the speed at which workers move out of the $X$ industry in response to unemployment in that industry.

The initial condition of the economy is assumed to correspond to the equilibrium position of the economy with a positive level of protection, $\tau_0$, granted to domestic producers of $X$, with the number of workers in $X$ equal to $L(\tau_0)$ and the number of workers in $Z$ equal to $\bar{N}(\tau_0)$. The problem for the social planner who controls commercial policy is to choose the path of the tariff rate that maximizes the present discounted value of the economy's final output, $V$, as given by

$$V = \int_0^\infty \{PF[L(\tau)] + G(\bar{N} - N)\} \exp(-rt) \, \mathrm{d}t$$

subject to the transition law

$$\dot{N} = -\beta[N - L(\tau)].$$

In this specification of the objective function of the social planner, it should be noted that the cost of unemployment is reflected, one-for-one, in the value of output of $X$ (measured as world market prices) that is lost as a result of unemployment of labor in that industry. (No unemployment

occurs in $Z$, so $L_Z$ is set equal to $\bar{N} - N$.) Thus, no allowance is made either for the excess social cost of unemployment above the value of output lost, or for the value that unemployed workers may derive from alternative uses of their time. Also, in the specification of the objective function, no allowance is made for the consumption distortion loss resulting from a non-zero tariff rate on imports of $X$. The specification of the objective function could be modified to take account of these factors with the cost of increased analytical complexity, but without altering the basic conclusions of the present discussion.

Since the number of workers in the $X$ industry, $N$, is a state variable of the dynamic optimization problem confronting the social planner, it is possible, using the relationship $U = N - L(\tau)$, to view the planner's control variable as the level of unemployment, $U$, rather than the tariff rate, $\tau$. Adopting this view (which no policy-maker would publicly admit), the problem for the planner is to maximize

$$V = \int_0^\infty [PF(N - U) + G(\bar{N} - N)] \exp(-rt) \, dt \qquad (17)$$

subject to the transition law

$$\dot{N} = -\beta U$$

by choice of the time path of $U$.

To determine the solution of this problem, we form the current value Hamiltonian

$$H = PF(N - U) + G(\bar{N} - N) + \lambda\beta U \qquad (18)$$

where $\lambda$ represents the shadow price of being a worker seeking work in $Z$ rather than a worker seeking work in $X$. ($\lambda$ is defined this way so that it will be positive along the adjustment path associated with trade liberalization.) The first-order condition for optimal behavior requires that $U$ be chosen so that

$$\partial H/\partial U = -PF'(N - U) + \lambda\beta \leq 0 \qquad (19)$$

with equality holding whenever $U > 0$. This condition says that, whenever $U > 0$, the level of unemployment must be such that the marginal benefit of unemployment arising from a more rapid movement of workers from seeking work in $X$ to seeking work in $Z$, as measured by $\lambda\beta$, must equal the marginal cost of unemployment arising from the value of lost output of $X$, as measured by $PF'(N - U)$. When the marginal benefit of unemployment is so low that this condition cannot be satisfied (i.e., when $\lambda < PF'(N)/\beta$), then the level of unemployment is zero. When $\lambda$ is greater than this minimum value, the level of unemployment is given by

$$U = N - F'^{-1} (\lambda\beta/P). \qquad (20)$$

From this result, it is apparent that the level of unemployment is an increasing function of λ when $\lambda > PF'(N)/\beta$.

Substituting the solution for the level of unemployment into the transition law governing the evolution of $N$, it follows that

$$\dot{N} = 0 \qquad\qquad \text{when } \lambda \leq PF'(N)/\beta$$
$$\dot{N} = \beta[F'^{-1}(\lambda\beta/P) - N] < 0 \quad \text{when } \lambda > PF'(N)/\beta. \tag{21}$$

This result is represented in the phase diagram shown in figure 4.3. The negatively sloped line along which $\lambda = PF'(N)/\beta$ is the upper boundary of the region in which the level of unemployment is zero and there is no movement of workers from seeking work in $X$ to seeking work in $Z$; i.e., in this region $\dot{N} = 0$. Above this region, the level of unemployment is positive and $\dot{N}$ is negative, indicating that workers are shifting from seeking work in $X$ to seeking work in $Z$.

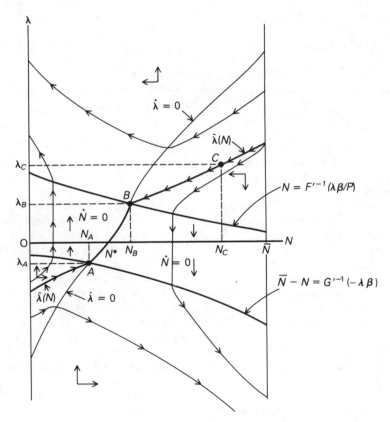

FIGURE 4.3 The optimal adjustment path for the distribution of workers between industries

The transition law for the shadow price $\lambda$ is given by

$$\dot{\lambda} = r\lambda - \partial H/\partial(-N) = r\lambda + PF'(N - U) - G'(\bar{N} - N). \tag{22}$$

Taking account of the solution for $U$ implied by (19), it follows that, when $\lambda < PF'(N)/\beta$ (and hence $U = 0$), the rate of change of $\lambda$ is given by

$$\dot{\lambda} = r\lambda + PF'(N) - G'(\bar{N} - N). \tag{23}$$

Thus, in the region of the phase diagram where $U = 0$ and $\dot{N} = 0$, the combinations of $N$ and $\lambda$ for which $\dot{\lambda} = 0$ are those for which

$$\lambda = [G'(\bar{N} - N) - PF'(N)]/r. \tag{24}$$

These combinations of $\lambda$ and $N$ are indicated by the section of the $\dot{\lambda} = 0$ locus in figure 4.3 that lies in the region *below* the line along which $\lambda = PF'(N)/\beta$. When $\lambda > PF'(N)/\beta$ (and hence $U = N - F'^{-1}(\lambda\beta/P)$), the rate of change of $\lambda$ is given by

$$\dot{\lambda} = (r + \beta)\lambda - G'(\bar{N} - N). \tag{25}$$

Thus, in the region of the phase diagram where $U > 0$ and $\dot{N} > 0$, the combinations of $N$ and $\lambda$ for which $\dot{\lambda} = 0$ are those for which

$$\lambda = G'(\bar{N} - N)/(r + \beta). \tag{26}$$

These combinations of $N$ and $\lambda$ are indicated by section of the $\dot{\lambda} = 0$ locus that lies in the region *above* the line where $\lambda = PF'(N)/\beta$. In general, in the region above the $\dot{\lambda} = 0$ locus $\dot{\lambda} > 0$, and in the region below the $\dot{\lambda} = 0$ locus, $\dot{\lambda} < 0$.

The distribution of workers that corresponds to the free trade equilibrium of the economy, indicated by $N = N^\star$, occurs where the value of the marginal product of labor in $X$, $PF'(N^\star)$, is equal to the value of the marginal product of labor in $Z$, $G'(\bar{N} - N^\star)$. If the social planner inherited this distribution of workers as the initial distribution at the start of the policy of trade liberalization (which is not possible if the economy was at equilibrium position corresponding to a positive tariff rate), the optimal policy for the social planner would clearly be to set $\lambda = 0$ and have the economy sit at its free trade equilibrium position. In the phase diagram, this policy is indicated by the point where $N = N^\star$ along the $N$-axis. Starting with $N = N^\star$, any choice of $\lambda(0)$ other than zero would clearly not be optimal, since it would place the economy on a dynamic path that would ultimately lead away from the free trade equilibrium and toward an equilibrium where either $N = \bar{N}^\star$ (if $\lambda(0) < 0$) or $N = 0$ (if $\lambda(0) > 0$).

It must be recognized, however, that the point where $N = N^\star$ and $\lambda = 0$ is not the only optimal steady state for the economy. In fact, any point on the $\dot{\lambda} = 0$ locus in the region of the phase diagram where $\dot{N} = 0$ is

an optimal steady-state position. In other words, if the economy inherits a distribution of workers with $N$ between the levels $N_A$ and $N_B$ illustrated in figure 4.3, the optimal policy is to set $\lambda(0) = [G'(\bar{N} - N) - PF'(N)]/r$ (which makes $\dot{\lambda} = 0$) and to hold the distribution of workers at the inherited distribution. This is the optimal policy because the benefit of shifting a worker from one industry to another, as measured by $\lambda(0)$, which is the present discounted value of the difference between the value of the marginal product of labor in the two industries, is smaller than the cost of the unemployment that must be created (or tolerated) to induce a worker to shift industries.

The largest number of workers in the $X$ industry consistent with an optimal steady state, $N_B$, and the associated value of $\lambda_B$ for this optimal steady state, satisfy the condition that

$$PF'(N_B)/\beta = \lambda_B = [G'(\bar{N} - N_B) - PF'(N_B)]/r. \tag{27}$$

If the level of protection previously granted to the $X$ industry was substantial, it is likely that the inherited number of workers in the $X$ industry, $N_0$, will exceed $N_B$. In this case, the optimal policy for the social planner is to choose $\lambda(0) = \lambda_C$ in order to place the economy at point $C$, which lies along the stable branch of the dynamic system illustrated in figure 4.3. With this choice of $\lambda(0)$, the economy moves gradually along the stable branch of that dynamic system until it arrives at the optimal steady-state position indicated by the point $B$. At this point, no further movement is desirable because the social value of shifting additional workers out of $X$ and into $Z$ does not repay the social cost of inducing such movement. Any other choice of $\lambda(0)$ would not be optimal since it would lead to a situation either where $N$ converged to $\bar{N}$ (if $\lambda(0)$ were $< \lambda_C$) or where $N$ converged to 0 (if $\lambda(0)$ were $> \lambda_C$). In either case, the transversality conditions of the planner's optimization problem would be violated.

To move the economy along its optimal path, the social planner does not directly set the unemployment rate. Rather, he sets the path of the tariff rate applied to imports of $X$. If the level of protection previously granted to the $X$ industry was so low that the planner inherits a number of workers in the $X$ industry that is within the range of optimal steady-state levels of $N$ (i.e., between $N_A$ and $N_B$), the planner simply holds the tariff rate constant in order to hold the demand for labor in $X$, $L(\tau)$, at the inherited level of $N$. (This requires a positive tariff rate if $N$ is between $N^\star$ and $N_B$ and a negative tariff rate if $N$ is between $N_A$ and $N^\star$.) If the level of protection previously granted to the $X$ industry maintained a level of employment $N_0 = L(\tau_0)$ that was greater than $N_B$, as illustrated in figure 4.3, then the planner must immediately cut the tariff rate to below its previous level, $\tau_0$, in order to reduce the demand for labor in $X$ to below $N_0$ and stimulate the optimal rate of movement of workers from seeking work in $X$ to seeking work in $Z$. Subsequently, the planner must manipulate the tariff rate to move the economy along the stable branch in figure 4.3 until the steady-state point $B$ is reached. The path of the tariff rate that

moves the economy along the stable branch is determined by the required level of unemployment at that level of $N$ along the stable branch; formally, this requires that

$$L(\tau) = F'^{-1} [\tilde{\lambda}(N) \cdot \beta/P] \tag{28}$$

where $\tilde{\lambda}(N)$ is the value of $\lambda$ that is associated with $N$ along the stable branch in figure 4.3. The tariff rate at the optimal steady-state position $B$ is the tariff rate $\tau_B$ that is determined by this requirement when $N$ is set equal to $N_B$ and $\tilde{\lambda}(N) = \tilde{\lambda}(N_B) = \lambda_B$.

To move the economy along its optimal path from $C$ to $B$, the tariff rate set by the social planner must be declining. This is implied by the fact that $\tilde{\lambda}(N)$ is declining as we move along the stable branch from point $C$ to point $B$. Thus, the optimal path for commercial policy during the period of trade liberalization requires "overshooting," in the sense that the tariff rate is initially cut below its inherited level $\tau_0$ to a level $\tau_C$ (associated with the point $C$ in figure 4.3) that is *below* its new steady-state value $\tau_B$. Subsequently, the tariff rate is *raised* in order to move the economy along its optimal path from point $C$ to point $B$. Indeed, if the inherited level of $\tau_0$ were sufficiently high, it is even possible that the optimal policy would be to cut the tariff rate initially to a level below the free trade level; that is, the optimal path for commercial policy would involve an initial period during which imports of $X$ would be subsidized to stimulate a rapid movement of workers out of the $X$ and into the $Z$ industry.

## Extensions and Modifications

It would be misleading to suggest that any of the specific implications of the model discussed in the preceding subsection have any substantial claim to generality. In particular, the conclusion that the optimal path of commercial policy in a trade liberalization involves "overshooting," in which the level of protection is initially reduced below its optimal steady-state level (and perhaps made negative), is a specific implication of that model, and not a general property of reasonably specified models of the influence of unemployment on the optimal timing of trade liberalization. To obtain a better notion of the range of conclusions consistent with sensible economic models, it is useful to consider variations of the above model which preserve its simple two-industry, one-factor structure but allow for modifications in the objective function of the social planner or in the specification of the transition law that relates the rate of redistribution of workers to the level of unemployment.

With respect to the planner's objective function, one important modification would be to take account of the consumption distortion loss resulting from a tariff. Assuming, for simplicity, that the consumption distortion loss is a function $D(\tau)$ of the tariff rate, the objective of the social planner would become the maximization of

$$V = \int_0^\infty \{PF[L(\tau)] + G(\bar{N} - N) - D(\tau)\} \exp(-rt) \, dt \tag{29}$$

by the choice of the time-path of $\tau$, subject to the transition law

$$\dot{N} = -\beta \, [N - L(\tau)].$$

Without going through the details of the formal analysis of this problem, the following modifications of the results of the preceding subsection should be noted. Since the consumption distortion loss of the tariff is second order of smalls for small values of $\tau$ (assuming no other distortions), we retain the earlier result that there is a region of optimal steady positions for the economy surrounding the free trade equilibrium point. The size of this region of optimal steady states, however, is reduced because taking account of the consumption distortion loss of a tariff implies a greater shadow value for shifting workers out of $X$ and into $Z$ at any level of $N > N^{\star}$; specifically, at any steady-state position (where $U = 0$ and $\dot{N} = 0$), $\lambda$ is now given by

$$\lambda = \{G'(\bar{N} - N) - PF'(N) + D'[L^{-1}(N)] \, L'^{-1}(N)\}/r. \qquad (30)$$

Comparing this result with (24), the additional term $D'[L^{-1}(N)]L'^{-1}(N)/r$ that appears in (30) represents the present discounted value of the gain from reducing the number of workers seeking work in the $X$ industry by one unit. More generally, along the stable branch of the dynamic system governing the evolution of $N$ and $\lambda$ (which corresponds to the optimal path for the economy), the value of $\lambda$ will now be the present discounted value of

$$G'(\bar{N} - N) - PF'(N - U) + D'[L^{-1}(N - U)]L'^{-1}(N - U)$$

rather than the present discounted value of

$$G'(\bar{N} - N) - PF'(N - U).$$

For this reason, for $N > N^{\star}$, the value of $\lambda$ along the optimal path will be greater than it was when no account was taken of the consumption distortion loss of the tariff. This, in turn, implies that, for any value of $N$ above the optimal steady-state region, the optimal level of unemployment will be higher and the optimum level of the tariff rate will be lower than it was when no account was taken of the consumption distortion loss of the tariff.

Modification of the planner's objective function to allow for social costs of unemployment other than the value of lost output can be dealt with in much the same way as the modification allowing for the consumption distortion loss of the tariff. If the social loss from unemployment is assumed to be less than the value of lost output because unemployed workers derive benefit from alternative uses of their time, to the extent measured by the function $W(U)$ (with $W(U) > 0$, $W'(U) > 0$, and $W''(U) < 0$), then the marginal social cost of unemployment is reduced from $PF'(N - U)$ to

$PF'(N - U) - W'(U)$. The first-order condition determining the optimal level of $U$ for given values of $N$ and $\lambda$ becomes

$$PF'(N - U) - W'(U) \leqq \lambda\beta \tag{31}$$

with equality holding whenever $U > 0$. It is apparent that the maximum value of $\lambda$ consistent with zero unemployment is now smaller than when unemployed workers were assumed to derive no benefit from alternative uses of their time. For $\lambda$ above the maximum, the level of $U$ determined by (31), say, $\hat{U}(\lambda\beta, N, P)$, is greater than the corresponding level of $U$, given by $N - F'^{-1}(\lambda\beta/P)$, determined in the preceding subsection. Since the transition laws determining the evolution of $N$ and $\lambda$ are still given by (16) and (22), it is relatively easy to establish that the optimal path of trade liberalization is modified in the following ways. The range of optimal steady values of $N$ around $N^\star$ is reduced because the marginal social cost of unemployment is increased and the optimal level of the tariff rate is reduced. The long-run steady-state level of the tariff that is reached starting from such an $N$ is lower and the rate of convergence of the tariff to its steady-state level is greater, implying a greater initial reduction in the tariff below the previously granted level of protection.

On the other hand, if the social cost of unemployment is assumed to be greater than the value of output lost, for any of the reasons previously discussed, then the conclusions of the preceding paragraph are reversed. The range of optimal steady-state values of $N$ and $N^\star$ is expanded. For any $N$ above this range, the optimal level of unemployment is reduced and the optimal level of the tariff rate is increased. The long-run steady-state level of the tariff that is reached starting from such an $N$ is higher and the rate of convergence of the tariff rate to this long-run steady-state level is slower, implying a smaller initial reduction in the tariff but not an elimination of the "overshooting" of the initial reduction in the tariff.

Another area in which it is important to consider modifications of the model analyzed in the preceding subsection is in the specification of the transition law that governs the rate at which workers move from seeking work in the $X$ industry to seeking work in the $Z$ industry. This transition law is important because it controls the marginal benefit associated with unemployment by specifying the relationship between the level of unemployment and the rate of redistribution of the workforce. In a more complete analysis than will be attempted here, it would be appropriate to consider how this critical transition law arises out of the economic and institutional arrangements that govern wage rates, employment levels, labor migration, and education and training of the workforce. For the present, it is desirable at least to consider alternative specifications of the transition law (16), which should be thought of as a reduced-form relationship that might be derived from a more detailed investigation.

A more general formulation of the transition law (16) would allow the rate at which workers move from seeking work in $X$ to seeking work in

$Z$ to depend upon both the level of unemployment experienced by workers in $X$ and the number of such workers, say,

$$N = -\phi(U, N), \quad \phi(0, N) = 0 \text{ for all } N, \tag{32}$$

with $\phi_U = \partial\phi/\phi U > 0$ and $\phi_N = \partial\phi/\partial N > 0$. An additional attractive assumption is that $\phi$ is a linear homogeneous, quasi-concave function, implying that equal proportionate increases in $U$ and $N$ (holding the unemployment rate for workers in $X$ constant) would result in a proportionate increase in the rate of movement of workers out of the $X$ industry. A specific form of $\phi$ that has this property is the Cobb–Douglas form

$$\phi = \beta \; U^\alpha \; N^\alpha, \qquad 0 < \alpha < 1 \; . \tag{33}$$

The original form of the transition law (16) may be thought of as the limiting case of this Cobb–Douglas Form with $\alpha = 1$.

Given the more general form of the transition law (32), the Hamiltonian for the social planner's optimization problem becomes

$$H = PF(N - U) + G(\bar{N} - N) - \lambda\phi(U, N). \tag{34}$$

The first-order condition that determines the optimal value of $U$, for given values of $N$ and $\lambda$, becomes

$$\partial H/\partial U = -PF'(N - U) + \lambda\phi_U(U, N) \leqq 0 \tag{35}$$

with equality whenever $U > 0$. The value of $U$ that satisfies this condition (and maximizes the value of $H$) may be written as a function of $\lambda$ and $N$, say,

$$U = \bar{U}(\lambda, N).$$

When $\bar{U}(\lambda, N) > 0$, its partial derivatives are given by

$$\partial\bar{U}/\partial\lambda = -\phi_U/(PF'' + \lambda\phi_{UU}) \tag{36}$$

$$\partial\bar{U}/\partial N = (PF'' - \lambda\phi_{UN})/(PF'' + \lambda\phi_{UU}). \tag{37}$$

The second-order condition for maximization of $H$ with respect to $U$,

$$\partial^2 H/\partial U^2 = PF'' + \lambda\phi_{UU} < 0, \tag{38}$$

implies that the denominators in the expressions for $\partial\bar{U}/\partial\lambda$ and $\partial\bar{U}/\partial N$ must be negative. Since $\phi_U$ must be negative at the value of $U$ that satisfies (35) (with equality), it follows that $\partial\bar{U}/\partial\lambda > 0$. In other words, an increase

in the shadow value of moving workers out of $X$ and into $Z$ always justifies an increase in the level of unemployment. In the case where $\phi$ is a linear homogeneous, quasi-concave function, we also know that

$$\phi_{UU}U + \phi_{UN}N = 0. \tag{39}$$

Since $U$ must be $\leqq N$, it follows that, in the linear homogeneous, quasi-concave case, $0 \leqq \partial\tilde{U}/\partial N \leqq 1$, with $\partial\tilde{U}/\partial N = 0$ only if $\phi_{UU} = \phi_{UN}$ (which is true for the transition law (16)), and with $\partial\tilde{U}/\partial N = 1$ only if $U = N$ (which is true only if all workers in $X$ are unemployed).

The determination of the optimum level of unemployment as a function of $\lambda$ and $N$ is illustrated in figure 4.4. In this figure, the number seeking work in $X$, $N$, and the number actually employed in $X$, $N - U$, are measured positively along the horizontal axis, starting from the origin O. Relative to the origin O, the curve labeled $PF'(N - U)$ shows the value of the marginal product of labor in $X$ as a function of the number of workers employed in that industry. For a given number of workers seeking work in $X$, $N_0$, this same curve, viewed from the perspective of an origin at $N_0$, shows the marginal cost of unemployment, with the level of unemployment measured negatively along the horizontal axis starting at $N_0$.

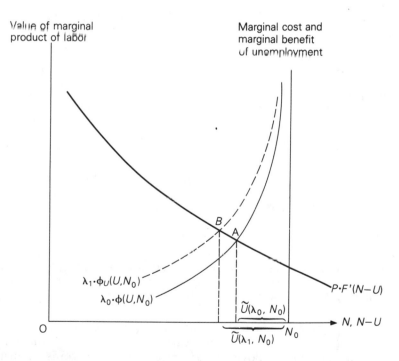

FIGURE 4.4   Determination of the unemployment rate

When $N = N_0$ and $\lambda = \lambda_0$, the marginal benefit of unemployment is indicated by the curve labeled $\lambda_0\phi_U(U, N_0)$, which is also plotted relative to the origin at $N_0$. The shape of this curve reflects the assumption that $\phi_{UU} < 0$; that is, the marginal response of the rate of redistribution of workers to an increase in the level of unemployment is assumed to decline as the level of unemployment rises. The intersection of the marginal cost and marginal benefit curves at the point $A$ determines the optimum level of unemployment $\tilde{U}(\lambda_0, N_0)$. An increase in $\lambda$ to $\lambda_1$ shifts this intersection point to $B$ and increases the optimum level of unemployment to $\tilde{U}(\lambda_1, N_0)$.

With the modification of Hamiltonian for the social planner's optimization problem, the rule governing the evolution of the shadow price $\lambda$ becomes

$$\dot{\lambda} = r\lambda - \partial H/\partial(-N) = r\lambda + PF'(N - U) - G'(\bar{N} - N) + \lambda\phi_N(U, N).$$

(40)

Setting $U = \tilde{U}(\lambda, N)$ in this differential equation and in the transition law $\dot{N} = -\phi(U, N)$, which determines the evolution of $N$, we obtain the differential equation system that governs the joint behavior of $N$ and $\lambda$.

One important issue concerning the nature of this differential equation system concerns the circumstance under which it will have a range of optimal steady-state values of $N$ and $\lambda$, where $\dot{N} = 0$ and $\dot{\lambda} = 0$, as was illustrated in figure 4.3. This situation arises when the "marginal product" of unemployment, in increasing the rate of redistribution of workers, $\phi_U(U, N)$, is bounded as the level of unemployment approaches zero. The reason is that, with an upper bound on the limiting value $\phi_U(U, N)$ as $U$ approaches 0, the limiting value of the marginal benefit of unemployment, $\lambda\phi_U(U, N)$, for small values of $\lambda$ is less than the marginal cost of unemployment, $PF'(N - U)$. This means that, in the neighborhood of the distribution of the workforce $N^\star$ that corresponds to the free trade equilibrium, where the value of $\lambda$ associated with the stable branch of the dynamic system governing $N$ and $\lambda$ must be small, we cannot satisfy the first-order condition (35) with a positive level of $U$. Hence, within a region around $N^\star$, $\dot{N}$ will be zero, implying that, once we reach this region, it is not optimal to incur the costs associated with any positive level of unemployment in order to enjoy the benefits of moving closer to free trade. In contrast, when the limit of $\phi_U(U, N)$ as $U$ approaches zero is unbounded, the only optimal steady-state position will be the free trade equilibrium position.

Another important issue concerning this differential equation system is the path of the tariff rate along the path of convergence to an optimal steady-state position, starting from a level of $N$ that is above the range of optimal steady-state levels of $N$. In this regard, it should be recalled that, for the transition law $\dot{N} = -\beta U$, examined in the preceding subsection, the optimal path of the tariff rate involved "overshooting," in the sense that the tariff rate was initially reduced to below its new steady-state level (which was below its inherited level) and then gradually raised to this

steady-state level. Since the tariff rate is directly related to the actual level of employment in $X$, through the function $L(\tau)$ described in the preceding subsection, the path of the tariff can be inferred from the path of $L = N - U$. Whenever the initial $N$ is above the range of optimal steady-state values of $N$, it follows that the tariff rate must initially be cut to below its inherited level in order to start the economy moving toward its optimal steady state. If $L = N - U$ is rising along the subsequent path of convergence to this steady state, it follows that the tariff rate must be rising along this path, and hence that the tariff rate must initially be cut to below its new steady-state level; that is, there must be "overshooting" in the optimal behavior of the tariff rate. On the other hand, if $L$ declines along the path of convergence to the optimal steady state, the tariff rate must be declining along this path and, hence, must be reduced initially by only a fraction of its ultimate reduction. This might be described as the case of "gradual adjustment" of the tariff rate.

After some rather tedious manipulations (the details of which are omitted), it is possible to show that the rate of change of employment in $X$ along the path of convergence to the steady state is given by

$$\dot{L} = \Omega \left[\lambda\phi(\phi_{UU} + \phi_{UN}) + \phi_U\dot{\lambda}\right] \tag{41}$$

where

$$\Omega = 1/(PF'' + \lambda\phi_{UU}) < 0 \tag{42}$$

Along this path of convergence, starting from an $N$ above the steady-state region, $\phi = -\dot{N}$ will be positive and $\dot{\lambda}$ will be negative. Hence, the prospects for avoiding "overshooting" of the tariff rate as an optimal policy depend on having $\phi_{UU} + \phi_{UN}$ negative and sufficiently large that $\dot{L}$ is positive. For the transition law $\phi(U, N) = \beta U$, examined in the preceding subsection, this condition cannot possibly be met, since $\phi_{UU}$ and $\phi_{UN}$ are both zero. In the case where $(U, N)$, is a linear homogeneous, quasi-concave function, we may use the fact that

$$\phi_{UU} + \phi_{UN} = (1/N) \left[(N - U)\,\phi_{UU} + U\phi_{UU} + N\phi_{UN}\right]$$
$$= \left[(N - U)/N\right]\phi_{UU} < 0$$

to conclude that the term $\lambda\phi(\phi_{UU} + \phi_{UN})$ contributes to the possibility that the initial reduction in the tariff rate will not overshoot the ultimate steady-state reduction in the tariff rate. More specifically, in the Cobb–Douglas case, where $\phi(U, N) = \beta U^\alpha N^{1-\alpha}$, it can be shown that, starting from an $N > N^*$, the tariff rate will ultimately be reduced to a steady-state value of zero (free trade equilibrium will be reached), and that the tariff rate will be declining along the optimal path of convergence to free trade at least in the region where

$$G'(\bar{N} - N) < (1/\alpha)PF''(N). \tag{43}$$

Since $G'(N^\star) = PF'(N^\star)$, it is apparent that this region necessarily includes a range of values of $N$ immediately above $N^\star$. When $\alpha$ is small, and when the marginal product of labor in the two industries is not very sensitive to changes in the levels of employment, the region where gradual convergence of the tariff rate is assured tends to be quite large.

An explanation of the result of gradual convergence to free trade in the Cobb–Douglas case may be given as follows. With the Cobb–Douglas specification of the $\phi(U, N)$ function, the marginal product of unemployment in stimulating workers to move from $X$ to $Z$, $\phi_U = \beta\alpha(N/U)^{1-\alpha}$, becomes indefinitely large as the level of unemployment is reduced toward zero. This implies that, even with a low shadow value for shifting a worker when we are near the free trade distribution of the workforce, the value of the marginal product of unemployment, $\lambda\phi_U$, will be able to equal the marginal cost of unemployment at some positive level of $U$. Hence, it always pays to tolerate at least a small amount of unemployment to move the economy in the direction of its free trade equilibrium. The marginal product of unemployment in stimulating redistribution of the labor force, however, is a sharply declining function of the level of unemployment, especially at relatively low levels of unemployment (i.e., when $\phi_{UU} = \beta\alpha(1-\alpha) N^{1-\alpha}U^{\alpha-2}$ is large and negative for small values of $U$). This means that there is an incentive to provide the stimulus required to induce workers to move to the free trade distribution of the labor force by having very low levels of unemployment spread over long periods rather than higher levels of unemployment for shorter periods. Hence, the optimal path for the tariff rate does not involve a large initial cut that would generate a high initial level of unemployment and stimulate a rapid initial rate of convergence of $N$ toward $N^\star$. Rather, the optimal policy calls for a small initial cut in the tariff rate to stimulate a small amount of unemployment, and then a gradual reduction in the tariff rate to maintain a small but decreasing level of unemployment along the adjustment path to the free trade equilibrium.

### Suggested Conclusions

As previously noted, concern about the economic and institutional arrangements underlying the assumed reduced-form relationship between the level of unemployment in the previously protected industry and the rate at which workers shift out of this industry casts some doubt on the validity and generality of the analysis based on this reduced-form relationship. If, however, we accept the hypothesis that there is such a reduced-form relationship that remains stable for variations in the commercial policy regime (and for variations in other related policies), then some general conclusions may be seen to follow from the preceding analysis concerning the influence of unemployment on the appropriate path of commercial policy in a program of trade liberalization.

First, there are circumstances in which it is not optimal, because of the social cost of unemployment, to push trade liberalization all the way to

what would be the first-best optimum in the absence of these costs. These circumstances arise when the marginal social cost of unemployment in the previously protected industry is positive and bounded away from zero at low levels of unemployment in that industry, and when the "marginal product" of unemployment in stimulating a more rapid movement of workers out of the previously protected industry does not become very large as the level of unemployment becomes small. When these conditions are met, it is not optimal to reduce the level of protection below a certain finite level because the social cost of the unemployment generated by further reductions is greater than the present discounted value of the gain in allocative efficiency from inducing workers to shift out of the previously protected industry.

Second, the circumstances under which a finite, permanent level of protection would be justified by the social costs of temporary unemployment resulting from reductions in the level of protection would not arise if it were possible to maintain a finite rate of redistribution of the workforce with a very low level of unemployment in the previously protected industry. In particular, adapting the model of capital redistribution used in section I to the present discussion of labor force redistribution, new workers entering the labor force might be assumed to locate outside of the previously protected industry in response to the incentives associated with even a very low level of unemployment in this industry; whereas workers already employed in the protected industry would move only in response to a much higher level of unemployment. In this situation, it would be optimal to generate, through reductions in the level of protection, at least the very low level of unemployment necessary to induce new workers not to locate in the protected industry until the first-best equilibrium is achieved.

Third, the behavior of commercial policy along the path of convergence to the optimal steady state depends critically on the shape of the reduced-form relationship between the level of unemployment in the protected industry and the rate at which workers are shifting out of this industry. In the case analyzed above, where we have a proportional response of $N$ to $U$, we find that it is optimal for the initial reduction in the tariff rate to overshoot the long-run steady state and for the tariff rate to rise (subsequent to this initial reduction) along the optimal path of convergence to its (positive) steady-state level. However, in the case of the Cobb–Douglas response function the optimal initial reduction in the tariff rate is smaller than the optimal steady-state reduction (to zero), and the tariff rate declines along the optimal path of convergence to its steady-state value.

Fourth, it is possible to argue, at least heuristically, that the properties exhibited by the Cobb–Douglas response function $\phi(U, N) = U^\alpha N^{1-\alpha}$ are probably more reasonable than the properties exhibited by the proportional response function $\phi(U, N) = \beta U$. The argument is that, even with a low level of unemployment in the protected industry (when the level of protection in this industry is not too high), most new workers will see the

advantage of seeking jobs outside of this industry, especially if the prospect is for further reductions in the level of protection. Hence, even with a low level of unemployment in the protected industry (relative to the average in the economy) there will be a fairly high net rate of movement of workers out of this industry as older workers retire and few new workers enter the industry. At higher levels of unemployment in the protected industry, even fewer new workers will decide to enter, and some older workers will decide to shift industries before retirement. However, the rate of worker redistribution will rise far less than proportionately with increases in the level of unemployment in the protected industry because most new workers will be affected even at low levels of unemployment, and because the number of older workers who decide to shift in response to an increase in unemployment tends to decrease as the level of unemployment rises.

Finally, if this heuristic argument about the form of the $\phi(U, N)$ function governing the response of the rate of worker movement to the level of unemployment in the protected industry is accepted, then it follows that concern with controlling the social costs of unemployment arising from reductions in the level of protection provides a valid rationale for a gradual policy of trade liberalization.

## APPENDIX

This appendix presents some of the formal details of the analysis of the dynamic process governing the adjustment of the economy for the model described in section I. We consider an economy that produces two goods, $X$ and $Z$, in accord with standard, neoclassical, linear homogeneous production functions, using two inputs, capital and labour:

$$X = F(L_X, K_X) \tag{A1}$$

$$Z = G(L_Z, K_Z). \tag{A2}$$

Labor is assumed to be mobile between $X$ and $Z$ production, but capital is specific, at least at a moment of time, to producing output in the industry where it is located.

There is an adjustment process through which capital can be moved from one industry to another over the course of time. Such capital movement is "costly" in the sense that it requires use of some of the economy's supply of mobile labor, in accord with the labor requirements function for capital movement:

$$L_M = \psi(|M|), \qquad \psi(0) = 0 \qquad \psi'(0) = 0, \ \psi'' > 0 \tag{A3}$$

where $M$ denotes the rate at which existing capital is being moved out of $Z$ and into $X$. The specification of $\psi$ as a function of the absolute value of

$M$ implies that the cost of moving existing capital is independent of the direction of the movement.

In addition to movement of existing capital, adjustment occurs through depreciation of existing capital, at an exponential rate of $\delta$ common to capital located in both industries, and through investment in new capital that may be located (initially) in either industry. Investment requires the use of some of the economy's supply of mobile labor in accord with the investment labor requirements function,

$$L_I = \phi(I), \qquad \phi(0) = 0, \ \phi'(I) > 0, \ \phi''(I) > 0, \qquad \text{(A4)}$$

where $I$ is the rate of production of new capital.

Taking account of investment in new capital, and depreciation and movement of existing capital, the rates of change of the capital stocks in the two industries are given by

$$K_X = I_X - \delta K_X + M \qquad \text{(A5)}$$

$$K_Z = I_Z - \delta K_Z - M \qquad \text{(A6)}$$

where $I_X \geqq 0$ and $I_Z \geqq 0$ are, respectively, the amounts of investment allocated to $X$ and $Z$, which add up to total investment in new capital; i.e.,

$$I_X + I_Z = 1. \qquad \text{(A7)}$$

The total amount of mobile labor available to produce final goods, to produce new capital, and to produce the service of movement of existing capital is the economy's endowment of labor, $\bar{L}$. Assuming that is fully employed, the constraint on the total use of labor is expressed by the requirement

$$L_X + L_Z + L_I + L_M = \bar{L}. \qquad \text{(A8)}$$

It is assumed that the behavior of the economy is governed by a social planner whose objective is to maximize the present discounted value of the economy's output of final goods, $V$, where $V$ is defined by

$$V = \int_0^\infty (PX + Z) \exp(-rt) \, dt. \qquad \text{(A9)}$$

It is assumed that the relative prices of $X$ in terms of $X$, denoted by $P$, and real interest rate measured in terms of units of $Z$ per year, denoted by $r$, are fixed exogenously (by conditions in world goods and capital markets). This assumption of exogenously determined values of $P$ and $r$ could be relaxed with some increase in the complexity of the analysis, but without altering any of its basic conclusions. The social planner's behavior is constrained by the relationships expressed in (A1)–(A8).

To determine the solution to the social planner's optimization problem, it is convenient to define the current value Hamiltonian

$$H = PF(L_X, K_X) + G(L_X, K_Z) + \mu_X(I_X - \delta K_X + M)$$

$$+ \mu_Z (I_Z - \delta K_Z - M) + \omega[\bar{L} - L_X - L_Z - \phi(I_X + I_Z) - \psi(|M|)].$$
(A10)

In this Hamiltonian, $\mu_X$ represents the shadow price of a unit of capital located in $X$, $\mu_Z$ represents the shadow price of a unit of capital located in $Z$, and $\omega$ represents the shadow wage rate, all measured in terms of units of $Z$ at time $t$. The first-order conditions for optimal behavior at time $t$ require maximization of $H$ by choice of the current control variables $L_X$, $L_X$, $I_X$, $I_Z$, $M$, and $\omega$. Assuming an interior solution, the associated first-order conditions for the maximization of $H$ are given by

$$\partial H / \partial L_X = PF_L - \omega = 0 \tag{A11a}$$

$$\partial H / \partial L_Z = G_L - \omega = 0 \tag{A11b}$$

$$I_X (\partial H / \partial I_X) = I_X (\mu_X - \omega \phi') = 0 \tag{A11c}$$

$$I_Z (\partial H / \partial I_Z) = I_Z (\mu_Z - \omega \phi') = 0 \tag{A11d}$$

$$\partial H / \partial M = \mu_X - \mu_Z - \omega \sin (M) \psi' = 0 \tag{A11e}$$

$$\partial H / \partial \omega = \bar{L} - L_X - L_Z - \phi(I_X + I_Z) - \psi(|M|) = 0. \tag{A11f}$$

The condition (A11a) determines the amount of labor employed in $X$ through the requirement that the value of the marginal product of labor in $X$ must equal the shadow wage rate. It follows that

$$L_X = K_X \ell_X(\omega/P), \qquad \partial \ell / \partial(\omega/P) < 0 \tag{A12a}$$

where $\ell_Z(\omega)$ is the labor demand function (the inverse of the marginal product of labor schedule) for a firm with one unit of capital located in $X$. Similarly, condition (A11b) determines the amount of labor employed in $Z$ through the relationship

$$L_Z = K_Z \ell_Z(\omega), \qquad \partial \ell_Z / \partial \omega < 0 \tag{A12b}$$

where $l_Z(\omega)$ is the labor demand function (the inverse of the marginal product of labor schedule) for a firm with one unit of capital located in $Z$.

Conditions (A11c) and (A11d) jointly determine the level of investment in new capital and its distribution between $X$ and $Z$. Except in the special case where $\mu_X = \mu_Z$, satisfaction of these two conditions requires that all newly produced capital be allocated to the industry which has the higher

shadow price of capital, and that no new capital be allocated to the industry with the lower shadow price of capital; that is,

$$I_X = \phi'^{-1}(\mu_X/\omega) \quad \text{if } \mu_X > \mu_Z$$
$$I_X = 0 \qquad\qquad\quad \text{if } \mu_X > \mu_Z \tag{A12c}$$

$$I_Z = 0 \qquad\qquad\quad \text{if } \mu_X < \mu_Z$$
$$I_Z = \phi'^{-1}(\mu_Z/\omega) \quad \text{if } \mu_X < \mu_Z. \tag{A12d}$$

In the special case where $\mu_X = \mu_Z$, the aggregate level of investment is determined by $I = \phi'^{-1}(\mu_X) = \phi'^{-1}(\mu_Z)$, and the distribution of investment between $X$ and $Z$ is determined by conditions other than the first-order conditions for maximization of the current value Hamiltonian.

The rate and direction of movement of existing capital between industries is determined by condition (A11e), which says that the marginal cost of moving capital from $Z$ into $X$, $\omega \, \text{sign}(M) \, \psi'(M)$, should equal the marginal benefit of such movement, as measured by the difference between the shadow price of a unit of capital located in $X$ and the shadow price of a unit of capital located in $Z$. Solving this condition to determine $M$, we find that

$$M = \text{sign}(\mu_X - \mu_Z) \, \psi'^{-1}(|\mu_X - \mu_Z|/\omega). \tag{A12e}$$

Thus, $|\mu_X - \mu_Z|/\omega$ determines the rate at which existing capital is moved between industries, and the sign of $\mu_X - \mu_Z$ determines the direction of that movement.

The appropriate value of the shadow wage rate is determined by condition (A11f), which is simply the labor-market-clearing condition. Using (A12a)–(A12e) to substitute into (A11f), it follows that this value of the shadow wage rate must satisfy

$$K_X \ell_X(\omega/P) + K_Z \ell_Z(\omega) + \phi\{\phi'^{-1}[\max(\mu_X,\mu_Z)/\omega]\}$$
$$+ \psi[\psi'^{-1}(|\mu_X - \mu_Z|/\omega)] = \bar{L}. \tag{A12f}$$

This condition can be solved for the optimum value of $\omega$ as a function of the state variables $K_X$ and $K_Z$ and the co-state variables $\mu_X$ and $\mu_Z$ (with the aggregate labor supply suppressed as an argument); viz.

$$\omega = \tilde{\omega}(K_X, K_Z, \mu_X, \mu_Z) \tag{A13}$$

where the partial derivatives of $\tilde{\omega}$ with respect to each of its arguments is positive. Using the function $\tilde{\omega}(K_X, K_Z, \mu_X, \mu_Z)$ to substitute for the variable $\omega$ that appears in (A12a)–(A12e), we may determine the values of the other current control variables, $L_X$, $L_X$, $I_X$, $I_Z$ and $M$, as functions of the state variables $K_X$ and $K_Z$ and the co-state variables $\mu_X$ and $\mu_Z$. These

functional relationships, which are implied by the first-order conditions for maximization of the current value Hamiltonian, are indicated by a tilde above the respective variable; e.g., $\tilde{L}_X(K_X, K_Z, \mu_X, \mu_Z)$ denotes the level of labor employed in $X$ as a function of the state and co-state variables of the social planner's maximization problem.

Optimal behavior by the social planner also requires that the state variables $K_X$ and $K_Z$ and the co-state variables $\mu_X$ and $\mu_Z$ evolve in accord with the appropriate transition laws. Specifically, for $K_X$ and $K_Z$, we require that

$$\dot{K}_X = \partial H/\partial\mu_X = \tilde{I}_X(K_X, K_X, \mu_X, \mu_Z) - \delta K_X + \tilde{M}(K_X, K_Z, \mu_X, \mu_Z)$$
(A14a)

$$\dot{K}_Z = \partial H/\partial\mu_Z = \tilde{I}_Z(K_X, K_Z, \mu_X, \mu_Z) - \delta K_Z - \tilde{M}(K_X, K_Z, \mu_X, \mu_Z).$$
(A14b)

For the co-state variables, $\mu_X$ and $\mu_Z$, we require that

$$\dot{\mu}_X = r\mu_X - \partial H/\partial K_X = (r + \delta)\,\mu_X - PF_K[\tilde{L}_X(K_X, K_Z, \mu_X, \mu_Z), K_X]$$
(A14c)

$$\dot{\mu}_Z = r\mu_Z - \partial H/\partial K_Z = (r + \delta)\,\mu_Z - GK\,[\tilde{L}_Z(K_X, K_Z, \mu_X, \mu_Z), K_Z].$$
(A14d)

In addition, for the social planner to have chosen the optimal path for the economy, $K_X$ and $K_Z$ must have the initial values determined by the initial levels of capital in the two industries, and the paths of the state and co-state variables must satisfy the non-negativity constraints and the relevant transversality conditions.

Since the dynamic system that characterizes the evolution of the state and co-state variables is a (nonlinear) fourth-order system, the usual graphical techniques (phase diagrams) that are applied for systems with one state variable and one co-state variable cannot be applied in the present case. There are, however, three important features of the present system that can be described relatively easily.

First, taking the forward-looking solutions of the differential equations (A14c) and (A14d) that characterize the evolution of the shadow prices of capital in the two industries, we find that

$$\mu_X(t) = \int_t^\beta PF_K(s)\exp[-(r + \delta)(s - t)]ds + B_X\exp[(r + \delta)t]$$
(A15a)

$$\mu_Z(t) = \int_t^\infty G_K(s)\exp[-(r + \delta)(s - t)]\,ds + B_Z\exp[(r + \delta)t].$$
(A15b)

The transversality conditions for the social planner's optimization imply that the constants $B_X$ and $B_Z$ in (A15a) and (A15b) must both be zero. Thus, the shadow price of capital located in each industry at time $t$ is equal to the present discounted value of the future return to a unit of capital in that industry, as determined by the value of the marginal product of capital in that industry, discounted at a rate equal to the market interest rate plus the depreciation rate. When the economy is controlled by private agents, these shadow prices calculated by the social planner are replaced by the prices of units of capital located in the two industries which are calculated by private agents.

Second, at the steady-state position of the economy for a given (constant) relative price of $X$ in terms of $Z$, the value of the marginal product of capital must be the same in the two industries. Assuming that production is non-specialized, it follows that steady-state wage rate, $\omega^*(P)$, and the steady-state rental rate on capital, $R^*(P)$ (both measured in terms of the numeraire $Z$), correspond to the equilibrium wage rate and rental rate determined in the standard two-sector (Heckscher–Ohlin–Samuelson) model in which labor and capital are assumed to be perfectly mobile between industries. The steady-state wage rate and rental rate, therefore, depend only on the relative commodity price, $P$. In the present model, however, the size of the capital stock is not fixed, and its steady-state level depends on the relative commodity price. Specifically, the steady-state size of the capital stock, $K^*$, is determined by the requirement that

$$\omega^*(P)\psi'(\delta K^*) = R^*(P)/(r + \delta) = \mu^*  \tag{A16}$$

where $R^*/(r + \delta)$ corresponds to the common steady-state value of $\mu_X$ and $\mu_Z$, denoted by $\mu^*$. From the properties of the standard two-sector model, it is known that, if $X$ production is relatively capital-intensive, $R^*(P)/\omega^*(P)$ is an increasing function of $P$. It follows that, in the present model, if $X$ production is relatively capital-intensive, then the steady-state capital stock will be an increasing function of $P$. The converse obviously holds if $X$ is relatively labor-intensive. The steady-state distribution of the capital stock also depends on $P$: specifically, it can be shown that $K_X^*(P)$ is an increasing function of $P$ and $K_Z^*(P)$ is a decreasing function of $P$.

Third, with respect to the adjustment process, it is important to note the difference between the factors that determine the rate of investment in new capital (and the distribution of that investment between industries) and the factors that determine the rate of movement of existing capital between industries. For the rate of investment, what matters is the maximum of $\mu_X$ and $\mu_Z$, and any small difference between $\mu_X$ and $\mu_Z$ leads all new capital to be located in the industry with the higher shadow price of capital. Changes in the shadow price of capital for capital with the lower shadow price have no effect on the rate of investment in new capital or on its distribution between industries, so long as this shadow price remains the lower of the two shadow prices of capital. In contrast, the rate

of movement of existing capital depends on the difference between the shadow prices of capital in the two industries. Common changes in the levels of $\mu_X$ and $\mu_Z$, therefore, have no effect on the rate of movement of existing capital.

The nature of the adjustment process subsequent to a permanent reduction in the level of production (which reduces the relative price of $X$ in terms of $Z$ seen by domestic producers and consumers) may be understood with the aid of figure A4.1. This figure is constructed for the case where the protected industry, $X$, is relatively capital-intensive. Since only relative commodity prices matter, it is clear that this analysis applies equally well to a permanent increase in the level of protection of the $Z$ industry which is assumed to be relatively labor-intensive.

In figure A4.1, the line labeled $L^*L^*$ shows the combinations of $K_X$ and $K_Z$ for which the long-run level of labor demand is equal to the available labor supply, as expressed by the requirement that

$$K_X \ell^*_X + K_Z \ell^*_Z + L^*_{\mp} = \bar{L}. \tag{A17}$$

where

$$\ell^*_X = \ell_X[\omega^*(P)/P], \ \ell^*_Z = \ell_Z[\omega^*(P)], \text{ and } L^*_{\mp} = \phi\{\phi'^{-1}[\mu^*/\omega^*(P)]\}.$$

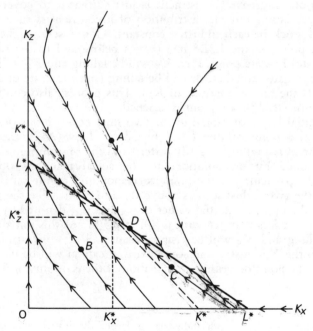

FIGURE A4.1   The paths of adjustment of capital in the two final goods industries

The nature of the solution of the social planner's optimization problem is such that the economy reaches this line precisely when $\mu_X$ and $\mu_Z$ are equal to each other and equal to $\mu^\star$. Once this line is reached, $\mu_X$ and $\mu_Z$ remain equal to $\mu^\star$ ($\dot{\mu}_X$ and $\dot{\mu}_Z$ are both equal to zero), the amount of labor devoted to investment remains constant at $L_I^\star$, the shadow wage remains constant at $\omega^\star(P)$, and aggregate investment remains constant at $I^\star = \phi(L_I^\star)$. The distribution of aggregate investment changes in order to keep (A17) satisfied; that is, $\dot{K}_X$ and $\dot{K}_Z$ jointly satisfy the conditions

$$\dot{K}_X \ell_X^\star + \dot{K}_Z \ell_Z^\star = 0 \tag{A18a}$$

$$\dot{K}_X + \dot{K}_Z = I^\star - \delta (K_X + K_Z). \tag{A18b}$$

From these conditions, it follows that, when the economy is at a point along the $L^\star L^\star$ line above and to the left of the optimum steady-state point ($K_X^\star$, $K_Z^\star$), $K_X$ is rising, $K_Z$ is falling, and the aggregate capital stock $K_X + K_Z$ is rising (since the rate of increase of $K_Z$ is greater than the rate of decrease of $K_X$). This process continues until the economy reaches the optimum steady-state position ($K_X^\star$, $K_Z^\star$), which depends on the given value of the domestic relative price of $X$ in terms of $Z$. At this optimum steady-state position, aggregate investment is just sufficient to cover aggregate capital depreciation and the distribution of investment is such as to keep the capital stock in each industry constant. Conversely, if the economy starts at a point on the $L^\star L^\star$ line that is below and to the right of the optimum steady-state point, then $K_X$ will be falling and $K_Z$ will be rising, and the aggregate capital stock will be falling (since the rate of decrease of $K_X$ exceeds the rate of increase of $K_Z$). This process also continues until the optimum steady-state point is reached.

If the initial levels of capital in the two final goods industries place the economy at a point off the $L^\star L^\star$ line defined by (A17), the optimum initial value of $\mu_X$ will necessarily differ from the optimum initial value of $\mu_Z$ determined by the solutions to the social planner's optimization problem. In particular, if the point corresponding to the initial levels of capital in the two industries lies above the $L^\star L^\star$ line, like the point $A = (K_X^A, K_Z^A)$, the optimum initial values of $\mu_X$ and $\mu_Z$, denoted by $\mu_X^A(0)$ and $\mu_Z^A(0)$, must be less than $\mu^\star$ with $\mu_X^A(0) > \mu_Z^A(0)$. At this initial point, $K_Z$ will be falling and $K_X$ will be rising because all new investment will be devoted to the $X$ industry and some existing capital will be moving from $Z$ to $X$.[16] The point describing the position of the economy in figure A4.1,

---

[16] If the capital stock in both industries is large, the initial level of aggregate investment together with the rate of capital movement may not be sufficient to compensate for depreciation of capital in $X$. In this case, both $K_X$ and $K_Z$ will be declining at the economy's initial point.

therefore, will be moving downward and to the right along a path leading to a point on the $L^*L^*$ line (or on the $K_X$ axis). As the economy moves along this path, both $\mu_X$ and $\mu_Z$ will be rising and $\mu_X$ will be rising more rapidly than $\mu_Z$. When the $L^*L^*$ line is reached, $\mu_Z$ will equal $\mu_X$ and both will equal $\mu^*$. Henceforth, the economy will move along the $L^*L^*$ line in the manner previously described.

If the initial levels of capital in the two industries place the economy at a point such as $B = (K_X^B, K_Z^B)$, which is below the $L^*L^*$ line, the optimum initial values of $\mu_X$ and $\mu_Z$, denoted by $\mu_X^B(0)$ and $\mu_Z^B(0)$, will be greater than $\mu^*$, with $\mu_X^B(0) < \mu_Z^B(0)$. At this initial point, $K_X$ will be falling and $K_Z$ will be rising because all new investment will be devoted to the $Z$ industry and some existing capital will be moving out of $X$ and into $Z$. The point describing the position of the economy, therefore, will be moving upward and to the left along a path leading to the $L^*L^*$ line (or to the $K_Z$ axis). As the economy moves along this path, both $\mu_X$ and $\mu_Z$ will be falling, with $\mu_Z$ falling more rapidly than $\mu_X$. When the $L^*L^*$ is reached, $\mu_X$ will equal $\mu_Z$ and both will equal $\mu^*$. Henceforth, the economy will move along the $L^*L^*$ line in the manner previously described.

If the initial position of the economy is the steady-state equilibrium position corresponding to a higher relative price of $X$ (sustained by the previous tariff protection granted to the $X$ industry), then this position must be at a point like $C = (K_X^C, K_Z^C)$, which lies below the $L^*L^*$ line and below and to the right of the new steady-state equilibrium point $(K_X^*, K_Z^*)$.[17] At this initial point $C$, the total capital stock, $K^C = K_X^C + K_Z^C$, must be greater than the new steady-state equilibrium capital stock, $K^* = K_X^* + K_Z^*$. This is indicated in figure A4.1 by the position of the point $C$ above the $K^*K^*$ line which shows the combinations of $K_X$ and $K_Z$ for which the total capital stock is equal to $K^*$. Starting at $C$, the rules governing the adjustment of the economy are those described in the preceding paragraph: $K_X$ falls and $K_Z$ rises, and both $\mu_X$ and $\mu_Z$ fall until $L^*L^*$ line is reached, at which time $\mu_X = \mu_Z = \mu^*$. Point $D$, at which the $L^*L^*$ line is reached (starting from $C$), must lie below and to the right of the new steady-state equilibrium point $(K_X^*, K_Z^*)$. Subsequent adjustment along the $L^*L^*$ line, therefore, involves a positive $K_Z$ and a negative $K_X$, with these levels of net investment converging to zero as the steady-state equilibrium position is reached. The path of adjustment from point $C$ to the new steady-state equilibrium position at $(K_X^*, K_Z^*)$ is the path of adjustment in response to an immediate trade liberalization that is discussed in the main text.

[17] The old steady-state equilibrium position must lie along the line described by (A17) for a higher value of $P$. Using the properties of the standard two-sector model, it may be shown that the old $L^*L^*$ line must lie below the $L^*L^*$ line in figure A4.1 which is drawn for a lower value of $P$.

# REFERENCES

Harris, J. and Todaro, M. (1970), "Migration, Unemployment and Development: A Two-Sector Analysis," *American Economic Review*, 6, 126–42.

Jones, R. W. (1971), "A Three Factor Model in Theory, Trade, and History," in J. N. Bhagwati and R. W. Jones (eds), *Trade, the Balance of Payments, and Growth*. Amsterdam: North Holland.

Lapan, H. E. (1976), "International Trade, Factor Market Distortions, and the Optimal Dynamic Subsidy," *American Economic Review*, 66 (3), 335–46.

Leamer, E. E. (1980), "Welfare Computations and the Optimal Staging of Tariff Reductions in Models with Adjustment Costs," *Journal of International Economics*, 10 (1), 21–36.

Martin, R. and Selowsky, M. (1982), "On the Optimal Phasing of Consumer Price Subsidies," unpublished manuscript, June.

Mayer, W. (1974), "Short-run and Long-run Equilibrium for a Small Open Economy," *Journal of Political Economy*, 82 (5), 955–67.

Mussa, M. L. (1974), "Tariffs and the Distribution of Income: The Importance of Factor Specificity, Substitutability, and Intensity in the Short and Long Run," *Journal of Political Economy*, 82 (6), 1191–1203.

Mussa, M. L. (1978), "Dynamic Adjustment in the Heckscher–Ohlin–Samuelson Model," *Journal of Political Economy*, 86 (5), 775–91.

Mussa, M. L. (1982a), "Imperfect Factor Mobility and the Distribution of Income," *Journal of International Economics*, 12 (1), 125–41.

Mussa, M. L. (1982b), "Government Policy and the Adjustment Process," in J. N. Bhagwati (ed.), *Import Competition and Response*. Chicago: University of Chicago Press.

Neary, J. P. (1982), "Intersectoral Capital Mobility, Wage Stickiness, and the Case for Adjustment Assistance," in J. N. Bhagwati (ed.), *Import Competition and Response*. Chicago: University of Chicago Press.

van Wijnbergen, S. (1983), "Tariffs, Employment and the Current Account: The Role of Real Wage Resistance," unpublished manuscript, July.

# Comment 1

*Trent Bertrand*

Michael Mussa's discourse is in two parts. The first deals with market adjustment during a liberalization process, defines conditions under which these adjustments will be optimal, and then identifies the sources of a failure in market processes in supporting an optimal adjustment process. The second part deals with a model of the adjustment process with a crucial role being played by adjustment of the tariff system. I like the first part, but have reservations about the second.

The first part represents substantial progress in sorting out the apparent confusion between the time dimensions of policy change and the time dimensions of an adjustment to the policy change. Factors that may be very important for how long it takes the economy to adjust to a policy change are not necessarily relevant for the question of how quickly the policies should be changed.

How would a market economy adjust to a policy change? Mussa has established a strong presumption that this market adjustment to an immediate change to an optimal policy regime would in turn be optimal and would not require further guidance by government intervention. Once he has done it, this "Adam Smith in a dynamic world" theorem may be fairly straightforward and self-evident. Nevertheless, it is very important. It gives us a framework for analyzing where this "invisible hand" may fail because of various market failures or distortions in the economy.

This is where research should be concentrated. What are these market failures? Mussa does an excellent job in analyzing the distortions that may be important. After reviewing these factors, he concludes that there are no general rules one way or the other. I'm not so sure about this. The implications of many of the distortions that he analyzes appear to suggest that there may be a presumption that the "distorted" market adjustment might be slower than the optimal. However, there could well be many exceptions to this, and this is where further research is required.

The second part does not get us very much further. The framework established in the first part is dropped. The model is not built on an adjustment process based on reasonable market behavior by economic agents. We are given a highly artificial model in which unemployment is the driving force in the adjustment process with the government controlling

this by its one policy tool, the tariff rate. The expected trade-off then occurs between costs in forgone output with unemployment, and its benefit in driving the reallocation of resources between sectors. Since market failures that speed up or slow down the adjustment process are not well defined, it is hard to evaluate the usefulness of different time-paths for the change in the policy tool. It is hard to imagine that such changes would be the first-best solution to realistic distortions in the adjustment process.

# Comment 2

*Sweder van Wijnbergen*

I think this is a good discussion and well structured, despite its length. Mussa starts by giving a rather lengthy example of what is really the first theorem of welfare economics. We know that under a certain set of conditions (perfect competition, a full set of markets, etc.) a free market equilibrium, if it exists, will be Pareto-efficient. Furthermore, it is well known that commodity taxes are superior to trade intervention as redistributive government instruments.

Mussa's lengthy example in the first part is simply an application of these basic theorems. Most people would agree that the necessary conditions are not satisfied in practice; in the second part Mussa takes us on a guided tour around some of these conditions and discusses what happens when they are violated.

One argument presented here on the optimal time pattern of trade reform needs more careful analysis. Mussa tells us that, if private discount rates are "too" high, future benefits of adjustment are not sufficiently taken into account, so that adjustment to changes in trade policy are "too" slow. His policy advice is actually to overshoot liberalization, cut tariffs more initially, and climb gradually up to the desired steady-state level which may be zero.

However, if private discount rates are above the social discount rate, private savings are too low. We know from recent work on macro-effects of tariffs (Razin and Svensson, 1983; van Wijnbergen, 1983) that a one-shot cut in tariffs will not affect private savings, which are already too low, thus exacerbating the costs of the initial distortion. This could very well change Mussa's policy rule.

Mussa's argument about the minimum wage is more interesting. For one thing, he looks at fixed real product wages. Rigid real consumption wages have better empirical and theoretical support. This is relevant, since a cut in tariffs will immediately raise real consumption wages for given real product wages. What happens to real consumption wages after all the general equilibrium effects have worked their way through is well known from basic trade theory and does not need repetition here.

The next point taken up is income distribution, which has an unusual focus: preservation of the status quo between owners of sector-specific

factors. We usually think of income distributional concerns as concavity in the social welfare function; we dislike some people being poor and others being rich—a very different issue. Another angle on income distribution which might be of relevance is Peter Hammond's discussion of *ex ante* versus *ex post* analysis: it is all very well to be promised, *ex ante*, a 5 percent higher real wage in sunrise industries to compensate for a 5 percent chance of not getting a job once I have moved out of a sunset industry; but if, *ex post*, I end up being among the 5 percent unemployed (not getting anything), it will be of little comfort to realize that the other 95 percent who did get jobs get 5 percent higher wages to compensate for my unemployment. A case for trade adjustment assistance could be made along these lines, and may be for gradualism if no other instruments are available.

The main part of Mussa's contribution, presented in a somewhat apologetic fashion, deals with unemployment. I think it is an interesting part. True, a lot depends on arbitrarily imposed wage rigidity and gradual migration functions. However, we do not have a generally accepted theory of unemployment which is both empirically plausible and has satisfactory micro-foundations. Until one is found, one can do worse than make plausible but admittedly ad hoc assumptions and proceed from there, as opposed to not addressing such issues at all. I do have a problem with the assumption of wage equalization across sectors in the absence of instantaneous labor mobility to enforce it. I suspect instead that, if sectoral wages were allowed to diverge in line with his assumption of zero *instantaneous* labor mobility (sectoral labor *stocks* are fixed at any moment in time but move gradually over time), one of his two main results would not survive—namely, the case for stopping short of free trade—as flexible sectoral wages would eliminate the unemployment costs a marginal tariff change has in Mussa's analysis. There would still be the allocational inefficiencies caused by gradual rather than instantaneous labor mobility, so that, I suspect, his other main result on the time pattern of liberalization would survive this modification.

REFERENCES

Razin, A. and Svensson, L. (1983), "An Asymmetry Between Import and Export Taxes," *Economic Letters*, 13, 55–57.
van Wijnbergen, S. (1983), "Tariffs, Employment and the Current Account: The Role of Real Wage Resistance," Warwick Economic Research Paper no. 248.

# 5

# On Compensation for Losses and Policy

*Simon Rottenberg*

## I ANALYTICS

Public policy may affect the efficiency of resource use by altering the relative price sets governing the constellation of commodities and services that the economy produces and the proportions in which factors are combined.

Policy may cause relative prices to differ from the set which expresses the social scarcity values of commodities and resources. If it does, the economy's output will be smaller than if appropriate prices prevailed in markets. In that case, an alteration of policy might cause resources to be put to more efficient uses and economic output might thereby be enlarged.

Policies may also affect the distribution of income and wealth. They imply taxes and subsidies which may be explicit or implicit. They may cause the distribution of income and wealth to be different from that which would prevail if a different set of policies were designed and applied. Policy and policy changes may produce gains for some vectors of the population and losses for others.

The distribution effect of policy change may appear all at one time in the form of a lump sum, simply altering the relative levels of different population vectors. Usually, however, policy change alters relative income streams over time. Diminished income streams for some and enlarged income streams for others can be transformed to lump-sum equivalents by capitalizing them.

The capitalized value of the incremental (positive or negative) income streams produced by public policy is of different magnitudes for different policies. If a policy has a positive capital value for some vector of the community's population, resistance will be offered to its change. The larger the private capital value of a unit of public policy, the stronger will be the resistance to its change.

It has been proposed that, when a policy change causes the use of resources to be more efficient, and when there is resistance to the change from those whose income would be relatively diminished, compensation

for these losses may lead the losers to accept that change. It is argued that this is an efficient arrangement, so long as the quantity of compensation necessary to secure consent is smaller than the quantity by which the community's output would rise as a consequence of the policy change.

Both efficiency and equity defenses have been offered for such a compensation arrangement. Analytical examination of the topic and a review of the experience of actual compensation policies, however, raise serious questions about these apparently rational defenses for compensation.

A policy of paying compensation in order to secure concurrence with the making of policy change seems very attractive. If a policy change can be expected to improve the efficiency in the uses to which the community's resources are put, and to increase the community's output of commodities and services by some magnitude, it would clearly seem to serve the community's purpose to make transfer payments that would assure the adoption of the policy change, if the required payments are not larger than the quantity by which the policy change enlarges economic output.

Public policies may have both output and distribution effects; few policies are neutral in these respects. Policies have output effects either because they tend to cause resources to be put to their most highly valued uses, or because they tend, oppositely, to cause resources to be put to lesser valued uses. Policies that are neutral in their allocational effects are those allowing prices of commodities and services to express their social scarcity values and permitting both the supply and the demand sides of markets to be responsive to the relative price parameters encountered in markets If market prices are inflexible, policies that cause prices to achieve socially optimal levels have favorable effects upon output.

Policies may have distribution effects because they may produce income and wealth distribution consequences — sometimes within a country and sometimes internationally — that are different from the consequences of other policies. Policy changes, therefore, may generate gains for some and losses for others.

Suppose a policy change would cause the aggregate real income of a community to be enlarged but would distribute the increment non-uniformly among a relevant population. Or suppose it would cause the whole enlarged real income to be distributed among the population in a way that diminishes the income of some, while enlarging it for others, in a different fashion than if the policy change had not occurred. In such a case, and especially if the gain of each of a large number of gainers is small while the loss of each a small number of losers is large, a policy change may not be affected, even if that change would result in a real income increase for the aggregate of the whole community.

The frustration of the change may occur either because the losers coalesce and promote political opposition to the change, or because the community's sense of equitable standards is done violence to by a redistribution of the type that has been defined.

It has been suggested that the frustration of the change can be mitigated by associating with the policy change an explicit or implicit arrangement

for identifying the losers, estimating the magnitudes of their losses, and compensating them, in whole or in part, for the losses caused by the policy change. If the compensation is smaller in magnitude than the aggregate output gain affected by the change, the aggregate community is made better off. Then the compensatory transfer payments from gainers to losers make the change politically viable by securing the losers' consent to the change, and assuaging the conscience of the community.

In this context, it is important to understand that equity is not necessarily achieved by distributional equality, and that the community's perception of equity is not necessarily the same as distributional equality. What may be perceived by the community to be equitable is income and wealth distribution that is proportional to effort, or to investment in the acquisition of skill, or to correct foresight of the future, or even to personal qualities like kindness or gentleness. If the properties thought to be the proper criteria for measuring the equitable quality of income distribution are not equally distributed in the population, then it may be that less, and not more, equal income distribution is considered equitable.

Compensatory arrangements may take the form of either money payments or complementary policy changes that have redistribution effects offsetting those of a given policy. Thus, if one policy change implicitly taxes vector A, a complementary policy change might also be made that implicitly subsidizes vector A. Money transfer payments may be made from revenues derived from general taxation or from revenues derived from the taxation of defined population vectors; those vectors may or may not consist of gainers from the relevant policy change. Compensatory arrangements can also take the form of legal rules that tax some forms of private adjustment to public policy changes and subsidize others.

Compensatory arrangements may or may not have effects upon efficiency and income distribution. Suppose money compensation payments are made from revenues generated by excise taxes. The prices of the taxed commodities will then diverge from their production costs; the prices will be distorted. This produces inefficiency in the sense that the marginal benefits produced by the consumption of the taxed commodities will not be equal to their marginal costs. Suppose, alternatively, that money compensation payments are made from revenues generated by income taxes. Then the price of leisure, which is the forgone income from the marginal choice of leisure over work, will diverge from the marginal product of labor; the price of leisure will be distorted. This will be inefficient in the sense that time will be allocated between work and leisure in proportions that cause the marginal utility of leisure to be unequal to the marginal productivity of labor.

Suppose compensation occurs in the form of subsidization of the consumption of some commodities. Relative price sets confronting those making commodity basket consumption choices will be distorted; they will not reflect relative production costs. Inefficient commodity baskets will be consumed.

Suppose a system of legal rules provided for payments to be made from

some to other private individuals and firms by defining a set of liabilities or duties to pay which are triggered by some defined behavioral set. For example, suppose firms were required to make compensatory payments to workers dismissed for some defined causes. In this case, redistribution cannot occur so long as payers and receivers are parties to transactions — either in the form of explicit contracts or in the form of implicit contracts, as in market transactions — and the transactions have multiple properties. If one of the properties of a transaction is specified (e.g., the terms upon which dismissal can occur), then adjustments will be made in the residual properties of the transactions, the dismissal terms will be taken into account, and the compensation arrangement will be rendered nugatory.

It is necessary, in order that compensation arrangements such as these be made inconsequential, that the rules defining the events triggering payments be known *ex ante*; it is then possible for the market, or for the parties to a negotiated contract, to make the adjustments in other terms of transactions that will frustrate redistribution. If compensation payments are required, however, by legal rules that are formulated and enforced *after* transactions have been consummated, then, of course, the rules *can* produce redistribution. After consummation of the transactions, it is too late to adjust other terms of a transaction to take account of compensatory payments, and in those circumstances compensation arrangements can have real effects.

Even if they are known *ex ante*, compensation arrangements by legal rules that impose duties to pay can be effective when the payments are made between strangers, i.e., those who are not parties to transactions in formal contracts or in markets.

Policy change is not distinguishable in its effects upon the distribution of income from the persistence (non–change) of policy, either in principle or in its pragmatic consequences; only the signs of the effects will be different.

Devaluation of an overvalued currency will benefit those engaged in the export trades, those with physical or human capital specialized to the production of export commodities, and those who produce subsitutes for the export commodities. Devaluation will harm those in the import trades, those with strong preferences for imported commodities, and those with capital assets that are complementary to imported goods. Alternatively, the persistence of overvaluation will benefit the first set and harm the second set.

Therefore, exporters et al. will exert political pressure for devaluation, while importers et al. will exert political pressure for persistence of the currently existing exchange rate policy.

If devaluation does not occur, exporters will suffer losses and will want to be compensated for those losses in exchange for their consent to the persistence of the condition of overvaluation. If devaluation does occur, importers will suffer losses and will want to be compensated for their losses to secure *their* consent to devaluation. This quality of symmetry

means that a compensation arrangement opens a Pandora's box of income and wealth transfers.

Public policy and policy change invariably generate complex networks of gains and losses. Consider, for example, the simple case of the introduction of withdrawal of the policy of clearing snow and ice from the public roadways by dispersing salt over the surface.

The first-order consequence of a policy change in this field would be expected to be a diminution or increase in the accident rate, a diminution or increase in the quantity of fuel consumed in vehicular transport, and an increase or diminution in the rate of vehicular corrosion.

The number of vectors whose incomes might be affected is large. They include the owners of vehicles; providers of medical services of a variety of kinds and their suppliers; those who make, maintain, and repair automobiles and their suppliers; those who make and apply anti-corrosive agents; those who insure automobiles against corrosive and accidental damage; and those who make, transport, and distribute fuel, as well as the makers, transporters, and sellers of road salt.

Losses/gains generated by the policy change are in some respects transitory while adjustment occurs. The policy will determine the locus of demand schedules for commodities and services; prices will fall or rise. Earnings will change. Exit and entry will occur at the margin. Some activities will become smaller or larger in volume. But, after time has passed for adjustment, earnings for similar labor will be the same in all activities and the return on capital will be normal in all activities.

Still, human and physical capital that is specific to the relevant contracting activities will experience a diminution in their values, and their owners will suffer losses. If the market correctly estimated the length of the period that would run before the policy change caused the capital to have a lower value, those who had invested in the acquisition of the capital would already have been justly compensated for the costs of their investments in the form of higher prices paid, during the period of their employment, for the services of their capital. If the market overestimated the length of the period that would run before policy change diminished the value of capital, the policy change would produce real losses for the investors. Real losses are defined as those that occur when the rate of return on investment is lower than normal; nominal losses occur when transfer payments or rents are not received.

The magnitudes by which capital values (and, therefore, the magnitudes of the real losses) are diminished will vary and will depend upon the available substitutes for the capital and the degree of capital specificity.

Suppose that the market's estimate of the length of run of a policy was confirmed by experience. In this case, if the policy had persisted and had had a longer run, capital would not have diminished in value and investors would have continued to receive higher earnings for their capital services. They would have received higher earnings than those necessary to attract the appropriate supply of capital to the market; in effect, they would

have received rents. They would have been overcompensated for their investments. A policy change in that case will also produce losses, but they will be nominal, not real, losses.

A compensation policy based on equity principles would find it necessary to identify the full complex of those who would be affected. Once identified, the intensity to which they are affected will vary among vectors and among individuals within each vector, and will depend directly upon the degree to which physical and human capital assets are specialized to the relevant activity. Non-specialized assets can move to other activities at low cost when a policy change causes a decline in volume; specialized assets will suffer large changes in their values. The complexity of assigning values to losses, even in such a simple case as this, is immensely difficult.

If a compensation policy is based not on equity principles, but on pragamatic imperatives, so that compensation is paid not to all losers but only to those whose assent is essential to the introduction of the policy, and if the magnitude of compensation is not measured by the magnitude of losses but is of a size just sufficient to secure assent from the relevant vectors, then the compensation policy will invoke protest. Such a compensation policy signal would make it worthwhile to put resources to rent-seeking activities that would be lost to alternative socially valuable uses.

The equity defense for a policy of compensating losers when policy changes rests upon a weak reed. Many kinds of phenomena produce losses. These include natural disasters like hurricanes, earthquakes, floods, pestilence, plant and human diseases, as well as wars, the discovery and exhaustion of natural resources, technological discoveries, and changes in consumer preference sets — and changes in public policy.

On grounds of equity, it does not seem warranted to select isolated public policy changes from this set as a trigger for making transfer payments. The existence or intensity of suffering is independent of its cause.

It might be argued that one can hedge against losses from those other causes by self-insuring or by buying commercial insurance. But hedging against losses from policy change can also occur, as by forming general capital that is not intensely specific to an activity, is less vulnerable to damage from policy change, and is capable of transfer to other uses if a policy change makes the utilization of the capital unprofitable in its current use.

It might be argued that other occurrences that generate losses can be hedged against because they can be estimated, but that estimates of the probability of policy change are much more tenuous. It is not clear that this is true. Legislatures are forever enacting legislation, and each legislative act constitutes a policy change. Everyone knows that policy is not immutable. That probability estimates are made of the length-of-run of policies is evident from the rise and fall of capital values in markets, as they are affected by policy. For example, let a rent control statute be adopted in a city and the value of relevant real property will fall; there will then be variance in the value over time, depending upon estimates of the intensity of enforcement of the statute, of the level at which the control will be

fixed, of the viability of methods of strategic evasion, and of the probability of repeal of the statute. Thus, estimational incapacity does not appear to be a circumstance that would frustrate hedging in the policy change case.

The pricing adjustments that appear in markets also raise a question about the equity defense for a compensation policy. Suppose a policy that is favorable for an activity is expected to have, alternatively, a short life and a long life. In the former case it is estimated that the policy will be changed (will be rendered less favorable to the relevant activity) after only a short period; in the latter case it is estimated that the policy will be changed only after a long period. The different estimates of the duration of policy in the two cases should be expected to affect prices in the relevant markets. A favorable policy that is expected to have a short life will have less market value than the same policy that is expected to have a long life. The values of rights exchanged in markets will take account of the expected duration of the policy.

Similarly, a policy change that is unfavorable to an activity, and that produces losses for those who are engaged in the activity, should also have been estimationally anticipated in markets. Prices in those markets will be affected. If the market works well, those who enter an activity that is likely to be unfavorably affected by a policy change will have been paid prices for the services of their assets (including human capital assets) that will already have justly compensated them for the risk that the unfavorable policy change will be adopted. In such a case, a compensation policy which makes transfer payments to losers will compound the compensation for the risks they run that they will be adversely affected by a policy change. A transfer payment to them pays them doubly for their risk.

If the market cannot correctly estimate the probability of the losses arising from policy changes, there is no reason to assume that the market will systematically underestimate the risk; it might overestimate. The prices paid for running the risk of unfavorable effects from policy change may be too high as well as too low. In the absence of a systematic underestimation of risk, the payment of explicit compensation for losses is not clearly defensible.

There is still another reason for questioning the equity defenses for payment of compensation to losers from policy changes. Suppose the losses are rents. Suppose the price paid for services in an activity was high because free entry into that activity was stopped by policy. Suppose, further, that the policy of frustrating entry was promoted by the pressures of incumbents in the activity. Now suppose policy changes are imposed so that entry into the activity is made less costly. Clearly, incumbents in the activity will then suffer losses: their capital will be diminished in value; the prices paid for their services will diminish. Should they be compensated for the losses they encounter because policy has changed? It is not clear that principles of equity warrant such payments. Prior to the change, they had been in privileged positions. They were being paid rents. Their privilege and their rents had their origins in the rent-producing activities of those who now lose those rents. It is not clearly warranted that the community

should transfer income to losers of privilege who, because of policy changes, are now deprived of that privilege and made equal to others.

It should be noted in this connection that, if entry and exit in an activity are free, policy can have favorable or unfavorable effects upon practitioners in an activity, or upon owners of assets engaged in the activity, only in the short run, while adjustments to the policy are being made. In the long run, when sufficient time has passed for appropriate adjustments, the policy turns out to have no effect upon income and wealth. A policy that subsidizes an activity, either explicitly or implicitly, will cause the volume of the activity to grow as new entrants respond to the subsidy; in the end, when the entry of those who have come to receive the subsidy is completed, the prices that are paid for services in the activity will be the market rate for such services in an activity, and the rate of return on investment in the activity will be normal. Similarly, a policy that taxes an activity, either explicitly or implicitly, will cause the volume of the activity to decline as marginal incumbents leave; when adjustment has been completed, the prices of services and the rate of return will again be normal.

If, with free entry and exit, the long-run effects of policy on prices of physical and human capital services are zero, policy can have non zero, favorable effects only if there are constraints on entry. Constraints on entry produce rents. Thus, compensation for losses produced by policy change must, in the long run, take the form of reimbursement for the loss of rents. The question is made more complex by the existence of markets for rights that produce rents.

For example, the right to grow tobacco for commercial sale has no value if entry into the industry is free. Services employed in the industry will receive only normal returns. The right to grow tobacco has a positive value only if entry is checked. A policy change that permits free entry into the industry, where entry had previously been constrained, would cause the value of the right to grow tobacco to fall to zero. Those who paid a price for the right will now find that right to be valueless. The rents had been captured by previous owners of the rights. The current owner of the now worthless right has suffered losses as a result of the change in policy. It can be argued, that it was always known that the right *might* be rendered nugatory by the repeal of the legislation establishing it. If so, the price paid by the current owner for the right to receive rents as a privileged producer of tobacco would have taken account of the probability of the extinction of the right. He would have been compensated, in the lower price that he paid for the right to produce tobacco, for the risk that the right would be eliminated.

The equity defense for compensation sometimes takes the line that compensation should be paid to losers because a change in public policy implies a breach of contract. Those who enter the industry under the old policy, it is argued, are informed of the implications of that policy; they perceive that the policy will persist. When policy is changed, the "rules of the game" are altered without their consent. The contract has been breached, and reimbursement for their ensuing losses is ethically warranted.

The counter-argument can be made that the perception of the persistence of the old policy was false and delusionary. It is widely known that no policy persists to infinity without change. There is no contract; therefore no contract was breached, and reimbursement for losses is unwarranted.

Even if it is not formally coupled with a compensation arrangement, a policy change might, nonetheless, trigger payments from private sources, as when the policy change precipitates the decline of employment in an industry in which either the law or a collective agreement provides for severance payments from firms to redundant and dismissed workers.

The policy change will have no effect if it was correctly anticipated by the market. The firm will incur no incremental cost. The price paid for the services of the workers, in the time during which they were employed by the firm, will have taken account of the prospective severance payment outlay. The severance payment is effectively derived from deferred wages. What would have been paid out over the time of employment is withheld and paid in lump sum at the time of dismissal.

If, on the other hand, the policy change was not anticipated, a severance payment arrangement of this kind would be a tax on the dismissal of workers. It would constitute a real cost to the firm. Fewer dismissals will occur; an inappropriate combination of factors will be encouraged; and some workers will continue to be employed in one industry when they would be more productive in another. Changes in policy with compensation for losses paid by firms can be expected to have unfavorable efficiency effects.

If workers are dismissed when the firms or industries in which they worked contract as a result of change in public policy, they become unemployed for a time. During that period, they command non-market time which has value for them. If they were compensated for the adverse effects of policy change by being given the whole of lost earnings during the period of unemployment, they would be made better off than workers who had not been dismissed; they would be able to command the same bundle of commodities as those who had retained continued employment, *and* they would receive an increment of non-market time as well. Any compensation policy that replaced all lost earnings would be expected to produce incentives for the prolongation of essentially voluntary unemployment.

The politically pragmatic defense for compensation payments rests on the claim that salutary public policy change sometimes cannot be made unless those who suffer losses are "bought off." Members of the legislature, sensitive to their estimates of voter behavior, may not adopt even those changes which benefit the aggregate of the whole community, unless assent is given by those upon whom losses are concentrated.

However, there is no certainty that making transfer payments will, in fact, forestall pressure campaigns in opposition to the change. It appears, for example, that trade adjustment assistance payments to US workers who have suffered from the competition of imported goods after trade liberalization have not prevented trade unions from persisting in campaigns

to limit imports of those goods. Workers in the relevant industries are clearly better off for having both payments to those who are dismissed and continued constraints on imports. In a society in which political discussion is open and free, compensation payments cannot be made conditional upon silence and withdrawal from the arena of dialogue. In a society which is closed to political discussion, compensation payments to losers might be superfluous or, at least, less cost-effective than other strategies for achieving acceptance of a policy change.

There is another sense in which compensation may fail as a political instrument for effecting policy change. Transfer payments are a "tax" on the exchequer. But public revenues have alternative uses, so expenditures for compensation payments are lost to other uses and produce opportunity costs for government. The legislature may be less willing to make policy changes that require budgetary expenditures than to make changes not requiring such expenditures. Therefore it does not necessarily follow that policy change is facilitated when it is associated with transfer payment arrangements; such an association might, rather, tend to forestall change.

The question of compensation for losers when policy changes occur is usually dealt with as though there is a dichotomized set of choices. That binary perception is incomplete. There are, in fact, at least three options: (a) let a high tariff on the importation of (say) shoes persist; (b) let there be a lower (including a zero) duty on shoe imports, and let shoe workers and shoe machinery owners be compensated for their loss; and (c) let there be a lower duty on shoe imports *without compensation* to workers and machinery owners.

Each of these options produces a different distribution of income and wealth. Therefore, each generates gains for some and losses for others; each causes the distribution of income to be different from what it would have been had other options been chosen.

It is not clear that, in every case, on either equity or politically pragmatic grounds, reduced duties with compensation are to be preferred to reduced duties without compensation. On the equity test, the option to be preferred depends upon which population vector it is desired to benefit at the expense of others; this *may* be current shoe workers and shoe machinery owners, but it need not be that vector. On the politically pragmatic test, the option to be preferred depends upon which vectors find it cheap to coalesce and articulate their interests, the intensity of those interests, and the rate at which, for each vector, shared interests transform to voting behavior; this *may* be shoe workers and shoe machinery owners, but it need not be that vector.

A policy of compensating those who are disadvantaged by policy change confronts four types of moral hazard. First, recipients may take their compensation and, nonetheless, continue their resistance to the policy change. Their gains are compounded by such a strategy: they receive both their compensation and whatever advantage is given them by the current policy, if their resistance to change is successful.

Second, firms and workers can be expected marginally to enter industries and economic activities whose incumbents are expected to receive compensation if change occurs. They enter not in response to expected investment yields, but only to place themselves in the relevant queue for compensation. Compensation effectively becomes, for them, not recompense for losses but, rather, rents.

Third, depending upon the formula for the determination of the amount of compensation, assets will be explicitly acquired by incumbents who expect compensation, in order to enlarge the compensation they will receive.

Fourth, false claims will be made to enlarge compensation. For instance, income stream expectations will be falsely enlarged if compensation is based upon income streams forestalled by the policy change; or human capital assets will be exaggerated if compensation is based upon the diminution of human capital values that occurs. Strategies which are calculated to establish eligibility to receive compensation payments and to cause those payments to be enlarged consume real resources in their contrivance and in the engineering of behavior for entry into the receiving queue. In addition to these organizing resources, other real capital assets are, to some extent, diverted from alternative uses in order to fulfill qualifying conditions and to affect the size of compensation payments.

If compensation payments are conditional and are paid out over time, there will be a tendency to spin out the fulfillment of the condition that triggers the payment of compensation. If compensation payments are made over time, for example, to unemployed workers whose lack of employment is determined to have been caused by a relevant policy change, and if the compensation payments are made only so long as the worker is unemployed, the duration of unemployment will be prolonged. Workers will be given a marginal incentive to refrain from active search for employment, because successful search will cut off the compensation payment stream.

This suggests that compensation payments should take the form of lump-sum payments. Lump-sum payments, however, may be transferred to rents. If unemployed workers receiving compensation payments find new employment as rapidly as unemployed workers who do not receive compensation payments, the payments may be perceived to be rents in the sense that their recipients suffered no extraordinary losses different from or larger than the losses suffered by workers unaffected by the policy change.

The proposals for associating compensation with changes in public policy are almost universally asymmetrical in quality. If policy change produces loss, it is proposed that losers be compensated. If, however, policy change produces gains, it is almost never proposed that gainers be required to disgorge their gains.

All policies have distribution effects. When policy increases rents for some, it diminishes rents for others; when policy increases the prices of

the services of some, it decreases the prices of the services of others. Policy might have explicit, deliberate redistributional objectives, or it might have efficiency objectives.

If redistribution is the objective sought by a policy change, it will tend to be frustrated if compensation is paid for the losses suffered as a consequence of the change; the compensation in part offsets the redistribution. If efficiency is the objective, policy should be designed that is allocationally neutral and the distribution effects of the policy should be ignored; if they are not ignored, there is a risk that the modification of policy to achieve desired secondary distribution effects will tend to frustrate the achievement of the efficiency purposes primary to the policy.

The literature on compensation for losses occasioned by policy change seems to assume that losses can be readily and explicitly attributed to changes in policy. This is, of course, false. Policy changes do not occur in otherwise static states of the world. Losses can be generated not only by policy changes, but also by many other factors. Alterations in the state of the world do not occur separately in time: they overlap. Furthermore, events can have multiple causes. The process of decomposition that would permit the consequences of policy change to be entirely separated out from the consequences of other phenomena would be very complex, perhaps impossible.

## II  EXEMPLARY CASES OF ADJUSTMENT COMPENSATION

### US Trade Adjustment Assistance

An arrangement for trade adjustment assistance was established in the United States by the Trade Expansion Act of 1962. The Act required that, in order to qualify, workers claiming adjustment assistance show that they had been injured by US liberalization of trade, and that liberalization was the major cause of injury. Very few workers received assistance under this standard of eligibility, and the Act was modified in the Trade Act of 1974. That Act provided for assistance to firms and workers injured by imports, whether or not resulting from trade concessions, and required that imports contribute *importantly* to the injury, but not that they constitute the major cause of the injury.

The 1974 Act produced a large increase in the number of workers receiving adjustment assistance. By early 1979, almost half a million workers had received $637 million in adjustment assistance. The assistance was of two types: money payments to compensate for earnings lost as a result of unemployment and diminished employment, and employment services to assist workers in finding new employment.

A study of recipients of trade adjustment assistance and a control group of other workers who had suffered unemployment for other causes was carried out in late 1979 (Mathematics Policy Research, 1979). The adjustment assistance recipients were heavily concentrated in a few industries,

mainly apparel, automobiles, and steel. Prior to the study, it had been assumed that workers who were adversely affected by imports would encounter a higher incidence of layoffs; that the duration of unemployment would be longer for those workers than for those unemployed from other causes; and that, because industries encountering import competition would be declining industries, job-specific skills of import-affected workers would diminish in value more than those of other workers, meaning that the earnings of those workers would decline more upon re-employment than would the earnings of other workers.

Most of those expectations were not borne out by the survey. Many workers receiving trade adjustment assistance were recalled to the jobs they held before receiving assistance. The unemployment experience of workers receiving assistance because they were adversely affected by imports was similar to that of workers unemployed for other causes.

Principles of distributional equity suggest policies that make compensatory transfer payments proportional to the injuries suffered. In this case, it was found that workers adversely affected by imports suffered injuries of roughly equal intensity and magnitude to those suffered by workers injured by other causes. While there seemed to be no warrant, on equity grounds, for giving larger transfer payment compensation to one set of workers, the legislation did make substantially larger payments available to import-impacted workers than to those adversely affected by other phenomena (see Richardson, 1982).

## Adjustment Assistance to Firms

Governmental assistance to firms to promote adjustment to policy change, and to other causes that affect them adversely, frequently subsidizes the persistence of inefficiency. This assistance is a kind of compensation for losers. There is a considerable history of North American and Western European experience in adjustment assistance for firms (see Vargo, 1971; US General Accounting Office, 1979).

The assistance often takes the form of promoting mergers, cooperative arrangements among firms, managerial reorganization, product diversification, and the increase in the mean size of firms by the elimination of smaller firms.

Assistance takes the form of loans at less than market rates or loan guarantees, tax incentives, and technical assistance. The rhetorical rationale for assistance refers to the necessity of "industrial restructuring and rationalization of industry."

The premise of this assistance is that government knows better than those who engage in market transactions the socially appropriate size of firms, the commodity mix that should be produced, the appropriate combination of factors, the proper location of economic activity, and the optimal pattern of production and marketing of commodities. Since wrong decisions were made in the market, governmental assistance is perceived to be an instrument for transforming them to right decisions; right decisions

are seen to be leading to survival of the firms in conditions of market competition. The premise on which adjustment assistance programs are based is, of course, questionable. There is no a priori justification for the belief that public officials are superior in their market judgments than are economic actors; indeed, the evidence of experience does not support that belief.

Where adjustment assistance has been administered, it has often had the negative effects of prolonging the life of inefficient firms that should be permitted to die; sub-optimally diminishing the rate of shrinkage of declining industries; retaining sets of managers who have already exhibited themselves to be incompetent and turning them to other governmentally assisted tasks; and locating capital and economic activity in socially inappropriate places (see Verreydt and Waelbroeck, 1982).

### US Urban Transit Job Protection

Arrangements for making compensatory adjustments for those who are perceived to be prospective losers when policy changes are introduced can lead to the introduction of inefficiencies. A case in point is the provision of protection of urban transit employees in the United States to eliminate or reduce losses they might incur as a result of federal subsidization of capital acquisitions and operating costs of urban transit systems.

After World War II, the number of riders on urban mass transit facilities in the United States declined sharply. In 1945 there were 18.9 billion transit passenger trips; by 1950, this had declined to 13.8 billion and by 1965, to 6.8 billion (American Public Transit Association, 1981, p. 52). The urban transit systems were replaced at a rapid rate by the private automobile as the preferred mode of transit. In 1975, 85 percent of all workers used private automobiles as their means of commuting to work and only 6 percent used mass transportation facilities; most of the rest either walked to work or worked at home (Meyer and Gomez-Ibanez, 1981, p. 38).

Until the end of World War II, most transit systems were privately owned. With the decline of ridership and the rise in operating costs, many systems were abandoned or else contracted their services. To permit the survival of urban transit services, many cities set up quasi-governmental authorities to acquire the systems and continue offering transit services. The urban transit systems of the country are now almost completely government-owned.

In order to facilitate the acquisition and rehabilitation of the transit systems by the governmental authorities, Congress enacted, in 1964, the Urban Mass Transportation Act, which made federal grants available for the acquisition of the systems and for capital improvements, such as the purchase of rolling stock and the building and improvement of garage and terminal facilities. The Act was amended in 1975 to provide also for federal grants to partially cover operating deficits. The fare revenues of the systems now cover only about one-third of the operating costs; the difference is provided by local, state, and federal subsidies.

When it was privately owned, the industry was heavily unionized and the terms of employment were defined by collective agreements. The unions were fearful that the acquisition of the transit systems by the public authorities would, in some cases, displace them as collective bargaining agents of the industry's workers and, in other cases, diminish the quantity of service, rendering some workers redundant; or that it would alter the nature of work done in the industry so that some crafts would become obsolete.

The unions offered political resistance to the congressional enactment of a federal grant program for the urban mass transit industry unless they were compensated by "job protection" clauses in the Act. Such protective clauses were inserted in the Act's Section 13(e). That section provided that "it shall be a condition of any assistance [given under the Act] that fair and equitable arrangements are made, as determined by the Secretary of Labor, to protect the interests of employees affected by such assistance." The protective arrangements were defined as including the preservation of rights, privileges, and benefits under existing collective bargaining agreements, the continuation of collective bargaining rights, the protection of individual employees against a worsening of their positions with respect to employment, priority of re-employment of dismissed workers, and paid training and retraining programs.

Grant assistance may not be given to a transit system unless the Secretary of Labor certifies that the relevant employees are protected. The Secretary of Labor has followed the practice of certifying only after the management of a system and the relevant trade unions have signed a "13(c) Agreement" providing for job protection for affected employees. The enactment of job protection arrangements to compensate transit employees for the risk they ran that the transit assistance program would affect them adversely has produced inefficiency in the industry.

The monopoly power of the workers of the industry was entrenched by providing for the survival of collective bargaining. A large proportion of the workers are bus operators. The ability to operate motor vehicles is commonly held; a very large fraction of the country's adult population has this skill, and the differences between operating automobiles and operating buses are sufficiently small that the skills can be learned in a few days. The large supply of operating skills implies that the competitive labor market price for bus operation would be relatively low. In fact, however, transit industry wages are not low. The average annual compensation of those workers in 1979 was $23,137; this compares with $14,376 for all private industry workers, $11,882 for automobile repair workers, and $13,841 for state and local government workers. Clearly, transit workers receive rents.

This results from the intensification of monopoly power produced by the compensatory legislation. Managers of the industry are held hostage; they know they cannot receive needed federal assistance grants unless the Secretary of Labor certifies that workers are protected, and that he will not certify unless the union signs a 13(c) agreement acceptable to them. Therefore, managers offer only weak resistance to demands for strong protective arrangements.

In addition to rents received in earnings of transit employees, the compensatory arrangement also generated other inefficiencies. The demand for transit services peaks sharply twice each working day. The difference between peak and trough demand is very large. The indicated supply response would be the employment of part-time labor, which would produce transit service during the peaks and would be released for other productive employment in the other hours of the day. The unions of the industry, however, put strong constraints on the number of part-time workers who are permitted to be employed. Workers are paid, therefore, for idle time or for make-work practices, and the output their employment could generate in other occupations in the trough hours is lost to the community.

The compensatory arrangement also inhibits the contraction of services from routes and during hours when the demand for service is trivially low; if workers must be paid full-time earnings in any case, the marginal savings from contracted services become small enough to forestall contraction. The subcontracting of the performance of, for example, rolling stock maintenance services to specialized performers is made impossible by union rules that prohibit subcontracting. The reduction of staff implied by contracting service, so that it can be performed by more efficient or more convenient transit modes, is forestalled by common requirements for redundancy, relocation, and retraining payments. The compensation arrangement in this industry also resulted in the unions' enforcement of lower work standards and stronger constraints on worker assignment.

The purposes of federal capital and operating cost subsidies of the urban mass transit industry were intended to be the improvement of productivity, increased service, reduction in fares, increased ridership, help to the poor, and the stimulation of certain favorable effects with respect to energy consumption, urban revitalization, improvement of the environment, and efficiency of land use. However, a study of the effects of the federal subsidy has found that 47 percent of the subsidy was siphoned off by transit labor — 28 percent in the form of increased labor compensation and 19 percent in the form of hours bought but not used for any productive purpose (Lee, 1983).

The introduction of labor protection clauses in the Urban Mass Transportation Act of 1964, to compensate workers and secure the consent of the union representatives, had the effect of introducing new, and entrenching old, practices that produced economic inefficiencies of diverse kinds.

## US Clean Air Act Compensation to High-sulphur Coal Producers

Another compensation case that produced inefficiency is that of the Clean Air Act Amendment of 1977.

The emission of suphur dioxide waste gases, especially by coal-burning power generating plants, converts to sulphuric acid in the atmosphere and falls in rain upon the north-eastern sections of the country, where it does environmental damage. Sulphuric acid emissions could be reduced by

moving from high- to low-sulphur coal, by washing coal before burning, or by installing scrubbers that remove the sulphur from the gases in the stacks.

Congress adopted legislation specifying clean air standards. It might have left to the producers of the waste the choice of the strategy for reducing sulphuric acidic emissions to the legal standard; they could have been expected to choose the lowest-cost strategy, which might have varied among emitters. But Congress did not do this. If it had, some power plants might have reduced their consumption of high-sulphur coal and increased their consumption of low-sulphur coal. Low-sulphur coal is produced in the western states and high-sulphur coal in the eastern states. Diminished consumption of high-sulphur coal in power generation would have diminished the employment of eastern coal miners and diminished the capital value of the assets of proprietors of eastern coal mines.

In order to compensate eastern coal interests for the policy change enforcing low sulphuric acid gas emissions, Congress specified that the only acceptable method of reducing waste gases would be the installation of scrubbers in power generating company stacks. Those scrubbers were required to be installed in the stacks of all new coal-fired plants, independently of whether they burned low- or high-sulphur coal. Scrubbing is often a high-cost method for reducing the acidic content of waste gases.

Thus Congress's compensation policy, designed to reduce the losses that eastern coal miners and mine-owners would incur as a result of the clean air legislation, produced inefficiencies in the economy. The compensation policy required the employment of high-cost methods of waste abatement and caused the output of the eastern coal industry and the employment of resources by that industry to be inappropriately enlarged (see Ackerman and Hassler, 1981).

### UK Assistance to Cotton Manufacturers

In the late 1950s, the United Kingdom employed compensation as an instrument for achieving a faster rate of decline of the country's cotton manufacturing industry than would have occurred if market processes had been permitted to determine the size of the industry. Since the industry's more rapid rate of decline hastened the rate of unemployment in the industry, dismissed workers were also compensated.

The scheme produced inefficiency by subsidizing the physical destruction of part of the country's capital stock that had a still-surviving residuum of useful economic life for the production of cotton goods, and it made transfer payments which were rents to both owners of physical assets specialized to cotton production and to workers in the cotton manufacturing industry.

The industry had been an early entrant in the industrial revolution. The UK was the first producer of cotton manufactures in mills, and in 1790 it produced the whole of the world's output of mill-produced cotton. Output of the industry peaked in 1910–13 and declined thereafter. The UK

contribution to the world cotton trade peaked for the last time at 82 per cent in 1882–4.

The British had a certain nostalgic affection for the industry, and since it was concentrated in two counties, Lancashire and Cheshire, where it was thought there were no large alternative sources of employment, a series of public policies sought to keep the industry alive. By about 1930 a consensus formed that the industry was suffering secular decline, and public dialogue developed over the question of the form of responsive public policy.

It came to be widely believed that the industry's problems derived mainly from an excess of capital equipment, some of which was operated intermittently in periods of revival of demand for cotton goods and of rising cotton goods prices; in trough periods some of this equipment was idled and some of it was sold for scrap. It was also thought that, although the industry's equipment was aged, and therefore of low productivity, there were only weak incentives for the purchase and installation of new, more productive equipment because the old equipment, long-since amortized, would produce cotton more cheaply than would new equipment, still to be paid for.

The British, therefore, settled in 1959 on a policy of subsidizing the scrapping of equipment and compensating dismissed workers. The number of spinning spindles and of looms in UK cotton peaked in 1924. In that year there were 63.4 million mule-equivalent spindles and 792,000 looms. In April 1959 there were in place 24 million mule-equivalent spindles, of which 8 million were idle; excess capacity was estimated to be 12 million. At the same, time there were 240,000 looms in place at running mills and excess capacity was estimated at 70,000 looms.

The government's scheme paid compensation upon the delivery of evidence that machinery had been physically destroyed. The highest rates of compensation were paid to operating mills that closed their doors, scrapping all equipment; the lowest rates were paid to firms that destroyed some equipment but did not close any of their weaving sheds or spinning mills.

The compensation rates were very generous; £66 was the mean rate of compensation for the destruction of a loom, the value of which in the second-hand machinery market just before the introduction of the scheme was only £5. The incentives to destroy machinery was strong, and machinery owners were very responsive to the government's offer. About half the spinning spindles and about 40 percent of the looms in place were destroyed. It was reported that machinery was moved from the storehouses of second-hand machinery dealers and from scrap yards back into the sheds and mills to be certified as having been destroyed in order to draw compensation payments.

The payment for the destruction of machines was covered by appropriations from the general exchequer and by levies on firms that survived the scheme. The compensation paid to dismissed workers was wholly covered by levies upon surviving firms.

By 1959 the UK produced only a small fraction of the world's cotton goods. There was free entry into the industry in other countries and in the UK as well. Dismissed workers were permitted to find their way back into employment in the industry. In these circumstances, neither surviving firms nor surviving workers could be advantaged by the higher rate of contraction of the industry that was induced by the government's schemes.

Clearly, the UK society was badly served by the policy. An inefficiently enlarged rate of contraction of the industry occurred. A piece of machinery has three uses: (a) to produce commodities continuously; (b) to produce commodities intermittently, as demand, costs, and prices fluctuate actively in use at times, and to wait idly at other times; and (c) to be reduced to scrap, melted down, and converted to other uses. The rational social rule is to shut down a machine when, at any output, it does not generate revenues that will cover variable cost; the rational social rule is to scrap a machine when its scrap value exceeds the discounted value of its estimated earnings stream, net of the cost of storage.

In well-informed, competitive markets, in which there are no significant external economies or diseconomies, machine owners will shut down (and re-open) and will scrap at the socially appropriate rates. The market rate of contraction of the industry will be at the socially appropriate level.

None of the defenses for the government's policy asserted that market participants were badly informed or that there were externalities. Yet the government, by subsidizing the enlargement of the rate of contraction of the industry, deprived the community of a warranted stream of commodities and adversely affected the efficiency of resource allocation and the output of the economy (see Rottenberg, 1964, pp. 575ff.; UK Board of Trade, 1959; Wiseman, 1959, pp. 1vff.).

## III CONCLUSION

Public policy, by distorting relative price sets of commodities and factors of production, can adversely affect efficiency and output in the economy. Changes in policy can, in this event, improve efficiency in resource use and cause the product of the economy to be enlarged. However, policy change may generate losses for some population vectors. Prospective losers may resist and frustrate the design and application of the change.

It has been proposed that an effective responsive strategy, in such cases, would be the compensation of prospective losers for the losses they will suffer if the policy change occurs, and the social welfare would be advanced by the employment of such a strategy.

Such a compensation strategy is attractive on its face. Closer examination, however, reveals that both its efficiency and its equity defenses might be derived from questionable premises.

# REFERENCES

Ackerman, Bruce A. and Hassler, William T. (1981), *Clean Coal/Dirty Air.* New Haven and London: Yale University Press.

American Public Transit Association (1981), *Transit Fact Book 1981.* Washington, DC: APTA.

Lee, Douglass B. (1983), "Evaluation of Federal Operating Subsidies to Transit, US Department of Transportation." Harvard University Staff Study no. SS–67–I/3/03, July 1983, mimeo.

Mathematics Policy Research (1979), "Survey of Trade Adjustment Assistance Recipients," Final Report. Princeton University, mimeo.

Meyer, John R. and Gomez-Ibanez, Jose A. (1981), *Autos, Transit and Cities.* Cambridge, Mass.: Harvard University Press.

Richardson, J. Davidson (1982), "Trade Adjustment Assistance under the United States Trade Act of 1974: An Analytical Examination and Worker Survey," in Jagdish N. Bhagwati (ed.), *Import Competition and Response.* Chicago: University of Chicago Press.

Rottenberg, S. (1964), "Adjustment to Senility by Induced Contraction," *Journal of Political Economy,* 72(6).

UK Board of Trade (1959), Reorganization of the Cotton Industry, Cmnd 744. London: HMSO.

US General Accounting Office (1979), Report to the Congress, *Considerations for Adjustment Assistance Under the 1974 Trade Act: A Summary of Techniques Used in Other Countries.* Vol. II, "Profiles of Adjustment Programs in Eight Countries." Washington, DC: GAO, mimeo.

Vargo, Franklin J. (1971), "How Others Do It: Trade Adjustment Assistance for Firms and Industries in Belgium, Canada, France, . . .". Washington, DC: US Department of Commerce, mimeo.

Verreydt, Eric and Waelbroeck, Jean (1982), "European Community Protection against Manufactured Imports from Developing Countries: A Case Study in the Political Economy of Protection," in Jagdish N. Bhagwati (ed.), *Import Competition and Response.* Chicago: University of Chicago Press.

Wiseman, J. (1959), "The Reorganization of the Cotton Industry," *The Times Review of Industry,* no. 31 (September).

# Comment 1

*Katherine Krumm*

Simon Rottenberg's arguments against compensation for loss arising from a policy change were quite eloquent. He was very comprehensive on the equity and efficiency and political pragmatic side, and pointed out a number of complexities and difficulties with a simplistic non-dynamic approach to compensation. At the same time, I feel that, in attempting to make these points, he has probably become too harsh in his case against compensation. The several points I would like to make do not really question the validity of Rottenberg's arguments, but rather try to balance them.

First, the presence of difficulties in developing a compensation policy is not in and of itself justification for not engaging in a compensation policy. Professor Rottenberg mentioned inefficiencies ranging from revenue collection to finance compensation. Ideally, some lump-sum method is used so as not to distort. This may not be possible, but it is not certainly the first or the last time that we have had to move into the theory of second- or third-best in taxation. One solution might be to make sure the costs of taxation distortion are taken into account when evaluating the costs and benefits of compensation.

Also, moral hazard problems were mentioned. Again, avoiding moral hazard problems is not necessarily superior to compensation policies designed to take them into account. If we are assuming that government action is predictable, we can probably assume that agents' behavior and their reactions to policies are predictable as well. In other contexts economists have developed incentive-compatible schemes, based on these reactions, to address the moral hazard problems. For example, we can learn from the insurance literature. Certainly moral hazard is present there; yet the insurance business continues to exist and has developed a number of contract features, such as deductibles or partial compensation.

Rottenberg mentions the complexity of government calculations necessary for compensation, identification of those affected, magnitudes, etc. We often underestimate the tasks that a government has to undertake, and certainly this is to be avoided. At the same time, we want some symmetry here. We can assume that agents can easily estimate policy change probability, and therefore can hedge. Certainly both government and private agents have complex decisions. (As an aside, I want to mention that the

assumption of rational expectations underlying a lot of this discussion is still being debated in the profession.)

A second point is that compensation for any expected change is not equitable because it would be doubly compensating. That is not an argument against compensation, nor is it an argument against taxation of the gainers for some type of unexpected shock. It is an empirical question as to what was and was not expected. Were the returns on this specific human capital, for example, abnormally high or low previous to the policy shock? On this equity question, society's concept of justice and equity may weigh status quo more heavily, regardless.

A third point is that compensation may have a reputation effect. If the current government's compensation for a former policy change suggests that there will be future compensation in the event of its policy being reversed, agents will be more willing to act in accordance with the new policy. It might be that the government wants its policy change taken seriously; it might want investment to go into sector-specific physical and human capital and not only into general capital; it may not want hedging to occur.

This raises the issue of lack of credibility, and the problems it poses in an attempt to liberalize. It might even be that the perceived probability of policy reversal is increased by the hedging behavior, and the credibility becomes endogenous. Likewise, the perceived probability of reversal might be decreased if the cost to government in changing back to the former policy is greater. If the society's policy is that a government has to compensate in the future, lack of credibility of the policy poses less of a problem. If there are imperfect capital markets for individual agents, a policy may be credible only if no group is going to suffer too much in the process of policy change. The cost in any one period cannot be too great for any one group; otherwise the policy will not be continued. In that case, it might make sense to compensate to affect expectations on the probability of policy reversal.

To conclude, Rottenberg has made a number of insightful points, on both the equity and the efficiency problems of compensation policy. Despite these, there may be times when it makes sense to compensate. Then we have to proceed with designing a compensation policy while keeping those problems in mind.

# Comment 2

*Demetris Papageorgiou*

Simon Rottenberg has examined the rationale for compensating factors of production for losses incurred as a result of policy change. He has searched for conditions, if any, under which such compensation is a sufficient or a necessary condition to the attainment of an improvement in welfare, provided that the policy reforms themselves are socially efficient.

I find it useful to subdivide my discussion into three components. The first analyzes the conditions under which monetary compensation to the (potential) losers of a new "efficient" policy is a sufficient requirement for a welfare improvement. For example, are there "efficient" policies for which compensation constitutes a sufficient condition for a welfare improvement, and other "efficient policies" for which compensation is irrelevant to the attainment of such an improvement? The second component discusses the efficient (optimal) ways of taxing and compensating, taking into account that losses have different time-paths from gains. The third component touches on the political considerations of both enacting new policies which inevitably will generate losers and of implementing new methods for taxation and compensation.

In the absence of any objective knowledge about the proper weights of welfare attached to various income groups, an efficient policy will guarantee a welfare improvement as well, if the losers are compensated for the monetary losses the policy imposes on them. This statement is correct regardless of the relative size of the income weights of the groups affected by the policy.

But what are the implications of this statement? Let us take the hypothetical example of a quota system for importing cars, which is effective in the sense that domestic prices of cars are considerably higher than they would be without the quota. Suppose now that the government changes its policy from quotas to tariffs, with rates lower than those implied by the prevailing quota system. This policy change stands to benefit the government, in the form of tariff revenues, and the consumers, in the form of lower prices, while the car-importers under the quota system and the domestic industry for car manufacturing are the losers. Are the old quota holders for cars entitled to compensation because of the policy switch? Are the owners of human and non-human capital employed in the

local industry of car manufacturing entitled to compensation? Entitlement here means "in order to guarantee welfare improvement."

In this hypothetical case, it is obvious that the unweighted gains from the increase in the consumer surplus, part of which is taxed away by the government, exceeds the unweighted losses of the importers under the quota arrangements and of the local car industry. This example allows an examination of some interesting situations. Consider the case in which there is a legal barrier to entry into the local car industry, so that there is only one firm realizing rents from the protection. Following the policy change, then, is compensation to the owners of the factors of production employed by the firm sufficient for welfare improvement? Or consider the case in which the holders of the quotas, or the owners of the factors of production employed by the firm, are earning their marginal product because they have paid the full price of the quota (either by buying the right of the quota in the market or by rent-seeking activities), or for the right to be in the local car industry. Are they, then, "more" entitled to compensation because of the new policy as compared with those of the previous case, for a welfare improvement? And furthermore, does the distinction really matter?

Moreover, is compensation warranted only for losses of quasi-rents (producers' surplus, in this case), or also for the ensuing frictional unemployment of factors of production? What are the economically optimal rules for deciding on the level of compensation of such factors if frictionally unemployed?

Consider Rottenberg's argument that those agents in the economy who are affected by the change in policy have been making decisions all along on their own investment of time and money, aware of possible reversals or changes in general of government policies. In other words, in our hypothetical example, the market price of a transferable import quota for cars incorporates the agents' evaluation of the effects of future government policies on the stream of income to be generated from them. If this is true, is compensation a sufficient precondition for a welfare improvement if a new, efficient policy is implemented? And in what sense does a lack of objective knowledge of welfare weights suggest the use of non-uniform income distribution weights? If I don't have objective grounds to judge whether "society" values the welfare of car consumers any differently from that of car importers or manufacturers, am I not really saying that the welfare of each is of equal value? In this case, what are the economic arguments for compensation?

Suppose that we have concluded that compensation is necessary and have also decided on the proper amounts. The issue then becomes the form by which revenues will be generated for compensating the losers and the precise form under which compensation will be disbursed. Two interesting problems are normally related with compensation. One has to do with the identification of winners and losers, and the other with the form of taxation.

Is it always feasible, for example, to tax the winners in order to compensate the losers? Is it at all probable that some of the winners may also be losers? Is it always possible to identify the winners and losers? (For example, how does one distinguish those who lose jobs because of deregulation from those who would have left their jobs anyway?) What are the preferred ways of taxing the winners? Given the costs of tax collection, would it be preferable to tax transactions or incomes or both on the grounds of efficiency — namely, the minimization of the deadweight loss and collection costs for the amount of revenue required?

Moreover, how does one reimburse the owners of factors of production that have been negatively affected by the new policies? While a lump-sum payment is the efficient method, in that it does not prolong the employment of resources in activities which have been negatively affected by policy reforms, it does however raise the issue of government's ability to raise the required sums on the one hand, and to determine their precise distribution among those entitled to compensation on the other.

The preceding questions become even more complex when we consider the possibility that gains from efficient policy changes are generated over longer periods than losses; suppose not only that some of the gains of an efficient policy change would appear within five years, while losses are incurred within six months, but also that some of the winners will emerge for the first time five years hence. How, then, does one go about collecting taxes now on future gains and from future winners? Does the phasing of the policy implementation over time offer a possible answer? In the phasing period, the final winners are taxed to provide compensation to the losers, as would be the case in phasing policies aimed at reducing the level and variance of protection. The consumers, by paying higher prices now than at the end of the phasing, are thus taxed, and those protected, while less and less so over the phasing period, are therefore compensated. But, as Rottenberg correctly argues, what will ensure that those correctly and properly compensated for now will not raise their demands for the old pre-reform policy in the near future?

It seems to me that little, if any, economic rationale can be established in favor of compensation for losers owing to policy reforms. If, however, it is decided to compensate potentatial losers in order to gain their consent to policy reform, common sense would suggest that the amount of compensation should not exceed the present value of the net benefits of the reforms, and that the disbursement should be in a manner that will least inhibit the mobility of factors of production.

# PART IV

---

# Liberalization of the
# Capital Account

# PART IV

## Liberalization of the Capital Account

# 6

# Welfare Consequences of Capital Inflows

*Arnold C. Harberger*

## I INTRODUCTION

This chapter addresses the question of the welfare consequences of international indebtedness. The proximate objective is to determine whether there exists a presumption in favor of policy interventions in the process by which economic agents in a particular country enter into debt arrangements with foreign creditors. In the event of a positive answer to this question, the next step is to explore some of the attributes that such policy interventions should possess, given the nature of the diagnosis that argues for their existence. Throughout the paper, our attention will be focused on less developed countries (LDCs), and within this group rather more on the so-called middle-income countries than on the truly poor ones.[1]

In pursuing the indicated objective, we shall follow two lines of analysis. The first (in section II) is that of standard applied welfare economics; the question here arises whether "externalities" are present in the process of LDC borrowing, and if so what is their nature and how should they be dealt with. The second approach is more macroeconomic; it inquires whether the presence of substantial international indebtedness enhances the probability that the country will be beset by difficulties of a macroeconomic nature.

By way of a preview, the conclusion of section II is that the marginal cost of foreign borrowing does indeed exceed the average cost, and that the existence of this difference (as far as country risk, as distinct from individual borrower risk, is concerned) is not "internalized" by individual borrowers. This gives rise to a situation in which a well chosen tax on

---

[1] Lest readers misunderstand, our concentration in middle-income countries does not mean that this will be an empirical study. Quite the contrary: our treatment is strictly analytical. However, the models and scenarios presented have been constructed bearing in mind mainly the situations, capital market structures, and policy constraints characteristic of the middle-income group.

foreign indebtedness would help improve the general welfare by acting as a corrective to a pre-existing distortion.

Section III explores the macroeconomic panorama. It demonstrates (using a simple simulation model) how a smoother time-path of international borrowing will help produce smoother time-paths of such variables as output, home goods prices, and wages. The analysis suggests that policy devices that help smooth the flow over time of international borrowing might be beneficial. One schema that seems to have significant value while possessing few drawbacks consists of devices that give incentives to concentrating a country's international borrowings toward the longer end of the term structure. Ample precedents exist, particularly in regulations that require a certain fraction (higher for shorter-term loans) of the proceeds of international borrowings to be held on deposit at the central bank. This places an automatic tax on short-term loans and tends to shift private borrowings to the longer-term end of the spectrum.

## II ON COUNTRY RISK

The principles determining the premia for country risk are similar to those applying to individual borrowers. A borrower has certain attributes which either enhance or diminish his quality as a debtor; these determine the risk premium that applies to him even at low levels of (his) total debt. In addition, the greater the amount of his debt relative to his assets, income, etc., the greater will be his probability of default and hence the greater will be the risk premium demanded on loans to him.

### Rising Supply Price of Debt may Look Like Monopsony but is not

In a certain sense, therefore, each individual borrower faces an upward-rising supply curve of funds. But is he a monopsonist? Certainly not, if one interprets that term to mean that he has an influence on market rates of interest. The interest rate that *he* has to pay will rise as a function of his total borrowings, not the interest rate in the local, national, or international market. So it is too with LDCs. Any individual country is likely to be too small to influence the rates of interest prevailing in the world capital market; yet the greater is that country's indebtedness, the higher will be the premium over, say, LIBOR or the US prime rate that it has to pay. But even very large middle-income countries are not likely to have an influence on LIBOR or the US prime rate itself. (Brazil's GDP, for example, is larger than that of Illinois but smaller than that of Illinois plus Indiana.) Hence these countries, just like individual borrowers, face upward-rising supply curves of funds, without in fact being able to influence the levels of world interest rates.

How do we characterize such a situation, and how should countries (or individuals for that matter) react to it? Unfortunately, the central issue here turns out to depend on the attitudes of borrowers with regard to

default. If borrowers' attitudes were symmetrical to those of lenders, then they (the borrowers) would be just as happy about the act of not making a payment as the lenders are unhappy about not receiving it. Default risk would be incorporated into the stated yield of bonds, but would otherwise have no meaning.[2]

### Something Like a Quasi-monopsony Situation may Arise from Differential Perceptions of Default Risk by Borrowers on the one Hand versus Lenders on the Other

One small step away from complete symmetry between borrowers and lenders occurs when borrowers and lenders, so to speak, look upon the phenomenon of default symmetrically, but assign different probabilities to it. Thus, if $i_f$ is the risk-free rate, $D$ is the amount of debt by a given borrower, $\delta_L$ is risk premium as assessed by lenders, and $\delta_B$ is the risk premium as assessed by the borrower, then the stated supply price funds to the given borrower will be

$$i_S(D) = i_f + \delta_L(D).$$

But the borrower will assess the time risk premium at $\delta_B$, and will act as if funds made available to him along the curve

$$i_B(D) = i_f + \delta_B(D)$$

were actually costing him simply the risk-free rate $i_f$.

He (the borrower) will be in a quasi-monopsony position when $\delta_L > \delta_B$. He will perceive the effective supply price to him to be upward-rising (for well-behaved curves) and to be equal to $i_f + [\delta_L(D) - \delta_B(D)]$. The marginal cost to him will then be

$$
\begin{aligned}
MC(D) &= \partial D[i_f + \delta_L(D) - \delta_B(D)]/\partial D \\
&= i_f + (\delta_L - \delta_B) + D\frac{\partial(\delta_L - \delta_B)}{\partial D}.
\end{aligned}
$$

---

[2] A classroom example I have often used concerns a perpetuity of $10 per month. At a rate of discount of 12 percent this would sell for $1,000. Suppose now that it were specified that each month a coin would be flipped, with the borrower paying $10 if it turned up heads and nothing if it turned up tails. Now the bond would (with only trivial qualifications) sell for $500. Its stated yield would go up to 24 percent, the additional 12 percentage points being "default risk." But everybody would presumably act as if the actual rate were 12 percent, and as if the actual situation were virtually identical to one which paid $5 with certainty every month. Here is a case in which borrowers and lenders have symmetrical attitudes with respect to default risk.

The above framework provides a "convenient" reason why supply curves of funds facing individual borrowers (or countries) might be upward-rising in the sense that the relevant cost to the borrower is indeed higher than the risk-free rate. It also shows why it is that in examples like the one given in note 2, where the perceptions of risk are the same for borrowers and lenders, it is indeed just the risk-free rate that represents the relevant marginal cost of funds to the borrower. However, it seems to me artificial (to say the least) to assume that the non-payment of debt, in the act of default, is viewed by most borrowers just as if it were any ordinary cash inflow (or reduction of any ordinary outflow, say, through a fall in the world price of an important input). On the whole, the act of default carries with it certain genuine costs—some of them concurrent in time with the default, and others extending over a number of future years because the credit standing of the individual (or country) is impaired.

In short, most borrowers do not perceive, in the act of default, a benefit equal to the amount they fail to pay. This means that the marginal cost of debt, as perceived by the borrower, will be equal to

$$MC(D) = i_f + (\delta_L - \delta_B) + D\frac{\partial(\delta_L - \delta_B)}{\partial D} + H(D).$$

$H(D)$ can be thought of as a "humiliation factor," but it must be emphasized (a) that it entails genuine financial costs as well as purely subjective ones, and (b) that it is likely also to be a rising function of any individual borrower's (or country's) debt, at least over a wide range within which the expectation of default rises as indebtedness itself increases.[3]

### Marginal Cost of Individual Borrower Risk is "Internalized" but that of Country Risk is not

An ordinary borrower will observe $(i_f + \delta_L)$—that is simply the supply price that faces him in the market. In addition, he will have his own perception of the probability of default, and his own judgment as to the extra costs $H(D)$ associated with default. Taking all these things into account, he will see $MC(D)$ as the marginal cost of debt that is relevant for his decisions, and will presumably act accordingly.

The situation is different when it comes to country risk. An individual Mexican or Brazilian borrower may today have ample collateral and little or no debt outstanding. Yet he will have to pay a healthy premium over LIBOR or the US prime rate in order to borrow in the international marketplace. That is, he would have to pay a $\delta_L$ for "country risk" even though, say, there is no serious individual risk. Moreover, with each increment of Mexican borrowing, this $\delta_L$ for country risk will increase,

---

[3] I will not attempt to deal with cases of debt levels so high that the probability of default approaches certainty.

giving rise to an externality quite similar to that associated with traffic congestion.[4] This externality—a cost which is borne by the economic agents of the country—will not normally be perceived or internalized by each marginal or incremental private borrower. It will consist of that tiny increment of cost that the fact of having more country debt imposes on all the country's borrowers.

### Guessing at the Size of the Country Risk Externality

The empirical analysis of country risk has been plagued by problems of two types: (a) especially for LDCs, the data are not of good quality; (b) the underlying economics of country risk dictates that the supply curve of funds facing a country shifts both upward (i.e., to a higher rate at any given quantity) and inward (to a lower quantity for given rate) as the country's situation becomes riskier. I state it this way intentionally—i.e, in spite of the fact that, for any upward-sloping curve, an upward and a leftward shift amount to the same thing geometrically—because I believe it reflects the way many participants in the capital market think. They think, or so it appears to me, both in terms of risk premia (in percentage points of interest per annum) and in terms of country debt limits.

As in many situations in economics, we may recognize the ultimate relevance of certain non-measurable items, but we end up working with what we can measure. So it is here. In the premium over LIBOR we actually *see* $\delta_L$, the risk premium demanded by lenders. We do not see $\delta_B$, the "risk premium" that borrowers perceive as a benefit to themselves, nor do we see $H(D)$, the "humiliation factor" that they perceive as a cost. We do know, however, that these two effects work in opposite directions, and we can hope that their net difference is small. Moreover, the quantification of the (in principle) measurable externality between $i_S = i_f + \delta_L(D)$ and $MC(D)$ is in any case an interesting exercise in its own right. We turn now to that task.

At any moment in time we can presumably observe, say, LIBOR ($i_f$) itself, together with the premium ($\delta_L$) that relatively low-risk borrowers (perhaps the government itself) in that country are paying (i.e., $\delta_L$ conceptually measures risk—individual borrower risk should in principle be added to it). We also know at least roughly the size of the (public plus private) international debt ($D$) of the country. These data permit us to locate points $A$, $B$, and $C$ in figure 6.1.

Now consider that the shape of a curve reflecting risk should be concave upward—otherwise the marginal cost of debt would tend ultimately to

---

[4] Additional cars on a highway slow down the average speed of all vehicles on that road, thus imposing costs on drivers other than those of the newly added cars. Similarly, adding new borrowers in a given country will, insofar as the country risk premium is an increasing function of total country debt (private plus public), cause other borrowers to have to pay higher rates, either immediately, or as old loans are rolled over and new ones incurred.

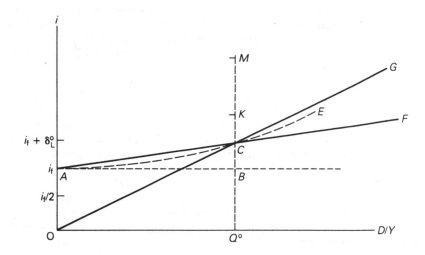

FIGURE 6.1    Upper and lower limits on the marginal cost of debt

decline with $x$. The plausible shape of the curve joining $A$ and $C$ would presumably be similar to $ACE$ as shown in figure 6.1. As it passes through $C$ this is necessarily steeper than $ACF$. I have also drawn it flatter than $OCG$. If indeed this is the case most of the time, we can "bound" the risk externality as lying between the "premium over LIBOR" ($\delta_L$) on the one hand and the actual real rate ($i_f + \delta_L$) on the other. Since the historic levels of real relatively risk-free rates have averaged in the range of, say, 2–3 percent per year, and since premia over LIBOR, for middle-income LDCs at least, have floated in the range of $\frac{1}{2}$ to, say, $2\frac{1}{2}$ percent per year, one can say that in a good case the country risk externality would be perhaps around $\frac{1}{2}$ to 1 percentage points, and in a bad case it might reach around 4 to 5 percentage points per annum.

These inferences follow simply from the geometry of the relationship between marginal and average curves. The line (also straight) which is marginal to the straight line $ACF$ will run through points $A$ and $K$, where $KC = BC$ from the standard relationship between marginal and average magnitudes when the average is a rising fraction of quantity. The externality at $Q^0$ is thus $CK$, which is equal to $BC$, the observed premium $\delta_L$. The line which is marginal to $OCG$ will pass through $O$ and $M$, where $Q^0C = CM$, once again from the standard marginal/average relationship. Economically, $CM$ would measure the externality for an average cost curve having the slope of $OCG$ at point $C$. But $CM = Q^0C$, which is simply $i_f + \delta_L^0$, the actual supply price of credit to the country (including country risk), measured at the quantity $Q^0$.

Hence, if the actual average cost curve passing through $C$ has a slope lying between that of $ACF$ and that of $OCG$, it follows that the actual

externality lies between $CK$ (which we identify with $\delta_L$) and $CM$ (which we identify with $(i_f + \delta_L)$. Assuming $i_f = 3$ percent, and $0.005 < \delta_L < 0.025$, this means that the risk premium would lie between $0.005$ (= min $\delta_L$) and $0.055$ (= $i_f$ + max $\delta_L$). My own sense is that the international credit market has tended to exhibit relatively greater supply elasticity where country risk was adjudged to be low, and relatively lower elasticity where country risk was considered to be high. Pursuing this line, one might construct an intermediate case with intercept at $i_f/2$, and consider that low-risk countries have $\delta_L$ between $0.005$ and $0.01$ and an intercept between $i_f/2$ and $i_f$, while relatively high-risk countries have $\delta_L$ between $0.010$ and $0.025$ and an intercept between zero and $i_f/2$. In this case the externality for the low-risk countries would run between $0.005$ (= min $\delta_L$) and $0.025$ (= $i_f/2$ + max $\delta_L$), while that for the high-risk countries would run between $0.025$ (= $i_f/2$ + min $\delta_L$) and $0.055$ (= $i_f$ + max $\delta_L$).

## Some Underpinnings for our Quantifications

In the area of policy economics with which we are dealing, there is little room for faintness of heart. Some sense of quantitative orders of magnitude is needed to get a reasonable diagnosis of the situation with which we are dealing. Yet formidable problems confront empirical work: the quantification of country risk premia is itself subject to great measurement or estimation error (which in turn tends to bias coefficients toward zero); moreover, many intangible factors enter into the assessment of country risk as among countries at any given time, and within a single country across different periods.

I hope that, given the fractious nature of the estimation problems involved, I will be forgiven for placing principal reliance on what appear to me to be plausible ranges for the relevant risk parameters. I feel very comfortable with an upper limit to the (risk-inclusive) elasticity of supply of funds that is based on a straight line like $ACF$ in figure 6.1. My confidence here rests mainly on my being firmly persuaded that the actual curve must get progressively steeper at higher quantities.

The upper limit is less easy to define. Certainly we do not seem to observe situations such as would be produced by elasticities of $\frac{1}{2}$ or less for the risk-inclusive supply curve. For example, at an elasticity of $\frac{1}{2}$, the actual interest rate charged would increase by 50 percent with a growth of just one-quarter in the $D/Y$ ratio. In the process, total interest cost would increase by a factor of nearly 2 ($1.25 \times 1.5 = 1.875$). I believe we have witnessed many increases of 25 percent in a country's $D/Y$ ratio, but never did they appear to come close to producing such an increase in interest cost. Such an elasticity would entail, in figure 6.1, an intercept on the vertical axis equal to $- (i_f + \delta^0)$. While the implications of such an intercept seem to be quite implausible and outside the range of our experience, I do not feel one can say quite the same for an intercept of zero and its implied unit-elastic supply of funds. Here the implications, while perhaps somewhat stretching our credulity, do not look on their face to be patently at odds with our experience.

*Some Thoughts on Country Debt Limits*

The qualms that I have about the approach taken here do not concern the problem of quantification of the risk premium as such, but rather the phenomenon of country debt limits. It seems quite clear that something like such limits exist, yet they are hard to pin down. In the first place, they are not formal limits, imposed by a specific entity. In the second place, there are usually new loans being made by some banks, even to countries conceived of as being at or near their debt limits. At this point one might be tempted to conclude that country debt limits are a figment of somebody's imagination. But then try to imagine an expansion of 25 or 30 percent in international credits to Brazil or Mexico, over the next year, to be accomplished strictly through ordinary financial operations with the international commercial banking community! I think one has to conclude from such an exercise that something like country debt limits do indeed exist.

But how does one deal with such limits in an analysis such as the present one? The most natural way of modeling a debt limit is to have the supply curve turn zero-elastic. But if we take this route we have to face something approaching an infinite marginal cost of debt—and with it an externality that also approaches infinity. Certainly, if the supply curve of funds is continuous, as it turns the corner to approach a vertical line, the curve marginal to it will diverge ever more widely from it, the externality being at every point $(1/\epsilon)$ $(i_f + 0_L)$, where $\epsilon$ is the elasticity of the (risk-inclusive) supply curve.

The problem is, I do not believe that we *see* externalities that even remotely approach an infinite cost. The analogy that I find most interesting is that of the sort of mats that one sometimes sees used as padding on gymnasium walls. The debt limits that exist in the real world are more like cushions than rigid walls. Some new loans are continually being made in the neighborhood of the limits, yet major expansions in total outstanding credit seem not to occur. If one were to try to trace the marginal or incremental cost associated with the loans that do occur when a country is at or near its debt limit, those costs are probably similar to the marginal costs of debt at other places along the supply curve of funds—more likely to be one or two times rather than three, four, five, or ten times the supply price of the funds involved. So I think of a supply curve of funds that behaves pretty much as described in our discussion surrounding figure 6.1, but against which is superimposed a cushiony debt limit. When the debt limit is penetrated, average and marginal costs derived from the supply curve are relevant. But penetrations of the debt limits do not take place at the volition of the borrowers, and do not occur with sufficient frequency to keep the term "limit" from having real meaning.

*Policy Implications of this Analysis*

For better or worse, simple and clear conclusions usually follow from simple and clear analysis. In the foregoing text, we have identified an externality—the difference between the marginal social cost of international credit and its average cost. The corrective for any such externality is something that will lead economic agents to internalize it. In the present case a tax would be the obvious instrument for accomplishing this task. A tax equal to the premium over LIBOR on, say, government debt in the country in question would do part but not all of the job. It would be an interesting tax, since it would vary appropriately with the situation, being high when the externality was high and low when it was low. It also has the advantage of being essentially independent of the actual or expected rate of inflation—expected inflation rates are incorporated into the interest rates on loans, not into the premia for risk on international obligations.

It seems to me that, just as the optimal congestion toll varies with the time of day and the season of the year, so too would an optimal "international borrowing tax" vary over time. Taking just the minimum tax implied by our analysis—an amount equal to the premium over LIBOR— it would vary rather dramatically as perceptions of country risk changed. At the level of theory at which we have been working, this means a tax that is high when the premium over LIBOR is high, and low when the premium is low. Arguing against this is the notion that people who enter into an obligation ought to know what they are getting into. I do not find this argument persuasive, especially since so much international credit has come to be lent at variable rates (LIBOR + $\delta$). But in the context of an actual legislative debate, I would consider the "first-best" position to be a tax which always collected $\delta_t$, the premium over LIBOR prevailing at time $t$ on loans with very low borrower risk. A "fall-back" position would be a uniform tax which tried to aim at $\bar{\delta}$, the prospective average premium over LIBOR on such loans.

Other devices for restricting foreign borrowing, such as direct licensing, etc., have less appeal, if for no other reason than because of their susceptibility to corruption, but in any event because of their likely high efficiency cost. (Whereas the efficiency cost of a tax of $T$ is $\frac{1}{2}T(Q_0 - Q_1)$, where $(Q_0 - Q_1)$ is the reduction in quantity occasioned by the tax, the efficiency cost of a quota limiting the quantity to $Q_1$ in a fashion independent of demand price is equal to $\frac{1}{2}T(Q_0 - Q_1)$ *plus* $\frac{1}{2} TQ_1$!)

## III MACROECONOMIC EXTERNALITIES

As a profession, we have yet to appropriately marry welfare economics with the monetary-macro area of our discipline. For example, we understate dramatically the welfare costs of inflation when we measure those

costs by the area under the demand curve for real cash balances between the quantities implied by the different inflation rates. Equally, we overstate the costs of cyclical unemployment by (often) implicitly assuming that the supply price of the unemployed is zero. This chapter is certainly not the place for me to try to resolve the perplexing issues that the above examples raise. But in any event, at a minimum, our profession seems to attach a negative value to economic fluctuations as such. That is, we prefer smoother paths to rougher ones—particularly where production and employment are concerned. It is from this rather minimal value judgment that I proceed in the remainder of the present section.

I may as well be frank, too, in revealing the origin of my recent interest in taking a macroeconomic view of the international lending process. During the late 1970s and into at least 1980, there was an obvious excess supply of international funds available to Chile. Actual lending was limited by a series of regulations—concerning the interest rates that foreigners could receive, concerning the amounts the Chilean financial institutions could borrow from abroad, concerning the "reserves" that such institutions would have to hold against their borrowings, etc. Uncharacteristically, perhaps, I found myself favoring, in principle, restrictions on the rate of Chile's international borrowing. My thinking in this case was motivated not by the notion of a permanent externality, such as was discussed in section II above, but rather by an instinctive fear of the consequences of "letting it all come in at once." I truly envisioned a capital inflow of 40 or 50 percent—or more—of a year's GDP, taking place within a 12-month period, if all restrictions and constraints would have been relaxed. I "knew" (or at least felt I knew) that with a free exchange rate there would have been an incredible appreciation of the peso had free entry of capital been allowed. And even with a fixed exchange rate, I warned against letting too much capital come in too fast. Ultimately, high rates of capital inflow did emerge, and the peso came to take on a highly appreciated value, but good economists to this day take different positions with regard to the causal chain involved.

Trying to set the stage for what will follow, let me say that I do not consider capital inflow as such to be a bad thing. I do, however, feel that any economic entity has a certain debt-bearing capacity, and that the equilibrium level of debt (or for a country, say, the equilibrium relationship of debt ($D$) to gross domestic product ($Y$)) is a number that has meaning and is to a considerable degree independent of the path by which the debt level was reached. My instinct tells me that reaching a given debt level by a smooth path is better than reaching it by a rough and bumpy one. I truly feel this to be so, without being able to "prove" it in terms of economic models that I consider to be deeply valid. The outcome of this situation is that I will present a model that I do consider to be deeply valid. Within the framework of this model, we will consider different paths by which a country might accumulate a given amount of debt, and will trace their consequences on the time-paths of output, prices, international reserves, etc. In judging these outcomes, we will consider smoother paths to be preferable to bumpy ones, other things being equal.

The model definitely does not belong to A. C. Harberger. It is the property of the economics profession, in the same sense that supply and demand belong to all of us. What the model has going for it is the principle of Occam's Razor. I do not believe you can devise a simpler model to handle the types of problem that this model does. We have two classes of goods: home goods (*H*) and tradables (*T*); the demand functions for these goods embody the notion that normally all income is spent (implicitly, the capital market is supposed to bring this result about); the supply functions are so designed as to be compatible with movements along a product transformation curve, but not to require that one always stays on such a curve; excess money (i.e., $M^s > M^d$) is spent in some pattern over time; and foreign borrowing (*B*) enters as a separate argument in the demand functions for goods.

The comparative static model incorporating these assumptions is set out below. The variables of the model are:

$H^d = H^s$      demand and supply of home goods

$T^d, T^s$      demand and supply of tradables

$B = T^d - T^s$      net foreign borrowing less net interest paid (= deficit in merchandise trade plus that in non-financial services)

$y = H^s + T^s$      aggregate output

$P_T =$      world price of tradables, taken as given and therefore equal to the exchange rate

$P_H =$      price level of home goods

$w =$      wage level (index of factor costs)

(Initial prices and wages are all assumed equal to unity, so that $dp_T$, $dp_H$, and $dw$ all represent percentage changes. Initial levels of $H^s$ and $T^s$ are each assumed to be equal to $0.5y$.)

$M^s = M^d$      money supply and demand (broad definition)

The equations of the model in its comparative static form are:

$$H^d = a_0 - a_1(p_H - p_T) + a_2 y + a_3 B \tag{1}$$

$$T^d = -a_0 - a_1(p_T - p_H) + (1 - a_2)y + (1 - a_3)B \tag{2}$$

$$H^s = b_0 + b_1(p_H - w) \tag{3}$$

$$T^s = c_0 + c_1(p_T - w) \tag{4}$$

$$y = H^s + T^s \tag{5}$$

$$B = T^d - T^s \tag{6}$$

$$M^d = ky[f_1 p_H + (1 - f_1)p_T] \tag{7}$$

$$w = f_1 p_H + (1 - f_1)p_T \tag{8}$$

$$w = w_0 + \beta[f_1(p_H - p_{H0}) + (1 - f_1))p_T - p_{T0})] \qquad \left\{ \begin{array}{l} \text{alternatives} \\ \text{to (8)} \end{array} \right. \qquad \begin{array}{l} (8a) \\ (8b) \end{array}$$

$$w = w_0$$

$$H^d = H^s \tag{9}$$

In the dynamic version we incorporate the following assumptions:
(a)    Last period's income is spent this period.
(b)    This period's foreign borrowings are spent this period.
(c)    Any excess supply of money coming out of last period is spent this period.
(d)    Any excess of foreign borrowing over the trade deficit is converted into money during the same period (money multiplier = 1).
(e)    The supply response of goods to changes in the price–wage relationships is spread out over five periods.

The equations that embody these assumptions are as follows (using $j$ as the time subscript):

$$H_j^d = a_0 - a_1(p_{Hj} - p_{Tj}) + a_2 y_{j-1} + a_3 B_j + a_1(M u_{j-1}^s - M_{j-1}^d) \tag{1'}$$

$$T_j^d = -a_0 - a_1(p_{Tj} - p_{Hj}) + (1 - a_2)y_{j-1} + (1 - a_{23})B_j$$
$$+ e_4(M_{j-1}^s - M_{j-1}^d) \tag{2'}$$

$$H_j^s = b_0 + b_1 \sum_{m=0}^{4} [2(p_{H,j-m} - w_{j-m})] \tag{3'}$$

$$T_j^s = c_0 + c_1 \sum_{m=0}^{4} [2(p_{H,j-m,} - w_{j-m})] \tag{4'}$$

$$y_j = H_j^s + T_j^s \tag{5'}$$

$$B_j = \text{foreign borrowing during period } j \tag{6'}$$

$$M_j^d = ky_j(f_1 p_{Hj} + (1 - f_1) p_{Tj}] = \text{money demand at end of period } j \tag{7'}$$

$$w_j = f_1 p_{Hj-1} + (1 - f_1) p_{Tj-1} \tag{8'}$$

$$w_j = w_0 + \beta[f_1(p_{Hj-1} - p_{H0}) + (1 - f_1)(p_{Tj-1} - p_{T0})] \qquad (8a')$$

$$w_j = w_0 \qquad (8b')$$

$$H_j^d = H_j^s \qquad (9')$$

$$M_j^s = M_{j-1}^s + \Delta R_j \qquad \text{(money supply fed by change in international reserves)} \qquad (10')$$

$$\Delta R_j = T_j^s - T_j^d + B_j \qquad \text{(reserves grow when foreign borrowing exceeds trade deficit)} \qquad (11')$$

Many different simulations were done using this model, but relatively few are reported here. The main point to be borne in mind is that the lessons to be derived from studying the results of all the simulations are essentially identical to those that derived from looking at the results presented here.

*Going from low to high elasticities*, we compare figure 6.2(a) with 6.2(b) (or column (1) with column (2) of table 6.1) and figure 6.3(a) with 6.3(b) (or column (5) with column (6) of the table). The periodicity of response remains identical, but, as should be anticipated, movements of prices are somewhat greater in the low-elasticity case, while movements of quantities (real output) are somewhat greater in the high-elasticity case.

*Making the time-path smoother*, while leaving its length the same, we compare figure 6.2(b) with 6.2(c) (or column (2) with column (3) of table 6.1) and figure 6.3(b) with 6.3(c) (or column (6) with column (7) of the table). This does virtually nothing—the cumulative divergence of both prices and output from their initial values remain virtually identical. It is only the timing which changes: as the peak inflow of capital moves from periods 9–12 to periods 5–8, the peaks of output, home goods prices, and international reserves also occur earlier. But nothing else of moment happens.

*Stretching the inflow of capital*, on the other hand, has a significant effect. Figures 6.2(d) and 6.3(d) have the same total capital flow as all the rest, but it is spread over double the period. The simplest comparison to make is between these figures and figures 6.2(c) and 6.3(c), respectively, for between members of these pairs the only difference is the length of time over which the given total capital flow is distributed. The notable result here is that, while the home goods price level rises by almost precisely half as much in case 6.2(d) (column (4) of the table) as in case 6.2(c), the *cumulative* deviations (both positive and negative) of output from its norm are cut in half. That means that we achieve more output stability by bringing in the same amount of capital over a longer time. If output stability is a desideratum, therefore, it is worth paying some price to avoid drastic changes in the rate of capital inflow. In the Keynesian case the effect

TABLE 6.1 Features of time paths of capital, output, prices, and reserves under alternative assumptions

| | Neoclassical elasticity[t] assumptions | | | | Keynesian elasticity[t] assumptions | | | |
|---|---|---|---|---|---|---|---|---|
| | Low (1) (from 6.2b) | High (2) (from 6.2a) | High (3) (from 6.2c) | High (4) (from 6.2d) | Low (5) (from 6.3a) | High (6) (from 6.3b) | High (7) (from 6.3c) | High (8) (from 6.3d) |
| **Capital inflow** | | | | | | | | |
| Peak level | 15 | 15 | 15 | 7.5 | 15 | 15 | 15 | 7.5 |
| First reaches peak[t] | 9 | 9 | 5 | 9 | 9 | 9 | 5 | 9 |
| End of peak[t] | 12 | 12 | 8 | 16 | 12 | 12 | 8 | 16 |
| **Real output** | | | | | | | | |
| Peak level | 103.4 | 104.5 | 106.6 | 102.2 | 114.2 | 116.8 | 117.1 | 108.7 |
| First < 100[t] | 13 | 13 | 9 | 16 | 16 | 16 | 15 | 28 |
| Cumulative > 100 | 23.8 / 224 | 33.3 | 33.1 | 18.2 | 117.0 | 137.1 | 134.7 | 133.1 |
| Cumulative < 100 | 23.8 | −32.2 | 32.3 | 18.0 | 4.3 | 4.9 | 2.4 | 0.7 |
| **Home goods price level** | | | | | | | | |
| Peak level | 1.27 | 1.19 | 1.19 | 1.10 | 1.19 | 1.10 | 1.10 | 1.05 |
| Period of peak[t] | 10 | 10–11 | 6–8 | 10,11,14,15 | 10 | 10,11 | 5,6 | 9–11,15 |
| First < 1.0[t] | 13 | 13 | 14 | 26 | 13 | 13 | 13 | 26 |
| **Foreign reserves** | | | | | | | | |
| Peak level | 50.9 | 48.0 | 48.8 | 44.0 | 47.9 | 49.5 | 50.4 | 44.7 |
| Period of peak[t] | 12 | 12 | 5 | 13 | 10,12 | 10 | 5–7 | 10,13 |
| First < 40[t] | 15 | 14 | 13 | 25 | 14 | 14 | 13 | 25 |

*Notes:*
Throughout, it is assumed that the marginal propensities to spend on tradables and nontradables are 0.6 and 0.4, respectively, out of income; 0.2 and 0.8 out of loan proceeds; and 0.25 (per period) out of $m^s$ and $m^d$.
Low elasticities of supply = 0.5 for tradables, 2.0 for nontradables.
High elasticities of supply = 1.0 for tradables, 4.0 for nontradables.
All elasticities of demand = −0.50; initial quantities of tradables and nontradables both = 0.5; initial price levels = 1.0, initial reserves = 40.

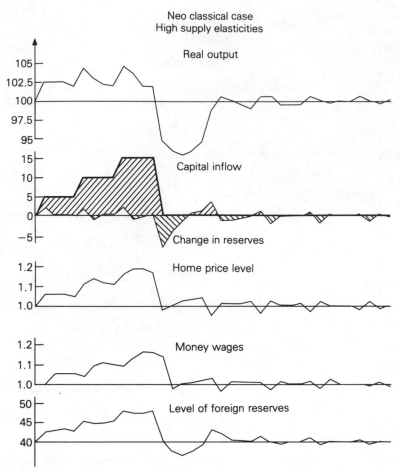

FIGURE 6.2(a)   Change in reserves: neoclassical case, high supply elasticities

is in the same direction but less dramatic—the same cumulative deviation of output is simply spread over twice the period.

*As between the Keynesian and the neoclassical versions of the model*, our prior expectations are substantially validated. As one would anticipate, the neoclassical version provides for no free lunch. Though a bulge in output does occur as the borrowings are spent, a later decline of output below its norm occurs to cancel out the gain. In fact, the cumulative sum (to $t = \infty$) of the deviations of output from its norm is exactly zero in all cases built on neoclassical assumptions (something I did not know at the time the assumptions were imposed).

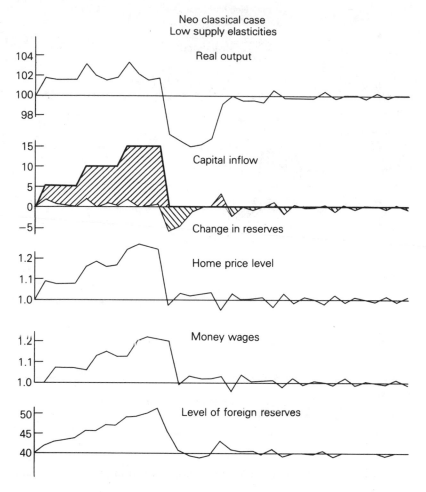

FIGURE 6.2(b)    Change in reserves: neoclassical case, low supply elasticities

On the other hand, the Keynesian assumptions do imply a (sort of) free lunch. The rise of output above its norm is not counterbalanced by anything like an equivalent shortfall later on. But, before rejoicing too much, recall that we have not provided for the repayment of the amounts being borrowed. If we introduced a separate pattern of repayment over a later span of years, we would find that the repayment cycle would entail, in the neoclassical case, just a shortfall of output counterbalanced later by an equivalent "surplus" of production. In the Keynesian case, however, the

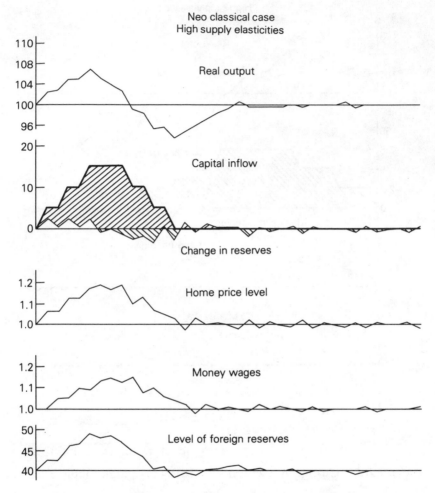

FIGURE 6.2(c)   Change in reserves: neoclassical case, high supply elasticities

predominant effect of repayment would be the shortfall of output, with no corresponding "surplus" to counterbalance it.

The lesson from the macroeconomic exercise that is relevant for this chapter is that, *if* we desire smooth paths of output and relative prices, we should be willing to incur some costs in order to help limit fluctuations in the rate of international capital flows. One has to tread carefully in this arena of policy, however, because all the results reported here stem from the fact that some share (in this case, 80 percent) of the loan proceeds is

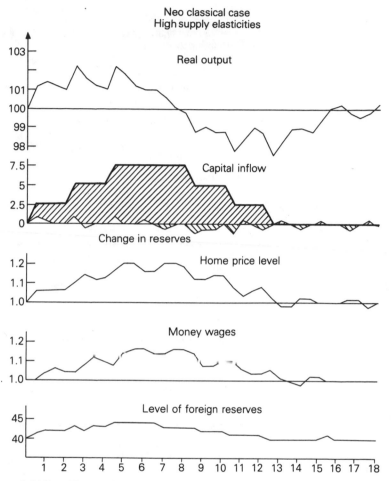

FIGURE 6.2(d)   Change in reserves: neoclassical case, high supply elasticities

assumed to be spent on nontradables. If the total proceeds were incrementally spent on tradables, there would be no effect on output, home goods prices, wages, or any such variable. It would be as if the country borrowed some Siemens generators or Mazda trucks and simply started working with them. One must thus be aware that any restriction we introduce, or any "distortion" that we impose, as a corrective for the ills of a too-variable rate of capital flow will be itself distorting (and non-corrective) to the extent that the capital flows are "spent" on tradables. Funds being fungible, we cannot hope to legislate disincentives to borrowing to finance one type of spending and not another. Hence we must simply be aware that, as we introduce policy measures designed to smooth the rate of capital flow, we will in certain circumstances be helping to correct a pre-existing distortion, while in other cases we will be introducing

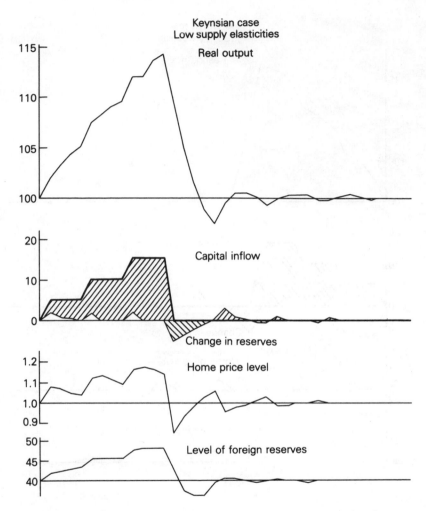

FIGURE 6.3(a)   Change in reserves: Keynesian case, low supply elasticities

a new distortion into an otherwise acceptable situation. (Because the pre-existing distortion is finite in the one case and zero in the other, we can always find a corrective distortion sufficiently small that its net effect is positive.)

Given this consideration, as well as the fact that we have not established more than an impressionistic case for the existence of a macroeconomic externality associated with international borrowing, I am prone to move cautiously with respect to policy measures.

The policy device that I find most appealing under these circumstances is one that several countries have actually used—a "tax" which varies

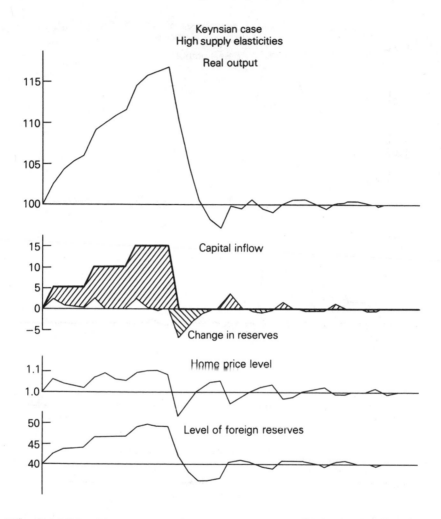

FIGURE 6.3(b)   Change in reserves: Keynesian case, high supply elasticities

inversely with the term of an international credit. Typically, this "tax" has taken the form of a requirement that a certain fraction of the loan proceeds be placed on deposit (either at a zero or at a less-than-market-interest rate) at the central bank. By varying this fraction (or, indeed, by simply placing a time limit on the period the deposit must be held), the cost to the borrower can be made to fall (as a fraction of the loan amount) as a function of the term to maturity of the loan.

    As I see it, this device is more of a safeguard against an abrupt cutting off of international credit than it is a smoother of the rate of inflow as

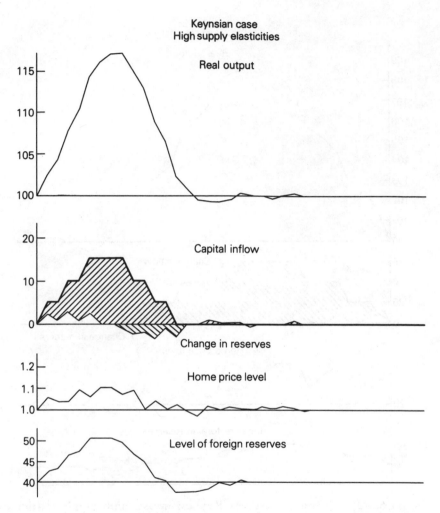

FIGURE 6.3(c)   Change in reserves: Keynesian case, high supply elasticities

such. It is my belief that the presence of legislation of this type should not significantly reduce the "country debt limits" that the international financial community (in its own rough way) imposes. Debt limits should depend on magnitudes like GNP, capital stock, exports, etc., much more than on the specific time-paths associated with the debt itself. Obviously, there are costs involved to individual borrowers who would prefer (or have easier individual access to) shorter-term credits. But I feel there can be little doubt that countries whose average term of debt has been longer have found it easier to surmount the difficulties involved in the recent tendency of the

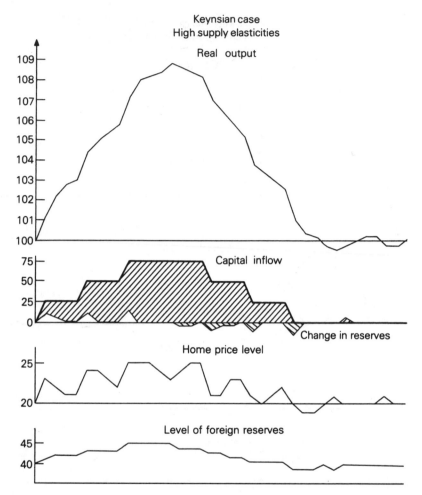

FIGURE 6.3(d)   Change in reserves: Keynesian case, high supply elasticities

international financial community to retrench the flow of credit to LDCs. And I do *not* have the sense that the countries with regulations tending in this direction have had to pay any obvious price for them in terms of significantly reduced total credit volumes.[5]

[5] Without trying to impugn the rationality of the international financial community, I feel nonetheless irresistibly tempted to note the degree to which the separate entities comprising that community tend to reach similar judgments at about the same time. At the very minimum, policy measures designed to lengthen the average term of a country's international indebtedness will limit the damage that could be done by the international financial community's all of a sudden deciding (with or without good reason) to withhold renewal of existing credits.

# Comment 1

*Liaquat Ahamed*

This contribution embodies the quintessential characteristics of what I call "the Harberger approach" to economic analysis. It involves taking very simple models and using them to illuminate current policy issues. I personally find this a very useful approach. It allows one to focus on policy issues in an analytical manner without having to embark on long-run programs of research. Nevertheless, it does have some pitfalls, and I shall refer to some of them here.

Let me turn to section II, which addresses microeconomic issues. Here I have a serious reservation: is it illuminating to think of problems of foreign borrowing in terms of demand and supply curves? Let me illustrate this with two examples. The first relates to the notion of country limits. One interpretation of country limits is the one vaguely proposed by Harberger that the supply curve for foreign capital becomes totally vertical. I must admit that I always conceived of these country limits as representing some degree of credit rationing, where interest rates are not allowed to play an equilibrating role. Therefore, when I think of country limits it is not that the supply curve becomes vertical, but that it steadily slopes upwards and stops dead in its tracks.

The second problem I have with thinking about foreign borrowing in terms of supply and demand curves is the traditional difficulty associated with partial equilibrium analysis—that the demand and supply curves depend on very much the same sorts of things. For example, let us suppose the probability of default declines with the rate of growth. Thus, when a shift in investment opportunities occurs, not only would the demand curve for foreign capital shift upward, but, because the probability of repudiation falls, the suppy curve would shift as well. You would get a rise in the debt-to-GDP ratio, but the risk premium could go anywhere.

By contrast, suppose you had a rise in the demand for foreign capital that emanated from a fall in savings. The demand curve would shift upwards, but the supply curve would shift backwards. Debt-to-GDP ratio could go any way, and you get a rise in the risk premium. Hence, if one were to look historically at relationships between the debt-to-GDP ratios and risk premia, you would have a hard time identifying a pattern, because supply and demand curves were shifting all over the place.

From a policy point of view, therefore, I think one would want to divide countries on the basis of whether or not they have been rationed. For a

country that is not being rationed in the international market, I suspect that the sort of considerations Harberger raises in his paper are quite relevant. A lot of the middle-income countries in the mid-1970s would fall into that category. However, I would hazard a guess that most developing countries, including a lot of the middle-income ones, are currently being rationed.

The major policy issue in countries that are being rationed relates to a different externality. Certain forms of expenditure or economic activity, by shifting the supply curve of the capital, provide an externality to the rest of the economy. Let us suppose that a country was able to raise its savings rate and increase its investment rate commensurately. The resulting acceleration in growth, by shifting the supply curve of foreign capital, would alleviate foreign borrowing constraints, and therefore would have a second-round effect on growth. The implications of this would be that one might want to subsidize savings. This is a very different form of externality from the one referred by Harberger.

Let me turn to section III, which is the macroeconomics section. Here one has to distinguish two very separate sets of issues. Suppose a country has a debt-to-GDP ratio of 10 percent, and an exogenous event occurs which warrants a shift of its debt-to-GDP ratio to 50 percent. The first issue is, how fast should it go from one position to the other? The second issue, which I think is somewhat confused with the first, relates to instability in annual flows.

Regarding the first question of how fast to adjust, I think the simulations do tell a story. I am not sure I quite believe the story, for precisely the same sorts of reasons cited by Dornbusch (1984). The best way of illustrating this is to look at one of the scenarios. Capital inflows steadily build up and then go to zero; the real exchange rate steadily appreciates by 25 percent and then suddenly collapses. Now, if it is known that a dramatic depreciation is going to happen in the last period, the residents of the country would have sold their real assets and moved the money abroad. So, for the sort of story that Harberger relates to be valid, one must assume some form of myopic private behavior. One way of rationalizing the story might be in terms of speculative booms. Essentially, an inflow of foreign capital drives up the real exchange rate; real estate prices start going up; everyone goes abroad and borrows more to invest more in real estate; and so on. I am perfectly willing to believe that the private sector does act in ways that destabilize the economy, but I do not think that has much to do with short-term capital.

Let me turn to the issue of instability in the flows of external capital from period to period. Here, I think, there is a case for a tax that varies inversely with maturity. I would like to make two points, however. One is that the instability of short-term capital is prone to being somewhat overrated. Certain forms of short-term capital—for example, trade credit—are probably more stable than medium-term credit.

Second, in periods when perceptions about a country's prospects start becoming gloomier, medium-term credit tends to dry up first, while banks

are still willing to provide short-term credit. I can evisage—though I have not thought this through very carefully—a tax on short-term borrowing leading to *more* instability in the availability of total credit than would be the case in the absence of such a tax.

# Comment 2

*Rudiger Dornbusch*

It is a pleasure to discuss the 1980s version of Harberger's earlier and influential work of economic policy in a dependent economy setting (see Harberger, 1964, 1974). The present contribution integrates two of Harberger's longstanding concerns and the oral tradition that he has created: along with the cubist elements (triangles, trapezoids, etc.) of his interest in applied welfare economics, we have the macro-issues of relative prices and employment in a small open economy.

Herberger raises two aspects of the capital inflow problem. First, the micro-question—are there externalities? He identifies the externality as the country risk premium. In an analogy to the traffic congestion problem, he recommends as a remedy a toll, or a corrective tax on foreign borrowing. Second, he addresses the macro-problem, noting that capital inflows tend to make waves and that those waves are disruptive from a stabilization point of view. Even if we cannot put down an exact model to judge the macro-costs of the disruption, Harberger follows common sense to suggest that we want to stretch out the flows and smooth and reduce their amplitude.

I will first consider the externality issue. In Harberger's model, a country encounters in world capital markets an increasing risk premium as it raises its debt-to-income ratio, but there is no incentive for the individual borrower to internalize this aggregate effect. In an analogy with the traffic problem, a congestion tax is required, but the question remains how large that tax should be. Here I differ with Harberger. I cannot see that a country faces an upward-sloping supply curve of funds. All theory and evidence run counter to this. We observe that countries can borrow at extremely moderate spreads over LIBOR—2 or 3 percent—or cannot borrow at all. There is no evidence that the risk premium varies systematically and sensitively with a country's external indebtedness. But we would expect this from the theory of credit rationing. Once we accept that the appropriate model is one that includes credit rationing, and, in addition, accept the possibility that a country may not be able to roll the debt owing to an external shock, the congestion costs must be reckoned in terms of this extended model, and the tax might well become prohibitive. Capital

controls would be optimal when external indebtedness is too large relative to the macro-risks of shocks-cum-rationing.

A second point in this context is to ask whether there are other distortions in the economy that have a bearing on the capital flows. In the Chilean context this was certainly the case. The exchange overvaluation implied a subsidy on investment with import content and a subsidy on imports of durables. The capital account surplus merely reflects the excessive, distortion-induced current account deficit. Given the real exchange rate, an additional, corrective capital import tax is appropriate.

Consider next the macro-problem. In Harberger's formulation a capital inflow is directly linked to spending: capital inflows raise spending one-for-one, thus introducing a most unfortunate and confusing lack of distinction between the capital account—trade in assets—and the current account, or the balance between income and spending. Consider two different experiments. Suppose the capital account is opened and the rest of the world goes bonkers over Chilean assets, leading to a massive capital inflow. Surely the Chilean authorities can respond by printing up Chilean securities (money or debt) and thereby can sustain the exchange rate, and shield the economy completely from the capital inflow by accumulating foreign assets. Capital inflows do not, by any means, create the necessity of an imported spending boom, real appreciation, and trade deficit. By contrast, consider an increase in aggregate spending. Overvaluation, brought about by exchange rate fixing in conjunction with mismanaged wage indexation, leads to dissaving and a massive shift into imported consumer and producer durables. The current account is financed by foreign borrowing. Which is the Chilean case? I have little doubt that it is the second, but even if it were the former, appreciation can only result as the consequence of mismanagement by the authorities.

But what should be the policy response to excessive current account deficits and real appreciation? Should the authorities limit the deficit? Should they do so even if the deficit reflects high investment owing to improved investment opportunities, as was the case, for example, with minerals in Australia? Unless we see an explicit distortion, we would be inclined not to interfere. But there are two specific points to bear in mind. One is macroeconomic adjustment costs stemming from inflexible money and/or real wages, which become important once the boom subsides and debt service and real depreciation become necessary. The second is the need to recognize, as Martin and Selowsky (1984) have shown, that domestic and real interest rates differ, because in the adjustment process the real price of home goods changes. If sufficient foresight makes the private sector overestimate its debt service ability, this may be an important source of aggregate difficulties and, hence, a reason to be concerned with excessive rates, both current and cumulative, of foreign borrowing.

Harberger's contribution is important in stepping back from the Latin American debt problems to ask whether there are lessons and good economic foundations for a very different policy approach. Even if he does not quite say it, he leads one to conclude that he firmly rejects the *laissez-faire*

approach to foreign borrowing. He would certainly impose some taxes, but, more importantly, he would have warning bells ringing from all the towers once real exchange rates and standards of living detach themselves from reality, as was the case in Chile and Argentina in 1980–1. This is an important lesson from a policy economist whose presumption runs strongly in favor of free markets.

## REFERENCES

Dornbusch, R. (1983), "Real Interest Rates, Home Goods and Optimal External Borrowing," *Journal of Political Economy,* February.
Dornbusch, R. (1984), "External Debt, Budget Deficits and Disequilibrium Exchange Rates." Unpublished manuscript, MIT.
Harberger, A. (1964), "Some Notes on Inflation," in W. Baer and I. Kersteneksky (eds), *Inflation and Growth in Latin America.* Homewood, Ill.: Richard D. Irwin.
Harberger, A. (1974), "The Case of the Three Numeraires," in H. Sellekaertz (ed.), *Economic Development and Planning: Essays in Honour of Tinbergen.* London: Macmillan.
Martin, R. and Selowsky, M. (1984), "Energy Prices, Substitution, and Optimal Borrowing in the Short-run," *Journal of Development Economics.*

# 7

# The Order of Liberalization of the Current and Capital Accounts of the Balance of Payments

*Sebastian Edwards*

## I INTRODUCTION

For many years, economists have argued that developing countries should rely more heavily on the market mechanism. In particular, it has been argued that liberalization processes, entailing the "freeing" of domestic markets and opening up of the economy to the rest of the world, should be implemented. A large amount of effort and resources have been devoted to the study of the relationship between the degree of market use, economic efficiency, and economic growth. These studies have resulted in the accumulation of an impressive body of empirical evidence that indicates that liberalized and export-oriented economies outperform — in terms of both growth and equitable income distribution — repressed and closed economies.[1] However, despite this evidence, and the widespread belief among economists in the merits of liberalizing the LDC economies, few serious efforts to that effect have been made by these countries. Many times liberalization attempts have been frustrated at different stages, wtih these economies reverting to repressed inward-looking developing strategies.

Why, then, if liberalization is so desirable, do we not observe more successful liberalization attempts? There are a number of possible answers to this question. First, even if a liberalization process results in an overall (for the economy as a whole) welfare gain, there are sectors that will gain and sectors that will lose from it. If the losing sectors are politically

---

[1] Harberger (1959); Little et al. (1970); Balassa (1976, 1982); Bhagwati (1978); Bhagwati and Srinivasan (1979); Krueger (1978, 1981, 1983a). On the order of liberalization see Edwards (1985b).

powerful they may frustrate these liberalization efforts.[2] This problem becomes more complicated once it is recognized that short-run winners and losers may differ from long-run winners and losers (see Mayer, 1974; Mussa, 1974). From a policy perspective, this fact suggests that the identification of different groups affected by the liberalization process, and the possible compensation of (short-run?) losers, could be important to generate a successful process.

Second, to the extent that there are short-run rigidities and adjustment costs, a liberalization process may result in short-run output (and welfare) losses. Even if these losses are more than compensated in the future — with the present value of the change in society's welfare being positive — governments may be reluctant to embark on a liberalization episode. The reason for this is that the time-horizon relevant to a government may be different (i.e., shorter) than that relevant to the economy as a whole. From a policy perspective, this problem indicates that the analysis of the dynamics of liberalization — differences between short- and long-run effects — is critical. Once this dynamic process is understood, policies aimed at reducing the short-run costs of the adjustment could be implemented.

Third, liberalization has often been attempted at a time when a major stabilization program, aimed at reducing inflation and solving a serious balance of payments crisis, is underway.[3] As a result of this, the costs of the liberalization process are confused with those of the stabilization program, with the consequent resistance to the liberalization effort.

Finally, sometimes the transition between a repressed and liberalized economy is mismanaged at a macroeconomic level, generating additional costs, which can become associated with the liberalization process itself.

It is clear from this discussion that the *dynamic* aspects of liberalization episodes are extremely important. The transition between a repressed state and a liberalized economy should be implemented carefully, in order to avoid the abortion of the liberalization attempt itself. Among these dynamic aspects, those related to the speed and order of liberalization are particularly important. With respect to the former, the main question is, how fast should an economy be liberalized? In analyzing this problem considerations related to (a) efficiency gains, (b) income distribution, (c) credibility of the liberalization reforms, and (d) feasibility of the attempt should be taken into account.[4] Regarding the order of liberalization, the main question is, which markets should be liberalized first? This is a complicated question which has both micro- (welfare) and macro-implications. At the micro-level typical second-best problems are present, while at the macro-level different orders of the liberalization process will imply different paths for

[2] This statement, of course, assumes away the possibility of fully compensating the losers of the liberalization effort.

[3] See Krueger (1978, 1981); Little (1982); Michaely (1982).

[4] On the speed of liberalization see Aizenman (1983), Leamer (1980), Pindyck (1982), Krueger (1983b), Mussa (1982).

the critical variables, including the real exchange rate, aggregate output, and unemployment.

This chapter deals with a particular aspect of the order of economic liberalization: the order of liberalizing the current and capital account of the balance of payments. It has generally been considered that the opening of the economy to the rest of the world is an integral part of any economic reform aimed at increasing the role of markets in LDCs. Until recently, however, very little discussion has been devoted to the order in which the current and capital accounts should be liberalized.[5] The recent experience of a group of countries from the Cone of South America — Argentina, Chile, and Uruguay — has generated new interest on the subject. These countries followed opposite orders — Argentina and Uruguay opened the capital account first, while Chile opened the current account first — with a common fate in the early 1980s: deep economic recession and (partial) reversal of the liberalization attempt. An important policy question that has emerged from these experiences has to do with defining liberalization policy packages (including a specific order) so as to increase the possibility that the reforms will indeed be undertaken and will not be reverted.

In this chapter some of the most important issues related to the order of liberalization of the current and capital accounts of the balance of payments are discussed. The organization is as follows. In Section II a positive analysis of the effects of liberalizing the capital and current accounts on production and income distribution is presented. The framework used for this discussion is a three-good–two-factor model with sector-specific capital in the short run. This analysis proceeds with great detail and shows that each reform on its own will tend to have opposite effects on production and income distribution. Section III presents a summary and concluding comments, plus some thoughts regarding future lines of research on the subject.

## II PRICES AND RESOURCE MOVEMENTS DURING CAPITAL AND CURRENT ACCOUNT LIBERALIZATION

The purpose of this section is to set up an analytical framework for analyzing the process of economic liberalization in a small economy. The discussion will focus on two different aspects of economic liberalization — (a) the liberalization of foreign trade, and (b) the liberalization of capital flows (i.e., allowing foreign borrowing) — and will emphasize price and resource movements during the liberalization episode. The analysis presented here is largely positive and develops a model of a simplified

[5] Of course, this question is only relevant in a world with market imperfections and/or externalities. In a world without externalities or frictions, the question of the order of liberalization is trivial: all markets should be liberalized simultaneously and instantaneously.

economy, with three goods and two factors. The discussion traces in detail how both reforms will affect prices, resource movements, and production in the short and the long run. The analysis is based largely on the extension of the Viner–Ricardo model for the case of three goods as presented by Corden and Neary (1982). The model used assumes that there is no capital accumulation. For this reason, the analysis of the effects of opening the capital account is somewhat simplified since it assumes that *all* funds obtained from abroad are used to increase present consumption. However, the framework presented here can be also used to deal with the more general case where capital accumulation is also allowed.

The main objective of the analysis presented here is to provide a clear picture of the *real* consequences of the process of economic liberalization, including changes in production and in income distribution. At the risk of being repetitive, the analysis proceeds slowly, trying to make clear every important step in the chain of events that follows a liberalization episode. The model developed shows that, as a result of each of these reforms on their own, resources and production will tend to move in opposite directions. Also, the effects on income distribution of both reforms will be the opposite. While a trade reform (i.e., the removal of tariffs) will result in resources moving into the exportables sector, the opening of the capital account will result in resources moving out of that sector. To the extent that resource movements involve some costs, this fact suggests that, from a policy perspective, some efforts should be made to coordinate the real effects of the two reforms. A general principle that should be considered when determining the order of these two reforms is that the (unnecessary) reversal of resource movements should be avoided.[6] Then, the opening of the two accounts should be synchronized in a way such that resources do not move in and out of a sector in a short period of time, since the economy would then incur an unnecessary cost.

### The Economy under Consideration

Assume the case of a small country that produces three goods: exportables (X), importables (M), and nontradables (N). Production is carried out using capital and labor. Production functions have the conventional properties, and it is assumed that in the short run capital is sector-specific, with labor being perfectly mobile between the three sectors.[7]

Imports are initially subject to a tariff, and external borrowing is not allowed. With respect to the labor market, it will be assumed that it is free

---

[6] It is important to note that in the real world this should be only *one* of the principles used for determining the correct ordering: others — not mentioned in this section owing to the nature of the model — refer to issues related to credibility and continuity of the reform.

[7] On sector-specific models see, for example, Jones (1971); Mayer (1974); Mussa (1974, 1978, 1982); Neary (1978a, b, 1982).

of distortions. However, the consequences of assuming the existence of an economy-wide minimum wage, which is binding in the short run, will also be investigated. The domestic capital market is free of distortions, with the rental rates of capital being equalized in the long run, across sectors. Regarding factor intensity, it will be assumed that importables have the highest capital–labour ratio. With respect to exportables and nontradables, alternative assumptions regarding factor intensities will be briefly discussed in the following subsection.

A critical assumption made in this section is that there is no capital accumulation and that consequently, once international borrowing is allowed, the proceeds of foreign loans are fully used to increase present consumption.[8] In that sense, then, it is assumed that at the initial point the rate of time preference exceeds "the" world rate of interest. The analysis presented here also assumes that there is no initial inflation, and that tariff proceeds are returned to consumers in a non-distorting lump-sum fashion. These two assumptions represent a simplification of the real-world characteristics of countries that have embarked on liberalization attempts. As has been pointed out by Krueger (1981, 1983b) and Little (1982), among others, most liberalization attempts by developing countries have started from crisis situations with high inflation. However, by ignoring inflation in the present section it is possible to focus on issues related to liberalization, abstracting from those of stabilization. On the relationship between stabilization and liberalization, however, see Krueger (1981).

### Trade Liberalization

In this section the effects of reducing (eliminating) tariffs in a three-good small economy are investigated. It is assumed, for analytical convenience, that initially there are no quantitative restrictions (or that they have been already replaced by tariffs), and that the exchange rate is fixed and equal to one. It is also assumed that capital is sector-specific in the short run, while it can move freely between sectors in the long run. The discussion will first deal with long-run effects; then the short-run effects and the transition toward the long run will be discussed. The analysis will concentrate on the behavior of goods prices, factor rewards (i.e., income distribution), and production. It is assumed that, while all prices are flexible in the long run, some of them (i.e., wages) may be rigid in the short run.

*Long-run effects of trade liberalization.* In this class of models of a small economy with three goods (importables, exportables, and nontradables), two factors (capital and labor), and the usual competition assumptions, long-run domestic prices are fully determined (under non-specialization) by world prices, technology, and tariffs. Equilibrium can be described in

---

[8] In that sense, then, this analysis derives from the possibility of negative welfare effects of allowing foreign investment in the presence of tariffs.

the following way. World prices of exportables and importables (plus the tariff) determine the rewards to both factors of production; these rewards, in their turn, and under the assumption of competition, determine the price of nontradables. Demand considerations for nontradables determine total output and nontradables and total factors used in their production. This leaves a certain amount of factors that are used in the production of exportables and importables in a traditional Hecksher–Ohlin fashion.

In the rest of the analysis the price of exportables will be taken to be the numeraire (i.e., $P_x = 1$). Consider now the effect of a reduction (elimination) of the level of the import tariff on the relative prices of final goods and on factor rewards. This effect will depend basically on the assumptions made regarding factor intensities. Two cases will be considered here: case 1 assumes $(K/L)_X < (K/L)_N < (K/L)_M$; while case 2 assumes $(K/L)_N < (K/L)_X < (K/L)_M$.

Consider first case 1, where imports are assumed to have the highest capital–labor ratio with exports having the lowest. The effect of a reduction of the tariff on factor rewards and the relative price of nontradables $P_N$ can be analyzed using figure 7.1, which is the dual to the well-known Lerner–Pearce diagram. The initial equilibrium is given by the intersection of the three isocosts $MM$, $XX$, and $NN$. These curves present the combinations of wages and rental rates of capital that result in a constant cost of producing these goods at the existing technology (see Mussa, 1979). The slopes of these curves are equal to the capital–labor ratio, and, as may be seen in figure 7.1, correspond to the assumptions of case 1. Initially, equilibrium is obtained at $A$ with a wage rate (relative to exports) equal to $W_0$ and a rental rate equal to $r_0$.

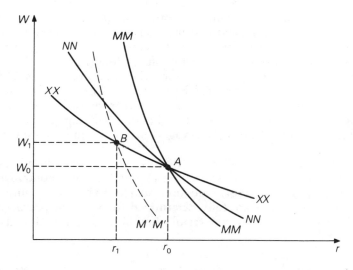

FIGURE 7.1

The reduction of the imports tariff will result in a leftward shift of the $MM$ curve toward $M'M'$. The reason for this is that now, in order to maintain equilibrium between domestic costs and the world price of importables, plus the tariff, lower combinations of wages and rental rates will be required. New long-run equilibrium will be obtained at $B$, where the new $M'M'$ curve intersects the $XX$ curve. As the Stolper–Samuelson theorem indicates, the reduction of the import tariff in an economy where exportables are labor-intensive will result in higher wages and lower rental rates (i.e., $W_1 > W_0$, and $r_1 < r_0$).

The new equilibrium point $B$ is below the $NN$ isocost, indicating that, as a consequence of the tariff reduction, the price of nontradables in terms of exportables will have to fall. This conclusion, of course, will not hold under case 2, where nontradables are more labor-intensive than exportables. In that case, the intersection of the $XX$ and $M'M'$ curves will be *above* the $NN$ curve, and for equilibrium to be restored in the nontradables sector their relative price will have to increase.[9] In order to simplify the discussion, through the rest of this paper we will focus on case 1, namely, $(K/L)_X < (K/L)_N < (K/L)_M$.

While the long-run (relative) price of nontradables is completely determined by technological considerations, the amount produced of this type of goods will also depend on the demand side. In particular, production of N will be such that, at the prevailing prices, the nontradables market clears. The production side of the model can be analyzed using a three-good Edgeworth–Bowley box as developed by Melvin (1968). Figure 7.2 illustrates the case where exportables are the most labor-intensive good.

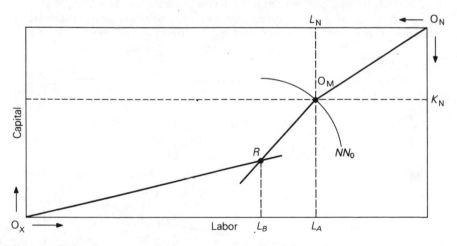

FIGURE 7.2

[9] Notice then that theoretically, depending on the assumptions regarding capital–labor intensity, the *real exchange rate*, defined as the domestic relative price of tradables to nontradables, may either increase or decline.

(See Corden and Neary, 1982, for an application of this diagram to a Dutch-disease type of analysis). In this diagram nontradables isoquants are drawn from origin $O_N$. At the initial prices the nontradable goods market clears at a level of production given by isoquant $NN_0$. The capital–labor ratio in nontradables production is given by the slope of $O_N O_M$. Production of exportables is measured from $O_X$, and that of importables by distance $O_M R$. In equilibrium the slope of $NN_0$ isoquant at $O_M$ equals the slopes of the corresponding isoquants for exportables and importables, which are tangent at $R$.

The discussion regarding factor rewards and relative prices (figure 7.1) showed that the reduction of the tariff will generate, in the long run, an increase in the wage rate relative to the rental rate. That means that all three sectors will now become more capital-intensive. This is shown in figure 7.3, where the broken rays depict the new (after-tariff reduction) capital–labor ratios. However, in order to determine the new equilibrium, it is necessary to know what will happen to the demand of nontradables as a consequence of the tariff reduction.

Assume first, in order to organize the discussion, that the quantity demanded for nontradables does not change after the import tariffs are reduced. This assumption will be relaxed later. In this case, the new equilibrium point in the production of nontradables will be obtained at the intersection of the new (higher) capital–labor ratio and the initial $NN_0$ isoquant, at point $O'_M$. Production of importables will be reduced to $O'_M T$, and production of exportables will increase to $O_X T$. This result was obtained under the assumption that the quantity of nontradables demanded was not affected by the reduction of tariffs. In general, however, this will not be the case. Moreover, given our assumptions regarding capital–labor intensity, it is expected that the demand for nontradables will *increase* as a

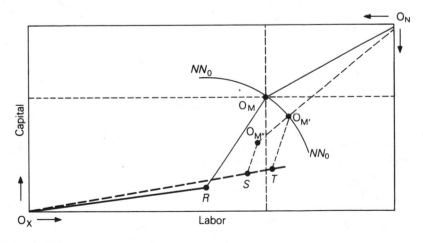

FIGURE 7.3

result of the liberalization. The reasons for this are two: (a) as shown in figure 7.1, after the liberalization of trade the (relative) price of nontradables will decline, producing a substitution effect in demand toward non-tradables; (b) the trade liberaliztion will generate a positive income effect as national income at international prices increases, which will also have a positive effect on the quantity demanded of N. If the demand for non-tradables increases, long-run equilibrium in figure 7.3 will be on the new capital–labor ratio ray to the left of the NN isocost. In terms of figure 7.3, this new equilibrium is obtained at $O''_M$, with production of exportables being equal to $OS$, production of importables having been reduced to $O''_M S$, and production of nontradables being equal to $O_N O''_M$.

In summary, under case 1 capital intensity assumptions, the *long-run effects* of a tariff reduction will be as follows::

(a)     Prices of nontradables, relative to exportables, will fall.
(b)     Wages, relative to all goods, will increase.
(c)     The rental rate of capital, relative to all goods, will decrease.
(d)     Production of exportables will expand.
(e)     Production of nontradables will expand.
(f)     Production of importables will decline.

*Short-run effects.* This section investigates the short-run effects of a tariff reduction under the case 1 assumptions about capital-labor intensity. It is assumed that in the short-run capital is sector-specific, while labor can move freely across sections. The representation used in this model, then, is an adaptation for a three-good case of the Viner–Ricardo models of Jones (1971), Mayer (1974) and Mussa (1974). (See the paper by Corden and Neary, 1982, for an application of this kind of model.)

The initial equilibrium situation can be illustrated using figure 7.4, which is adapted from Mussa (1974), for the case of the three goods. In this figure the horizontal axis measures total labor available in the economy, while the vertical axis depicts the wage rate in terms of exportables. $L_T$ is the demand for labor by the tradable goods sectors and is equal to the (horizontal) sum of the demand for labor by the exportable sector (which is given by $L_X$ in this figure) and the demand for labor of the importables sector. $L_N$, on the other hand, is the demand for labor of the nontradable goods sector. The initial equilibrium is characterized, then, by a wage rate equal to $W_0$, with $O_T L_A$ labor used in the production of exportables, $L_A L_B$ labor used in the production of importables, and $Q L_B$ used in the production of nontradables.

There are several differences between this short-run model and the long-run model discussed in the previous subsection. First, since capital is now sector-specific, the direct link between tradable goods prices and factor rewards is broken. For this reason the Stolper–Samuelson theorem does not hold (in the short run), and the price of nontradables will be determined by the intersection of the demand and supply schedules for these kinds of goods. The strategy is now to analyze the short-run effects of trade

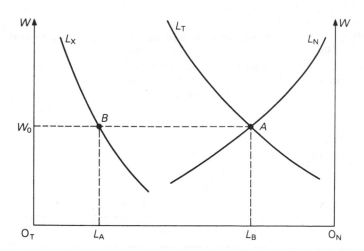

FIGURE 7.4

liberalization on prices, production, resource movements, and income distribution (i.e., factor rewards). This analysis is then combined with the long-run results already discussed in the previous section to find out the characteristics of the transition, in a way similar to that proposed by Peter Neary (1978a)

In the short run, the reduction of the tariff, under the assumption of sector-specific factors, will generate changes in the (relative) price of both importables and nontradables (see for example Dornbusch, 1974, 1980). While the price of importables will umambiguously fall, the behavior of the price of nontradables will depend on the assumption regarding substitutability and the magnitude of the income effects. Assuming that the three goods are gross substitutes in consumption and production, and that the income effect does not exceed the substitution effect, it can be shown that, as a result of the reduction of the tariff, the price of non-tradables will fall relative to that of exportables and will increase relative to that of importables.

The reduction in the level of the tariff will reduce the domestic price of importables, generating a downward shift of the $L_T$ curve (with the $L_X$ curve constant). In figure 7.5 the new $L_T$ curve will intersect the $L_N$ curve at $R$. However, this is not a final equilibrium situation, since, as already discussed, the tariff reduction will also result in a *decline* in the price of nontradables (relative to exports). As a consequence, $L_N$ will shift down-ward (by *less* than $L_T$) and final *short-run* equilibrium will be achieved at $S$. In this new equilibrium, production of exportables has increased — with labor used by this sector increasing by $L_A L_Q$. The production of nontradables may either increase or decrease, and production of importables

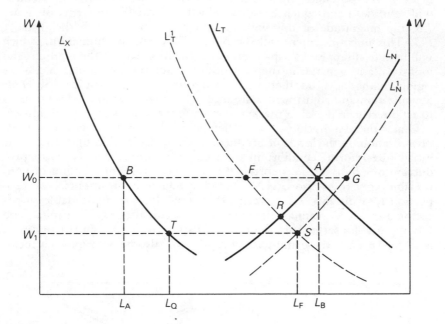

FIGURE 7.5

will fall. In the case depicted in figure 7.5, labor has moved out of the importables goods sector, into the exportable and nontradable sectors.

What has happened to factor rewards in the short run? Wages have declined in terms of the exportable good (from $W_0$ to $W_1$ in figure 7.5). Also, wages will decline in terms of the nontradable good, since the vertical distance between the $L_N$ and $L'_N$ curves is smaller than the reduction of $W$ from $W_0$ to $W_1$ (see Mussa, 1974). However, wages will increase relative to the importable good, since the domestic price of importables has fallen by more than wages. In the exportables sector, the rental rate of capital will increase in terms of all three goods, while the rental rates of the capital will decrease.[10]

The above discussion has assumed that all prices (of goods and factors) are fully flexible. However, this need not be the case. In a number of countries the labor market is usually characterized by the existence of (real) minimum wages. It is easy to see from figure 7.5 that if wages, expressed

[10] Formally, the rental rate of capital specific to the importable sector will decrease in terms of importables, and could either increase or decrease in terms of the other two goods.

in terms of exportables, are inflexibly downward, short-run unemployment will result as a consequence of the reduction of tariffs. In terms of figure 7.5, the magnitude of this unemployment will be equal to the distance *FG*. This unemployment will be only a short-run phenomenon, which will tend to disappear as capital moves between sectors in the medium and long run.[11] In general, in the presence of sector-specific capital and wage rigidity in the short run, there will be a second-best argument for slow trade liberalization and adjustment assistance. The first-best policy, however, is to act directly on the labor market, removing the sources of wage rigidity.[12]

Under the assumption of wage flexibility, the short-run effect of trade liberalization on the levels of production can be depicted in figure 7.6. The initial (pre-reform) equilibrium is given by points $A$ and $G$, with production of exportables proportional to distance $O_X A$, production of non-tradables given by isocost $NN_0$, and production of importables proportional to distance $GA$. Notice that, initially, the nontradable goods sector uses $O_N K_N$ capital, the exportables sector uses $O_X K_X$ capital, and the importables sector uses the rest ($K_N K_X$). Since in the short run capital is sector-specific, these amounts of capital will also be used by each sector

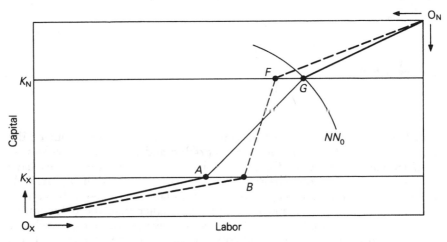

FIGURE 7.6

[11] See Neary (1982) and Edwards (1982) for discussions regarding trade liberalization, sticky wages, and unemployment. It is interesting to note that an effect of this type can be used analytically to derive short-run output losses following a trade liberalization process, as is done by Khan and Zahler (1983).

[12] In the specific case of Chile, the tariff reform proceeded at the same time as the minimum wage was *raised* in real terms. Elsewhere I have computed that the combination of the tariff reduction process and the increase in the minimum wage in Chile resulted in an increase in the rate of unemployment in Chile of approximately 35 percentage points (see Edwards, 1982).

after the tariff reform. This means that the new short-run equilibrium points will necessarily lie on the $K_N K_N$ and the $K_X K_X$ lines.

The tariff reduction will result in an increase in the use of labor (and thus in production, for given amounts of capital) in the exportables and importables sectors. This is shown in figure 7.6 by the movement of the equilibrium points to $B$ and $F$. The new capital–labor ratios are now given by the broken lines, and as may be seen, both the exportable and non-tradable sectors become relatively more labor-intensive, while the import-ables sector has become more capital-intensive. A comparison of figures 7.3 and 7.6 provides some indication of what the transition period will look like, with factors moving from their post-reform short-run allocation (figure 7.6) toward their long-run post-reform allocation (see figure 7.7, which combines figures 7.3 and 7.6).

In summary, for the general case with wage flexibility, the short-run effects of a tariff reduction on production, prices, and factors rewards are as follows:

(a)   Production of exportables increases.
(b)   Production of importables is reduced.
(c)   Production of nontradables increases.
(d)   Wages increase in terms of importables, and decline in terms of exportables and nontradables.
(e)   The rental rate of capital in the exportable sector increases relative to all goods.
(f)   The rental rate of capital in the importables sector will decrease relative to the importable good; it could increase or decrease relative to the other goods.
(g)   The rental rate of capital in the nontradables sector will increase relative to nontradable goods, and could either increase or decrease relative to the other two goods.

*The transition period after a trade liberalization.* According to the model used in this section, the main difference between short- and long-run effects of a trade liberalization is that in the short run capital is locked into its sector of origin. As time passes, however, capital will (slowly) move between sectors. In the present model, and in order to simplify the exposition, we assume that the movement of capital does not require the use of resources. However, the analysis could be modified by introducing a "moving indus-try," which uses labor and some specific factor, as in Mussa (1978).

The transition period will be characterized basically by factors (both capital and labor) moving between sectors, until the new long-run equi-librium (i.e., post-liberalization) capital–labor ratios and levels of pro-duction are attained. As discussed in the first subsection above, and as may be seen from figure 7.3, in the final long-run equilibrium all sectors will be more capital-intensive, with the exportable sector using more capital, in absolute terms, and the importable sector using less capital, in absolute terms, than prior to the trade reform. As may be also seen from figure

7.3, the nontradable goods sector could use either a larger or a smaller absolute amount of capital than before the tariff reduction. The nature of factor movements during the transition period can be seen in figure 7.7, which combines figures 7.3 and 7.6. Initial (i.e., pre-liberalization) equilibrium is given by points A and G. Short-run equilibrium is given by points B and F; while long-run equilibrium will be attained in points C and H. In order to avoid cluttering the diagram, only the post-liberalization capital–labor ratios have been drawn. The arrows between points B and C and F and H, respectively, show the way resources will move during the transition.

As may be seen in figure 7.7, for the particular case considered here, the transition will be characterized by the following:

(a)   Capital and labor will both move out of the importable goods sector.
(b)   Capital and labor will move into the exportable goods sector.
(c)   Capital will move into the nontradable goods sector, and labor will move out of the nontradable goods sector.

Table 7.1 summarizes the movement of resources that follows a trade liberalization. Column (1) depicts the movement of resources in the short run. Column (2) shows how resources move in the long run, when compared with the initial situation. This column is a summary of the situation described in the Melvin–Edgeworth–Bowley box in figure 7.3. Finally, in column (3) the movement of resources during the transition period is presented.

An important question that has not been discussed yet is related to the timing of these prices and resources movements. Broadly speaking, it would be expected that, following a tariff reduction, some time would

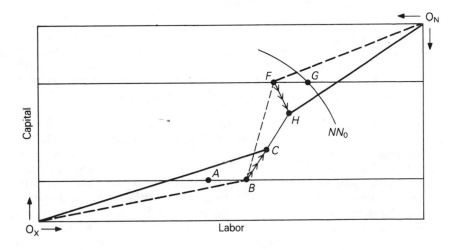

FIGURE 7.7

TABLE 7.1  Short- and long-run resource movements following a trade liberalization

| Sector | (1) Short-run vs. initial situation | | (2) Long-run vs. initial situation | | (3) Long-run vs. short run (transition) | |
|---|---|---|---|---|---|---|
| | K | L | K | L | K | L |
| Exportables | — | ↑ | ↑ | ↑ | ↑ | ↑ |
| Importables | — | ↓ | ↓ | ↓ | ↓ | ↓ ↑ |
| Nontradables | — | ↑ | ↑ | ↑ ↓ (?) | ↑ | ↓ ↑ (?) |

pass before goods arbitrage would result in relative price adjustments. In that sense the initial effect of tariff reductions on resource movements will not be instantaneous.[13] On the other hand, it is difficult to know a priori how fast the adjustment process between the short and long run will take. This is largely an empirical question whose answer will require country-specific analyses.

### The Liberalization of the Capital Account

In this subsection the model presented above is used to investigate how the opening of the capital account (only) will affect relative prices, income distribution, production, and resource movements. The analysis assumes that the importables sector is subject to a tariff and that the world relative price of exportables and importables is constant, so that these two goods can be aggregated into a single tradable good.

It is clear that the framework used in this section (a three-good–two-factor model) is not the most appropriate one to deal with intertemporal problems related to the financial sector, such as those generated by the opening of the capital account. However, this model is still rich enough to allow us to investigate how the opening of the capital account will affect the real side of the economy.[14] In order to do this, an approach similar to that suggested by McKinnon (1976) for analyzing a transfer-related adjustment is used.

[13] From a practical point of view, there are a number of considerations, such as the creation of the required infrastructure to increase imports, that tend to indicate that the actual reduction in domestic prices will take more time.

[14] Ideally, one would want a fully specified multi-period general equilibrium model of both the real and financial sectors of the economy. Clearly, however, a model of this kind is not analytically tractable. An alternative way to tackle the problem of the opening of the capital account is to use a simulation framework as in Khan and Zahler (1983).

It is assumed that, prior to the opening of the capital account, the domestic rate of time preferences exceeds the world rate of interest. This means that, once the capital account is opened, domestic agents will borrow from abroad in order to increase present consumption. It is further assumed that all of the foreign funds obtained, once the capital account is opened, are used to increase present consumption. Even though this is not a very realistic assumption, it simplifies the exposition. The case where the funds obtained when the capital account is used to increase investment is discussed in the next subsection; the discussion will then focus on the *adjustment problem* created by the inflow of foreign capital that will follow the opening of the capital account.

The analysis presented in this section assumes that, once the capital account is opened, foreign capital will flow into the domestic economy at a stable rate for some time. This means that, during a certain period of time, expenditure will exceed income and foreign debt will be accumulated.[15] For expositional convenience this discussion does not deal specifically with the following stage, where the foreign debt has to be paid. However, the analytical tools developed here can easily handle this stage of the problem. In this section, then, it is possible to say that the time-horizon for the analysis has been broken into three distinct runs: the *short run*, characterized by positive foreign borrowing and sector-specific capital; the *long run*, where there still is a positive inflow of foreign funds, but where capital can move between sectors; and the *long long run* (not specifically considered), where the foreign debt begins to be repaid.[16]

The basic effect of opening the capital account is that expenditure will exceed income during some period of time. In order to simplify the discussion, the core of this subsection assumes that the amount by which expenditure exceeds income (i.e., the current account deficit) is the same in every period. However, the case where there is an initial overshooting of the level of capital inflows is also briefly investigated. The relevance of this latter case stems from the fact that it has generally been observed that, following an opening of the capital account, there is a jump, and a consequent reduction (i.e., an overshooting), of the level of capital inflows (for example, Korea 1965; Chile 1980; Argentina 1978; Uruguay 1979).

*Long-run effects.* In the long run — when capital can move between sectors — relative prices of the three goods are completely given by world prices, technology, and the tariff.[17] For this reason, in the present model

---

[15] This idea responds to the notion, developed by Fischer and Frenkel (1972a, 1972b), among others, that there are stages of the different accounts of the balance of payments through which countries pass. In that sense, then, we assume that our country is in the stage of development where foreign debt is accumulated.

[16] Of course, once the foreign debt has to be repaid the analysis will be similar to what is discussed here, in the sense that a distinction between the period when capital is sector-specific and when it can move across sectors has to be made.

[17] However, as will be discussed below, in the short run there will be changes on the relative prices, generated by demand effects.

the opening of the capital account will have no long-run effect on relative prices of goods or factors. However, to the extent that a fraction of the new funds obtained from abroad are used to finance a higher consumption of nontradables, the production of these goods will increase. Since a higher production of N requires an increase in the amount of resources used in that sector, production of the two tradable goods will have to decline. The long-run effects of the opening of the capital account on production can be summarized in figure 7.8, which is a by-now familiar Melvin–Edgeworth–Bowley box. The initial equilibrium conditions are summarized by points G and A. Since in the long run the opening of the capital account has *no* effect on relative prices or factors rewards, the original capital–labour ratios are not altered. The increase in the demand for nontradables, however, requires a higher production of this type of goods. The expansion of the nontradable goods sector will then take place along the original capital-labor ratio $O_N G$, with new (after liberalization) production of nontradables proportional to distance $O_N G'_1$, and given by isoquant $NN_1$; new production of exportables proportional to distance $X_X A'$; and new production of importables proportional to distance $G'A'$. It can then be seen that the long-run effects of opening the capital account will be as follows:

(a) Production of nontradables will increase, with capital and labor moving into this sector.
(b) Production of importables will decrease, with capital and labor moving out of this sector.
(c) Production of exportables will decrease, with capital and labor moving out of this sector.
(d) Prices of goods and factors will *not* be altered.

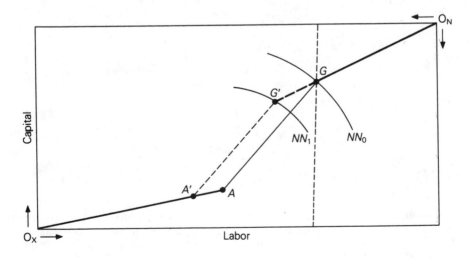

FIGURE 7.8

*The short-run effects.* In the short run, however, capital will be sector-specific, and the increase in the demand for nontradable goods will be reflected in an increase of their relative prices.[18] The short-run effects of a capital inflow on production can be summarized in a Salter-type diagram, as used by McKinnon (1976) in his analysis of transfers and the adjustments problem. In figure 7.9 the importable and exportable goods have been aggregated into a composite tradables good. $TT'$ is the (short-run) production possibilities curve between tradables and nontradables and has been constructed under the assumption that when relative prices change only labor can move between sectors. Initial equilibrium is attained at point $Q$, with the trade account being equal to zero and the nontradable goods market in equilibrium. The inflow of capital that takes place after the opening of the capital account has the property of allowing the consumption possibilities schedule to exceed the production possibilities frontier. The new consumption possibilities schedule is equal to $NT'$, which exceeds $TT'$ by the amount of the capital inflow, measured in terms of tradables (see McKinnon, 1976; Datta, 1983).

After the opening of the capital account, and assuming that $OE$ is the income–expenditure path corresponding to the initial relative price, consumption will tend to move to $S$, while production will remain at $Q$.

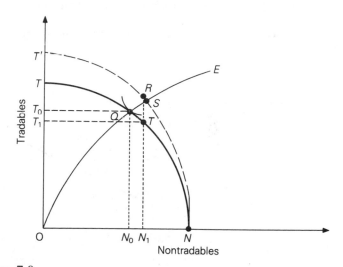

FIGURE 7.9

---

[18] Remember that we are assuming that the magnitude of the current account deficit is the same in the short and the long run. See the following subsection, however, for a brief analysis of the case where there is an overshooting of the level of capital inflows.

However, at this point there will be an excess demand for nontradable goods. As a result of this, the relative price of nontradables will increase until a new equilibrium situation, characterized by points R (consumption) and T (production), is attained. In this new equilibrium there is a current account deficit, and the nontradable goods market is in equilibrium. We can see, then, that in the short run the opening of the capital account will result in an *increase of the relative price of nontradables relative to tradables* — this is the real appreciation effect of opening the capital account pointed out by several authors.[19] The production of nontradables will increase from $N_0$ to $N_1$, and the production of tradables will decline from $T_0$ to $T_1$ in figure 7.9.

We can now translate the short-run effects of opening the capital account into a Melvin–Edgeworth–Bowley box. This will prove to be useful for the analysis of the transition. Figure 7.10 summarizes the short-run effects of opening the capital account. Initial equilibrium conditions are given by points G and A. Once the capital account is opened, expenditure will exceed income, with production of nontradables increasing and that of importables and exportables decreasing. New (short-run) equilibrium is attained at points H and B, which by definition are characterized by the fact that the same amount of capital is used in each sector as prior to the liberalization process. However, in order to increase its output, the nontradables sector becomes more labor-intensive; while both tradables sectors become more capital-intensive.

In the short run the wage rate increases in terms of both tradable goods and declines in terms of nontradables. The return to capital specific to the

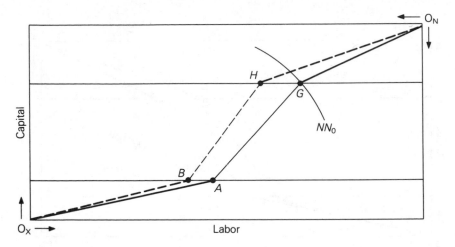

FIGURE 7.10

[19] See McKinnon (1973, 1976, 1982); Harberger (1982); Diaz-Alejandro (1981); Harberger and Edwards (1982); Edwards (1984a).

nontradables sector goes up in terms of all goods, while the return to capital in the two tradable goods declines.[20]

In summary, the short-run effects of the opening of the capital account are as follows:
(a) Relative price of nontradables increases in terms of both tradable goods.
(b) Production of nontradables increases.
(c) Production of both tradables declines.
(d) The wage rate increases in terms of both tradables and declines in terms of the nontradable.
(e) The rental rate of capital in both tradable goods sectors declines, in terms of all goods.
(f) The return to capital in the nontradable goods sector goes up in terms of all goods.

*Transition.* As in the case of the trade liberalization, the transition will be characterized by resources moving from their short-run equilibrium (figure 7.10) toward their long-run equilibrium (figure 7.8). As before, the best way to look at these resource movements is by combining the short- and long-run diagrams. This is done in figure 7.11. In this diagram *A* and *G* are initial (i.e., pre-liberalization) equilibrium points; *B* and *H* depict the short-run equilibrium after liberalization; and *A'* and *G'* are the long-run post-liberalization equilibrium points. It may be noted that the final equilibrium level of production of *N*, given by isoquant $NN_1$ (*G'*), exceeds the short-run level of production (given by the isoquant that passes through

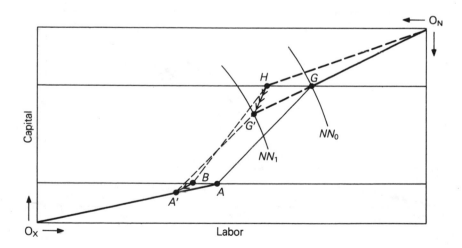

FIGURE 7.11

[20] This can be seen by following an analysis similar to that presented in figure 7.6.

point $H$). The reason for this is that, while the income effect — stemming from the higher absorption allowed by the opening of the capital account — is by assumption the same in the short and the long run, the relative price of nontradables is higher in the short run; consequently, the equilibrium level of production of nontradables will be higher in the long run.[21] If, however, it is assumed that in the short run the level of capital inflows will overshoot their long-run levels, the result will be somewhat different (see figure 7.12 p. 207).

Under the present assumptions — that the current account deficit is the same in short and the long run — the transition will be charactered by resources moving from $H$ to $G'$ and from $B$ to $A'$ in figure 7.11. Both capital and labor will move into the nontradables sector and out of the tradables sector. The production of nontradables will further expand during the transition, with the production of both tradables declining. Table 7.2 presents a summary of the short- and long-run resource movements that will follow an opening of the capital account, under the maintained assumptions. This table is equivalent to table 7.1 constructed for the case of the trade reform only. A comparison of the tables shows that both reforms, on their own, will tend to generate an *opposite* movement of resources. This, of course, is reflected by the fact that the real exchange rate will tend to move in opposite directions under each reform.

At this point it is important to recall some of the critical assumptions that have been made for this exercise. First, it was assumed that, as a consequence of opening the capital account, capital would flow into the domestic country, allowing absorption to exceed income. It was further assumed that this situation was sustainable for a (fairly) long period of

TABLE 7.2 Short- and long-run resource movements following a capital account liberalization

| Sector | (1) Short-run vs. initial situation | | (2) Long-run vs. initial situation | | (3) Long-run vs. short-run (transition) | |
|---|---|---|---|---|---|---|
| | $K$ | $L$ | $K$ | $L$ | $K$ | $L$ |
| Exportables | — | ↓ | ↓ | ↓ | ↓ | ↓ |
| Importables | — | ↓ | ↓ | ↓ | ↓ | ↓ |
| Nontradables | — | ↑ | ↑ | ↑ | ↑ | ↑ |

[21] The reason for this is that while in both cases (short- and long-run) the demand curve for nontradables will shift to the right by the same amount, the supply curve is more elastic in the long-run. Thus, the equilibrium output of nontradables will be higher in the long-run.

time, and that all the funds obtained from abroad were channeled into additional consumption. In that sense, the time-horizon of the analysis was broken into three distinct lengths: the short run, characterized by a positive foreign borrowing (absorption > income), and by capital being sector-specific; the long run, where again there is positive borrowing (absorption > income) but where capital can move between sectors; and the long long run, when the foreign debt has to be paid. It was assumed that the long long run takes place in the (distant) future, and was not analyzed.

A second important assumption made here is that, once the capital account is opened, a stable inflow of foreign capital takes place. In that sense, the possibility of an overshooting of the level of capital flows was ignored. This is not an innocent simplification, since, as has been mentioned, the stylized facts indicate that generally following the opening of the capital account there is an initial jump in the level of capital inflows. If such a behavior of capital flows were allowed, the analysis presented here would change, with more resources moving into the nontradable goods sector in the short run. This case is presented in figure 7.12, where short-run production of nontradables — given by isoquent $NN_2$ — exceeds long-run production of this kind of goods (given by isoquant $NN_1$). In this case the transition will differ from our previous analysis; as may be seen, while capital will move *into* the nontradable sector, labor will move *out of* the nontradable goods sector during the transition.

A critical question related to the effects of opening the capital account of the balance of payments concerns the *speed* at which these price and resource movements will take place. In general — and as has been emphasized by Frenkel (1982, 1983) it is expected that the inflow of capital following the opening of the capital account will be fast. In that case, it is expected that the short-run consequences of liberalizing this account of the balance of payments — in particular, the increase of the relative price of N and the tendency for labor to move into this sector — will be felt quickly. In fact, as will be argued below, and has been suggested by Frenkel (1983), the difference in the speed of adjustment of the capital and current accounts suggests that an appropriate order will consider opening the current account first. It will also be argued that the capital account should be opened *slowly*, following a multi-stage procedure.

### Summary

This section has presented a three-good–two-factor model to analyze the real effects — i.e., production and income distribution effects — of the liberalization of the current and capital account of the balance of payments. The analysis presented provided details on the characteristics of these processes, confirming prior conjectures: each reform on its own will result in *opposite* effects on resource movements and income distribution.

Abandoning the sphere of positive analysis, a critical question at this stage is whether there is anything to be learned regarding the appropriate order of liberalization from this discussion. The answer is a qualified yes.

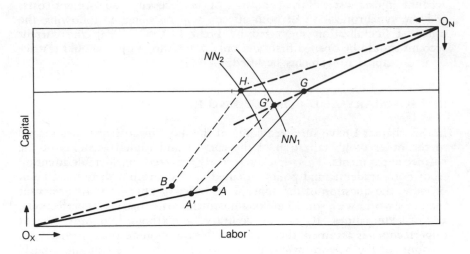

FIGURE 7.12

To the extent that in the real world resource movements across sectors are costly, there is a reason to try to avoid "unnecessary" shifts in resources.[22] A possible instance where these kinds of costs will occur is when, owing to a given policy, labor and capital move out of the exports sector and shortly afterwards, owing to a different policy, have to move back into this sector. These "unnecessary" adjustments costs could be avoided if resources were directly reallocated into their final sectors of use. This could be achieved by *synchronizing* the openings of the capital and current accounts, as has been suggested by Frenkel (1983).

At this point it could be argued that the principles of reducing the adjustment costs would call for a simultaneous opening of both accounts. In this case, the argument would go, resources would move directly into their final sectors without "unnecessary" switches. The problem with this reasoning, however, is that it assumes implicitly that the adjustment process following the opening of these accounts is equally fast. If however this is not the case, and the adjustment of the capital account is faster — as Frenkel (1982, 1983), Khan and Zahler (1983), and others have suggested — the simultaneous opening of both accounts will result in resources moving first into the nontradable goods sector and out of exportables and importables. In other words, if both accounts are opened simultaneously in the

---

[22] A possible way to model moving costs is through the existence of a "moving sector" as in Mussa (1978).

short run the capital account effects will tend to dominate. If the capital account adjusts faster,[23] the avoidance of "unnecessary" adjustment costs, and the synchronization of both effects, will be obtained following the order of liberalization suggested by Frenkel (1982, 1983): the current account should be opened first, and only when this is open should restrictions on capital movements be lifted.

## III.   SUMMARY AND CONCLUDING REMARKS

In this chapter I have surveyed some of the most important issues related to the order of liberalization of the current and capital accounts of the balance of payments. This topic has recently attracted considerable attention from both academic and policy-oriented circles. From a theoretical point of view, the question of the appropriate order of liberalization is relevant only in a world with some kind of adjustment costs, market imperfections, and/or externalities. If, on the contrary, a textbook economy free of imperfections is assumed, the answer to this question becomes trivial: both accounts of the balance of payments should be liberalized simultaneously and instantaneously. However, there are a number of reasons, both economic and political, why a simultaneous and instantaneous liberalization might not be feasible. In this context, then, the question regarding the order of liberalization becomes important.

The problem of the order of liberalization of the current and capital accounts of the balance of payments has become more interesting in light of the recent experience of a group of countries from the Cone of South America (Argentina, Chile, and Uruguay). These countries followed opposite orders — Argentina and Uruguay opened the capital account first, while Chile opened the current account first — with a common fate in the early 1980s: deep economic recession and (partial) reversal of the liberalization attempt. This Southern Cone experience has triggered greater concern over the issue of the adequate order of liberalization. At the present time there are no definite answers regarding these experiences and more research on the subject should be encouraged.

This chapter has focused exclusively on the analysis of some aspects of the order of liberalization of the capital and current accounts of the balance of payments. However, a number of important issues related to a broadly defined liberalization process deserve to be briefly mentioned. There are four major issues related to these reforms. First, if a liberalization will not fully eliminate all distortions, the question of welfare effects of partial reforms will become critical. Even though from a second-best perspective

---

[23] In terms of this model, a faster adjustment of the capital account means that interest arbitrage is faster than goods arbitrage, and that immediately following the opening of the capital account resources will be borrowed and absorption will exceed absorption. On the other hand, following trade reform, some time will pass before goods arbitrage will result in resource investment.

almost anything, in terms, of welfare, can happen as a consequence of a partial reform, there are well founded conjectures that the liberalization of some markets only will be welfare-improving.[24] Second, the question of the speed of liberalization is also important. In the absence of market imperfections and/or externalities, markets should be liberalized very quickly (now). If externalities are present, however, and the first-best policies to deal with them are not available, a gradual liberalization might be called for.[25]

Third, the relationship between liberalization and stabilization is crucial to understand the success or failure of liberalization reforms, since most liberalization attempts have been undertaken in conjunction with major stabilization programs.[26] The reason for this is that, in the first place, the initial imposition of restrictions and controls is usually related to an increase in the fiscal deficit and inflation. There are some important aspects of the relationship between these two policies — stabilization and liberalization — that deserve further attention. In particular, the desirability of implementing a major (almost full) liberalization at the same time as a stabilization program is on its way should be further investigated. And, fourth, the order of liberalization (i.e., which market should be liberalized first) is also important. There is generalized agreement among experts about some aspects of the order of liberalization. There is agreement, for example, that the capital account should be opened only after the domestic capital market is freed, and that this can happen only after the fiscal deficit has been substantially reduced. There has been less agreement, however, on the order of liberalization of the capital and current accounts. This is the topic that has been discussed in the present paper.

It is worth mentioning that, in the existing literature on the order of liberalization of the capital and current accounts of the balance of payments, the arguments can be grouped in three broad categories. The first line of argument is concerned with real exchange rate behavior and macro-economic stability during the liberalization effort. Some authors have argued that, to the extent that the opening of the capital account will generate destabilizing capital flows, the real exchange rate will be highly volatile after this account is liberalized; for this reason, the capital account should be opened only after the trade reform has been completed, and the new structure of production is "consolidated." Other authors, however, have argued that the best way to avoid undesired real exchange rate movements is by having a freely floating exchange rate with full convertibility. This exchange rate system, they argue, should be implemented before the trade reform. Consequently, according to this view, the capital account should be liberalized first.

[24] Krueger (1983b), Michaely (1982), Corbo and de Melo (1982).
[25] See Leamer (1980), Mussa (1982), Neary (1982), Edwards (1982), Michaely (1982), and Edwards and van Wijnbergen (1983).
[26] See Krueger (1978, 1981, 1983a), Little (1982).

In section II a *positive* analysis of the effects of liberalizing both accounts was presented. A three-good–two-factor model of trade was used to analyze how both reforms would affect production and income distribution in the short and long run. The model assumes that the short run can be characterized by a Ricardo–Viner setting, while in the long run a Heckscher–Ohlin framework is used. This discussion shows that both reforms, on their own, will tend to generate opposite effects on production and income distribution. To the extent that there are real costs related to resource movements, there is an argument for synchronizing the effects of opening both accounts, in order to avoid resources moving in and out of particular sectors. If, as has been suggested by Frenkel (1982, 1983) and Khan and Zahler (1983), among others, the speed of adjustment of the capital account is faster than that of the current account, this *synchronization of the economic effects* of opening both accounts will require that the current account is opened first.

The purpose of this chapter has been to survey the major issues related to the order of liberalization, presenting the different aspects of this problem in an organized fashion. While the analysis has not yielded a strong *theorem* regarding the appropriate order for liberalizing the current and capital accounts of the balance of payments, both the historical evidence and the theoretical considerations discussed suggest that a more prudent strategy would be based on liberalizing the current account first.

A central aspect of any reform package is related to the degree of credibility that the public has on the reform. If there is no credibility, agents will not make the decisions required for the new policy to have an effect on the economic structure. Moreover, in the particular case of the liberalization of the current and capital accounts of the balance of payments, the lack of credibility can result — as was the case of Argentina — in agents using foreign funds to increase investments in the "wrong" sector.[27] Of course, the degree of credibility of a reform package is not an exogenous variable, but will depend on a number of variables. One of the most important determinants of the degree of credibility is the perceived *consistency* of the proposed policies. If these policies are perceived as inconsistent, then agents will expect that the reform attempt will be discontinued or reverted. This is a basic but important principle, which should be kept in mind when implementing global economic reforms. In that sense, it may be argued that more important than determining the correct order of liberalization is the definition of consistent and credible policy packages that will support any particular order that is chosen.

---

[27] Of course, if the lack of credibility was founded, and the reforms are reversed, the investment was being done (from a private perspective) in the "right" sectors.

REFERENCES

Aizenman, Joshua (1983), "Dynamics of Trade Liberalization Policy," *Journal of Development Economics.*

Arriazu, Ricardo (1983a), "Policy Interdependence From a Latin American Perspective," *IMF Staff Papers.*

Arriazu, Ricardo (1983b), "Remarks on the Southern Cone," *IMF Staff Papers.*

Balassa, Bela (1976), "Principios de Reformas Arancelarias en Paises en Desarrollo," in *Estudios Monetarios IV.* Santiago: Banco Central de Chile.

Balassa, Bela (1978), *Development Strategies in Semi-Industrial Economics.* Oxford: Oxford University Press.

Balassa, Bela (1982), "Reforming the System of Incentives in Developing Economies," in B. Balassa (ed.), *Development Strategies in Semi-Industrial Economies.* Oxford: Oxford University Press.

Bertrand, T. S. and Flatters, F. (1971), "Tariffs, Capital Accumulation and Immisirizing Growth," *Journal of International Economics.*

Bhagwati, J. (1968), *The Theory and Practice of Commercial Policy: Departures From Unified Exchange Rates.* Princeton University Special Papers no. 8.

Bhagwati, J. (1978), *Anatomy and Consequences of Exchange Control Regimes.* New York: Ballinger.

Bhagwati, J. (1982a), "Directly Unproductive Profit Seeking Activities," *Journal of Political Economy.*

Bhagwati, J. (1982b), *Import Competition and Response.* Chicago: University of Chicago Press.

Bhagwati, J. and Srinivasan, T. N. (1979), "Trade Policy and Development," in R. Dornbusch and J. A. Frenkel (eds), *International Economic Policy: Theory and Evidence.* Baltimore: Johns Hopkins University Press.

Bhagwati, J. and Srinivasan, T. N. (1980), "Revenue Seeking: A Generalization of the Theory of Tariffs," *Journal of Political Economy.*

Bhagwati, J. and Srinivasan, T. N. (1983a), *Lectures in International Trade.* Cambridge, Mass.: MIT Press.

Bhagwati, J. and Srinivasan, T. N. (1983b), "On the Choice Between Capital and Labor Mobility," *Journal of International Economics.*

Blejer, M. and Landau, L. (1984), *Economic Liberalization and Stabilization in Argentina, Chile and Uruguay: The Monetary Approach to the Balance of Payments.* Washington: World Bank.

Blejer, M. and Mathieson, Donald J. (1981), "Preannouncement of Exchange Rate Changes as a Stabilization Instrument," *IMF Staff Papers.*

Branson, William (1983), "Remarks on the Southern Cone," *IMF Staff Papers.*

Brecher, R. A. (1974a), "Minimum Wage Rates and the Theory of International Trade," *Quarterly Journal of Economics.*

Brecher, R. A. (1974b), "Optimal Commercial Policy for a Minimum Wage Economy," *Journal of International Economics.*

Brecher, R. and Bhagwati, J. (1982), "Immiserizing Transfers From Abroad," *Journal of International Economics.*

Brecher, R. and Diaz-Alejandro, C. (1977), "Tariffs, Foreign Capital and Immiserizing Growth," *Journal of International Economics.*

Brecher, R. and Findlay, R. (1983), "Tariffs, Foreign Capital and National Welfare with Sector-Specific Factors," *Journal of International Economics.*

Bruno, Michael (1982), "Import Competition and Macroeconomic Adjustment Under Wage–Price Rigidity," in J. Bhagwati (ed.), *Import Competition and Response*. Chicago: University of Chicago Press.

Calvo, Guillermo (1981a), "Trying to Stabilize: Some Theoretical Reflections Based on the Case of Argentina," Columbia University Working Paper no. 128.

Calvo, Guillermo (1981b), "Devaluation: Levels vs. Rates," *Journal of International Economics*.

Calvo, Guillermo (1982), "The Chilean Economy in the 1970s," in K. Brunner and A. Meltzer (eds), *Economic Policy in a World of Change*, vol. 17, Carnegie-Rochester Conference Series.

Cavallo, D. and Mundlak, Y. (1982), *Agriculture and Economic Growth in an Open Economy: The Case of Argentina*. IFPRI.

Clark, Paul (1982), "Step-by-Step Liberalization of a Controlled Economy: Experience in Egypt." Unpublished paper.

Corbo, Vittorio (1982), "Recent developments of the Chilean Economy." Unpublished paper, prepared for the conference on "National Economic Policies in Chile," November 1982.

Corbo, Vittorio and Edwards, Sebastian (1981), "El Rol de Una Devaluacion en la Economia Chilena Actual." Unpublished paper.

Corbo, Vittorio and de Melo, Jaime (1982), "Liberalization with Stabilization in the Southern Cone." Unpublished paper.

Corden, W. M. (1981a), "The Exchange Rate, Monetary Policy and Northern Sea Oil," *Oxford Economic Papers*.

Corden, W. M. (1981b), "Exchange Rate Protection," in R. N. Cooper et al. (eds), *The International Monetary System Under Flexible Exchange Rates*. Cambridge, Mass.: Ballinger.

Corden, W. M. (1982), "Booming Sector and Dutch-Disease Economics: A Survey," Australian National University Working Paper no. 079.

Corden, W. M. and Neary, J. P. (1982), "Booming Sector and De-industrialization in a Small Open Economy," *Economic Journal*.

Datta, G. (1983), "Capital Importing Oil Exporters: Macroeconomic Issues in a Period of Rapidly Improving Terms of Trade." Unpublished paper, World Bank.

Diaz-Alejandro, Carlos F. (1981), "Southern Cone Stabilization Plans," in William R. Cline and Sidney Weintraub (eds), *Economic Stabilization in Developing Countries*. Washington, DC: Brookings Institution.

Diaz-Alejandro, Carlos F. (1983), "Good-Bye Financial Repression, Hello Financial Crash." Unpublished paper.

Dixit, Avinash and Norman, Victor (1980), *Theory of International Trade*. Cambridge: Cambridge University Press.

Dornbusch, Rudiger (1974), "Tariffs and Non-traded Goods," *Journal of International Economics*.

Dornbusch, Rudiger (1976), "The Theory of Flexible Exchange Regimes and Macroeconomic Policy," *Scandinavian Journal of Economics*.

Dornbusch, Rudiger (1980), *Open Economy Macroeconomics*. New York: Basic Books.

Dornbusch, Rudiger (1983a), "Remarks on the Southern Cone," *IMF Staff Papers*.

Dornbusch, Rudiger (1983b), "Real Interest Rates, Home Goods and Optimal External Borrowing," *Journal of Political Economy*.

Edwards, Sebastian (1982), "Minimum Wages and Trade Liberalization: Some Reflections Based on the Chilean Experience," Working Paper no. 230, Uni-

versity of California at Los Angeles Department of Economics.

Edwards, Sebastian (1983), "The Short-run Relation Between Grown and Inflation in Latin America: Comment," *American Economic Review*.

Edwards, Sebastian (1984), "LDC's Foreign Borrowing and Default Risk: An Empirical Investigation 1976–1980," *American Economic Review*.

Edwards, Sebastian (1985), "Stabilization with Liberalization: An Evolution of Ten Years of Chile's Experiment with Free Market Policies," *Economic Development and Cultural Change*.

Edwards, Sebastian (1986), "Economic Policy and Growth in Chile: 1973–1982," in G. Walton (ed.), *National Economic Policies in Chile*.

Edwards, Sebastian and Aoki, Masanao (1983), "Oil Export Boom and Dutch Disease," *Resources and Energy*.

Edwards, Sebastian and van Wijnbergen, Sweder (1983), "The Welfare Effects of Trade and Capital Market Liberalization: Consequences of Different Sequencing Scenarios," NBER Working Paper no. 1245.

Feldstein, Andrew (1980), "A General Equilibrium Approach to the Analysis of Trade Restrictions with an Application to Argentina," *IMF Staff Papers*.

Fellner, William (1982), "In Defense of the Credibility Hypothesis," *American Economic Review*.

Fischer, Stanley and Frenkel, Jacob (1972a), "Investment, the Two-Sector Model, and Trade in Debt and Capital Goods," *Journal of International Economics*.

Fischer, Stanley and Frenkel, Jacob (1972b), "International Capital Movements along Balanced Growth Paths: Comments and Extensions," *Economic Record*.

Fleming, J. M. (1974), "Dual Exchange Markets and Other Remedies for Disruptive Capital Flows," *IMF Staff Papers*.

Flood, Robert (1978), "Exchange Rate Expectations in Dual Exchange Markets," *Journal of International Economics*.

Frenkel, Jacob (1982), "The Order of Economic Liberalization: Discussion," in K. Brunner and A. H. Meltzer (eds), *Economic Policy in a World of Change*. Amsterdam: North-Holland.

Frenkel, Jacob (1983), "Remarks on the Southern Cone," *IMF Staff Papers*.

Fry, Maxwell (1978), "Money and Capital or Financial Deepening in Economic Development," *Journal of Money, Credit and Banking*.

Fry, Maxwell (1980), "Savings, Investment, Growth and the Cost of Financial Repression," *World Development*.

Fullerton, Don (1983), "Transition Losses of Partially Mobile Industry-specific Capital," *Quarterly Journal of Economics*.

Galbis, Vicente (1977), "Financial Intermediation and Economic Growth in Less Developed Countries: A Theoretical Approach," *Journal of Development Studies*.

Grossman, Gene (1983), "The Gains from International Factor Movements." Unpublished manuscript.

Hanson, James (1974), "Optimal International Borrowing and Lending," *American Economic Review*.

Hanson, James and de Melo, Jaime (1983), "The Uruguayan Experience with Liberalization and Stabilization," *Journal of Inter-American and World Affairs*.

Harberger, Arnold C. (1959), "Using the Resources at Hand More Efficiently," *American Economic Review*.

Harberger, Arnold C. (1976a), "Notas Sobre la Dinamica de la Liberalizacion del Comercio," in *Estudios Monetarios III*. Santiago: Banco Central de Chile.

Harberger, Arnold C. (1976b), "On Country Risk and the Social Cost of Foreign Borrowing by Developing Countries." Unpublished manuscript, University of

Chicago.

Harberger, Arnold C. (1978), "A Primer on Inflation," *Journal of Money, Credit and Banking*.

Harberger, Arnold C. (1980), "Vignettes on the World Capital Market," *American Economic Review, Papers and Proceedings*.

Harberger, Arnold C. (1982), "The Chilean Economy in the 1970s: Crisis, Stabilization, Liberalization, Reform," in K. Brunner and A. H. Meltzer (eds), *Economic Policy in a World of Change*. Amsterdam: North-Holland.

Harberger, Arnold C. and Edwards, Sebastian (1982), "International Sources of Inflation: Some New Results." Unpublished manuscript.

Johnson, Harry G. (1958), "The Gains From Freer Trade With Europe: An Estimate," *Manchester School of Economics and Social Studies*.

Johnson, Harry G. (1965), "Optimal Trade Intervention in the Presence of Domestic Dostortions," in R. Caves et al. (eds), *Trade Growth and Balance of Payments*. Chicago: Rand McNally.

Johnson, Harry G. (1967), "The Possibility of Income Losses from Increased Efficiency or Factor Accumulation in the Presence of Tariffs," *Economic Journal*.

Jones, R. J. (1971), "A Three-Factor Model in Theory, Trade and History," in J. Bhagwati (ed.), *Trade, Balance of Payments Growth*. Amsterdam: North-Holland.

Kapur, Basant (1983), "Optimal Financial and Foreign Exchange Liberalization of Less Developed Economies," *Quarterly Journal of Economics*.

Khan, Mohsin and Zahler, Roberto (1983), "The Macroeconomic Effects of Changes in Barriers to Trade and Capital Flows: A Simulation Analysis," *IMF Staff Papers*.

Krueger, Anne O. (1974), "The Political Economy of the Rent-seeking Society," *American Economic Review*.

Krueger, Anne O. (1978), *Foreign Trade Regimes and Economic Development: Liberalization Attempts of Consequences*. Cambridge, Mass.: Ballinger.

Krueger, Anne O. (1980), "Trade Policy as an Input to Development," *American Economic Review*.

Krueger, Anne O. (1981), "Interactions Between Inflation and Trade Objectives in Stabilization Programs," in W. R. Cline and S. Weintraub (eds), *Economic Stabilization in Developing Countries*. Washington, DC: Brookings Institution.

Krueger, Anne O. (1983a), *Trade and Employment in Developing Countries*. Chicago: University of Chicago Press.

Krueger, Anne O. (1983b), "The Problems of Liberalization." Unpublished paper, World Bank.

Krumm, Kathie (1983), "Credibility and Investment: Argentina's Attempted Liberalization 1976–1981." Unpublished paper.

Lal, Deepak (1982), "The Real Aspects of Stabilization and Structural Adjustment Policies — An Approach." Unpublished manuscript, World Bank.

Lanyi, Anthony (1975), "Separate Exchange Rate Markets for Current and Capital Transactions," *IMF Staff Papers*.

Leamer, E. E. (1980), "Welfare Computations and the Optimal Staging of Tariff Reductions in Models with Adjustment Costs," *Journal of International Economics*.

Little, Ian M. D. (1982), *Economic Development*. New York: Basic Books.

Little, Ian M. D., Scitovsky, T. and Scott, M. (1970), *Industry and Trade in Some Developing Countries*. Oxford: Oxford University Press.

Little, Ian M. D. and Selowsky, Marcelo (1982), "Energy Prices, Substitution and Optimal Borrowing in the Short-Run: An Analysis of Adjustment in Oil-importing Developing Countries," *Journal of Development Economics*.

Mayer, W. (1974), "Short-run and Long-run Equilibrium for a Small Open Economy," *Journal of Political Economy*.

McKinnon, Ronald J. (1973), *Money and Capital in Economic Development*. Washington, DC: Brookings Institution.

McKinnon, Ronald J. (1976), "International Transfers and Non-traded Commodities: The Adjustment Problem," in D. M. Leipziger (ed.), *The International Monetary System and the Developing Nations*. Washington, DC: US Agency for International Development.

McKinnon, Ronald J. (1979a), "Foreign Exchange Rate Policy and Economic Liberalization in LDCs." Unpublished paper.

McKinnon, Ronald J. (1979b), *Money In International Exchange: The Convertible Currency System*. Oxford: Oxford University Press.

McKinnon, Ronald J. (1980), "Financial Repression and Liberalization Problems in LDCs," in S. Grossman and E. Lundberg (eds), *The Past and Prospects of World Economic Order*. London: Macmillan.

McKinnon, Ronald J. (1982), "The Order of Economic Liberalization: Lessons from Chile and Argentina," in K. Brunner and A. Meltzer (eds), *Economic Policy in a World of Change*. Amsterdam: North-Holland.

McKinnon, Ronald J. and Mathiason, D. J. (1981), *How to Manage a Repressed Economy: Essays in International Finance*. Princeton: Princeton University Press.

Meade, J. E. (1951), *The Balance of Payments*. Oxford: Oxford University Press.

Melvin, James (1968), "Production and Trade With Two Factors and Three Goods," *American Economic Review*.

Michaely, Michael (1982), "The Sequencing of a Liberalization Policy: A Preliminary Statement of Issues." Unpublished paper.

Munoz, Oscar (1982), "Crecimiento y Desequilibrios en Chile," *Estudios Cieplan*.

Mussa, M. L. (1974), "Tariffs and the Distribution of Income: The Importance of Factor Specificity," *Journal of Political Economy*.

Mussa, M. L. (1978), "Dynamic Adjustment in the Heckscher–Ohlin–Samuelson Model," *Journal of Political Economy*.

Mussa, M. L. (1979), "The Two-sector Model in Terms of its Dual: A Geometric Exposition," *Journal of International Economics*.

Mussa, M. L. (1982), "Government Policy and the Adjustment Process," pp. 73–120 in J. Bhagwati (ed.), *Import Competition and Response*. Chicago: University of Chicago Press.

Neary, Peter (1978a), "Short-run Capital Specificity and the Pure Theory of International Trade," *Economic Journal*.

Neary, Peter (1978b), "Dynamic Stability and the Theory of Factor-market Distortions," *American Economic Review*.

Neary, Peter (1982), "Capital Mobility, Wage Stickiness and the Case for Adjustment Assistance," in J. Bhagwati (ed.), *Import Competition and Response*. Chicago: University of Chicago Press.

Nogues, Julio (1983), "Politica Comercial y Cambiaria: Una Interpretacion de la Experiencia Argentina 1976–1981." Santiago: Banco Central de Argentina.

Pindyck, Robert S. (1982), "The Optimal Phasing of Phased Deregulation," *Journal of Economic Dynamics and Control*.

Rodriguez, Carlos A. (1983), "Politicas de Estabilizacion en la Economia Argentina 1978–1982," *Guadernos de Economia*.

Rybczynski, T. M. (1955), "Factor Endowments, International Trade, and Factor Prices," *Economica*.

Schelling, Thomas (1982), "Establishing Credibility: Strategic Considerations,"

*American Economic Review.*

Sjaastad, Larry (1983), "Failure of Economic Liberalism in the Cone of Latin America," *The World Economy.*

Sjaastad, Larry and Cortes, Hernan (1981), "La Politica Economica de la Reforma Comercial en Chile," *Cuadernos de Economia.*

Squire, Lyn (1983), *Employment Policies for Developing Countries.* Oxford: Oxford University Press.

Srinivasan, T. N. (1983), "International Factors Movements," *Journal of International Economics* (May 1983).

Stockman, Alan C. (1982), "The Order of Economic Liberalization: Comment," in K. Brunner and A. H. Meltzer, *Economic Policy in a World of Change.* Amsterdam: North-Holland.

Svensson, Lars O. and Ragin, Arsaf (1983), "The Terms of Trade and the Current Account," *Journal of Political Economy.*

Taylor, John (1982), "Establishing Credibility: A Rational Expectations View," *American Economic Review.*

van Wijnbergen, Sweder (1984), "The Dutch Disease: A Disease After All?" *Economic Journal.*

# Comment 1

*Deepak Lal*

Reading about whether the capital account should be liberalized before the current account reminds me of a story of the young elephant who is learning how to walk. He has a very high IQ and has read all the manuals. He is cogitating: "Should I put my left foot forward? Well, there are lots of arguments for and against that. Well, should I put my right foot forward? Again, there are lots of arguments on both sides." He goes on in this fashion for about 15 minutes, until his mother gets fed up and just gives him a push. And lo and behold, he can walk!

I do not have very much to quarrel with in Sebastian Edwards's analysis, which is not surprising as I have used a similar mode of analysis in my paper which he has cited. However, as I am often a minority of one in seminars, I had better defend the minority position with which I am quite rightly identified in his paper.

I am still in favor of a *floating* exchange rate as an accompaniment to a trade liberalization program. The reason is that, unless one assumes omniscient authorities, even the direction of the nominal exchange rate in many trade liberalization programs can be very difficult to judge. I assume that the fiscal deficit is no longer a problem, and that the domestic capital market has been reformed. It seems to me that the adoption of a floating exchange rate could ease the transitional pains of a trade liberalization program.

There are two sorts of arguments, however, against the adoption of a floating rate. One is the feasibility of creating the forward exchange market that a floating rate requires. I find it difficult to understand why this should be infeasible. If six multinational banks were allowed to set up operation in most semi-industrial developing countries, they would be able to create a forward market. For instance, could Singapore, had it decided to float, do so? Could Hong Kong? Korea? Surely they could easily float their currencies if they wanted to. I do not think feasibility is the issue.

On the desirability of floating, we keep coming back to what can only be described as the queer cases which theory tells us *could* happen. I am not sure how seriously one should take these theoretical curiosa. I have a disadvantage in not knowing much about the Southern Cone; it has always seemed to me, from what purport to be behavioral descriptions of the

actions of agents in these countries, that to understand them, one needs to be a psychoanalyst. Frankly, I don't understand them. The country I normally have in the back of my mind when I think about these problems is India, and I cannot see that, if the capital account were liberalized, India's growth would be any lower than it is now.

There is a serious problem about the effects of capital flows on the real exchange rate. However, I am not persuaded by the argument that there is a good case based on informational lacunae for the equivalent of an optimal tariff on capital inflows, through some sort of sliding scale tax system. It depends, as do many other arguments for optimal intervention and fine-tuning, on assuming omniscient governments and myopic agents. But I do not accept either of these assumptions.

Finally, there is the point made by Ron McKinnon that one should not allow capital inflows, particularly short-run capital flows, during the transition to a liberal trade regime. On the one hand, economists go around telling countries that there is a tremendous shortage of capital. Now here we are saying, look it's terrible, you must stop this capital coming in. That is paradoxical. Although we can convince ourselves, given clear assumptions, that great harm will occur, I think we are exaggerating the harmful effects and forgetting the obvious advantage of capital inflows, given appropriate exchange rate policies, in easing the pains of the transition.

So, I am still an unrepentant floater! I think Edwards's use of the Melvin diagram was very useful. It brings out clearly that the unnecessary switches of resources which so concern Edwards are due to the assumption that private agents are myopic. Although nice in theory, it is difficult to believe that a private agent who is putting his own money into production decisions will not see that the initial real exchange rate is going to be changed.

The reason why many stabilization attempts fail may sometimes be the sequencing of policies, but, particularly in Latin America, the real problem appears to be the credibility of the authorities. Given their past behavior, only a fool would take everything that any government said seriously. What we have ultimately to explain is why certain governments are credible, which then leads to the question of why countries get the governments they do.

# Comment 2

## Ron McKinnon

Sebastian Edwards has done a very scholarly, if massive, job on economic liberalization and foreign capital flows. I won't be able to review it in its entirety here, so will concentrate on certain aspects of what he said.

Overborrowing in the course of a liberalization program is a problem of which our profession has become acutely aware from the recent experiences of Argentina, Chile, and Uruguay. However, the case of the Southern Cone in the 1970s is hardly very pure; in that period virtually all the less developed countries overborrowed, and then got themselves into a debt crisis. This era was complicated by recycling from the oil shock on the one hand, and then by what I consider to be a major breakdown in the public regulation of Western commercial banks on the other. The result was gross overlending by banks in the world economy at large, and to the Third World in particular.

A neater capsule experience that we could study, without these other distractions, is the South Korean liberalization experience of the 1960s. South Korea prior to that time had an export–GNP ratio of 3 percent — almost all foreign exchange earnings were US military counterpart or funds from USAID. It was considered to be an unsuccessful economy. Joan Robinson and the Cambridge Group used to compare North Korea very favorably to South Korea as a successful model for economic development!

But under pressure from the USAID in 1964, there was a major set of trade reforms in South Korea, a unification of the currency associated with a large exchange rate devaluation, and some liberalization of imports. Then in 1965, under the influence of my colleagues Ed Shaw and John Gurley, there was a major financial reform. The domestic capital market, which had been totally moribund, was suddenly brought back to life when interest rates were taken from very low pegs and put into very high pegs. This was accompanied by a major fiscal reform: there was no change in the tax law, but a different general was put in charge of the tax collection mechanism. Tax revenues doubled in the course of a year. Clearly, these reforms are very important, and they laid the basis for the South Korean success in subsequent years.

By the end of 1965, when these reforms had taken hold and exports had begun to grow rapidly, the domestic price level was actually stable. Both

the financial and foreign trade reforms were very successful. Prior to 1964–5 international lenders were accustomed to treating South Korea as a pariah; by the end of 1965, however, international lenders sharply changed their assessments of South Korea's prospects. These sharp shifts in banks' portfolios are not smooth — apparently because of the great herd instinct among international bankers.

Beginning in mid-1966, a large inflow of short-term capital suddenly hit the astonished South Koreans. An acute dilemma resulted for macroeconomic policy. If the South Korean government simply let the exchange rate appreciate, it would, of course, hit the country's nascent export industries very hard, something they found unacceptable. If they just hung on with the fixed rate, while being inundated with finance capital, they would lose control over the money base: inflation would come back. Which it did. Once lost, their price stability was never regained. In subsequent years, inflation and eventually devaluation proceeded, along with some degree of regression in their financial liberalization.

The question is, what should the South Koreans have done? Why, in a sense, did the international capital market fail in this period? Sebastian Edwards's analytical approach to this central point is not terribly satisfactory. Algebraically, his government starts as if it were actively restricting the inflow of capital, and then suddenly that restraint is relaxed. But, in fact, that is a deceptive way to look at it. What occurs at the time of the major liberalization in foreign trade and finance is that the true profitability of the economy increases, as perceived by foreign lenders and domestic borrowers. So, it is not as if the government had been keeping foreign capital out: nobody had wanted to lend to South Korea prior to 1964–5.

Once you undertake a successful stabilization-cum-liberalization program, where the true profitability of the economy suddenly rises, then there is a once-and-for-all attempt by foreign lenders to get a piece of the action and increase their claims — in this case, on the South Korean economy. This inundation with foreign capital is possible even in the case of a pure trade liberalization when there is no major financial stabilization occurring at the same time. But if there is a major financial stabilization, where you move interest rates from low pegs to high pegs, as the South Koreans did, then the inflow of capital is greatly exaggerated.

So what is the nature of the market failure here? Initial expectations of future profitability turn out to be wrong. People look at the real exchange rate and nominal interest rates immediately after the reform, and project some flow of profit into the future. They look at profitability myopically as individual lenders and borrowers, not taking into account what will happen if they all absorb foreign capital simultaneously. What seems profitable for any one of them will become unprofitable within a few years. You might say that this is irrational. People should be able to solve this system, and understand that the real exchange rate will turn against exporters once this capital flows in the aggregate. But this was a once-in-a-lifetime experience for the Koreans, and for most of the international

lenders at that time. Individuals cannot easily see through what will happen at the macroeconomic level.

This problem is made more acute insofar as the financial flow, even though it may be financing longer-term projects, is itself very short-term. When the real exchange rate starts to turn adversely against exporters, you might have to repay the short-term finance. So if this myopia exists in the international capital market, there is a very good case for doing what the Chilean government tried to do, namely, keep out short-term funds while allowing longer-term borrowing. However, the Chileans were not stringent enough in preventing the accumulation of short-term indebtedness.

In addition, we know that in any private capital market each individual borrower faces an upward-sloping supply curve for finance. This is not really a distortion; the more one borrows, the riskier the loan gets at the margin, as Harberger shows in chapter 6. The upward-sloping supply curve accurately reflects increasing riskiness.

Consider, instead, the world of the 1970s and 1980s, where governments guarantee all credit flows. The host government in the borrowing country guarantees private foreign credits — either officially or unofficially. In the lending countries we have the official export–import banks and deposit insurance for the commercial banks. Consequently, the normal upward-sloping supply curve for finance did not face *individual* private borrowers in the Third World in the 1970s: because of the government guarantees that were involved, they could then borrow at a virtually flat rate of interest.

If you combine this macroeconomic distortion with the macroeconomic myopia, capital inflows by private borrowers are further magnified at the time the liberalization occurs. Overborrowing in the Southern Cone in the 1970s was an order of magnitude worse than what happened to South Korea in the mid-1960s: the (impossible) attempt to absorb large amounts of foreign capital very quickly.

Where do we come out on this for policy? Well, at the very minimum, the World Bank should *not* try to buy a trade liberalization by giving aid. Never try to *bribe* someone into liberalizing, because you will be injecting capital at the time the liberalization occurs, and you will make that liberalization much harder to sustain. The abortive efforts to liberalize trade in Pakistan and India in the 1960s and 1970s, where aid was sometimes used as a lever to induce governments in the subcontinent to expand the flow of imports into the economy, may have indeed failed for this reason. If you allow this capital to come in, the real exchange rate turns against exporters and firms competing with imports and makes it unduly hard for them to adjust to the removal of protection.

As far as possible, trade liberalization and financial stabilization should be a "bootstrap" operation that a country does for itself — possibly with technical assistance from the World Bank. Exports and imports should remain in normal balance. However, a big injection of official capital at the time the liberalization occurs finances an unusual bulge in imports, and

throws out the wrong price signals in private markets. Remember that private lenders often magnify any such official injection by the World Bank or the IMF. Allow free inflows of foreign financial capital only at the tail-end of an otherwise successful program of liberalization. During liberalization, stringent controls on suddenly increased inflows of short-term capital are warranted.

In order to reduce the apparent need for external aid to begin liberalizing, it is quite helpful if the liberalizing economy is running a fiscal surplus rather than a deficit. I realize that the Chilean experiment ultimately broke down, as all Latin American economies got themselves into trouble in the early 1980s, even though Chilean fiscal policy was sound. However, there is a strong case for not requiring a big fiscal prop from some outside lender.

The need to bribe a country into opening its trade accounts often occurs because the country has an uncovered fiscal deficit; the international agency covers it for them if they agree to liberalize. Well, this is a bad combination if any liberalization is to be sustained for more than a few months or a year. Instead, be more like the Koreans in 1964–5: get fiscal policy under control *before*, or along with, the move to liberalize foreign trade *and* the domestic capital market.

Apart from these macroeconomic control problems within individual LDCs, there is the failure of the institutions of the international capital market per se. Government guarantees — both in the Western industrial economies that do the lending and in the borrowing countries — have created massive incentives to misallocate capital. How can one succinctly characterize the distortions involved?

(a) Neither private lenders in industrial countries nor private borrowers in LDCs see normal commercial risks. Good or bad projects get the same government credit guarantees.

(b) Western commercial banks have been unregulated in their risk-taking in international lending relative to much tighter regulations governing their domestic lending. This inadvertent regulatory loophole was, in part, associated with the development of the Eurocurrency market in the late 1960s. Moreover, public agencies in the industrial countries, such as the US Federal Deposit Insurance Corporation, give commercial banks undue incentive to take risks in the *unregulated* part of their loan portfolios without worrying about a run on their deposits. Consequently, commercial banks have completely pre-empted the inherently risky lending to LDCs. The dominance of commercial banks in the international capital market is an artifact of unbalanced regulatory policies in the industrial countries.

(c) Mainly as a consequence of (a) and (b), there has been virtually no development of a "normal" long-term primary securities market, where borrowers in LDCs sell bonds or equities to individual lenders in the wealthier economies.

Clearly, the private international capital market today looks very different from what it was prior to World War I. Then, the building of

American or Argentinian railways was financed largely by the issue of long-term sterling bonds in London. Tea or rubber plantations were financed by the flotation of equities. A major bankruptcy in, say, a railway project would put the bondholders out of pocket without jeopardizing the solvency of any major bank or the monetary system. Commercial banks were confined to discounting short-term trade bills associated with identifiable inventories or goods in transit. Merchant banks did the (risky) underwriting of bonds or equity flotations, and on occasion provided risk capital directly to overseas investment projects.

Although sounding anachronistic, I think that the international market in private financial capital in the 1980s should be encouraged to evolve back to something closer to its late nineteenth-century format. This would happen naturally, of course, if official guarantees of private credits were phased out, deposit insurance was circumscribed, and the regulation of the commercial banks' international and domestic activities were brought into better balance with respect to loan loss provisions, capital restraints on lending heavily to one borrower (or guarantor), and so on. The custodians of the national money supply, and the international payments mechanism, should not be in the business of long-term, high-risk lending.

Unlike what actually existed in the nineteenth century, however, official agencies such as the World Bank or the International Monetary Fund would still play an important role for those countries who remained poor credit risks if and when the private flows of international finance were so liberalized. The World Bank's technical assistance and long-term project support for poor countries would remain invaluable, as would the IMF's role as an international crisis manager on a shorter-term basis. Both would nicely complement the evolution of an active long-term international market in bonds and equities from which deposit-taking commercial banks were largely absent.

# PART V

## The Economic Liberalization of Chile: Did it Fail?

# 8

# What Went Wrong in Chile?

*James Hanson*

When I was asked to contribute to this topic along with Harberger and Edwards, two experts with a detailed knowledge of what has happened in Chile that far exceeds my own, I decided to concentrate on the areas of my comparative advantage — placing the Chilean experiment in the broader context of the experience of the rest of the region and commenting on some of the problems of Chilean political economy, especially those relating to the financial sector.

## I   A COMPARISON OF CHILEAN AND LATIN AMERICAN GROWTH EXPERIENCE

Figure 8.1 (top panel) shows the time-path of Chilean GDP from 1973 to 1982 on semilogarithmic scale, using a base of 1973 = 100.[1] The subject of this panel, the 1982 decrease of 14.3 percent in output, from an index of 133.5 to 114.4, stands out dramatically.

Chile's current depression is not, however, unique in Latin America, as anyone within reach of a newspaper or radio in the last 12 months could attest to on a moment's reflection. While Chile's decline was certainly the most precipitous, all of the Latin American countries have suffered some interruption in growth since 1980. This is shown in the rest of figure 8.1, which illustrates the GDP of the other major, non-oil-dependent countries during the period 1973–82, also using the 1973 base.[2]

---

[1] The Chilean data are the 1978-based real GDP, taken from the 1983 IFS. Use of the data from the 1982 IFS, which have an earlier base and thus weigh more heavily the inefficient, import-substituting industries, would imply a higher average growth rate (4.4 percent) in the period 1954–70 and a more pronounced cycle in 1973–6.

[2] All data are from the IFS 1983, except for Peru 1954–60 (IBRD, *Peru: Long-Term Development Issues*), Brazil 1954–63 (IFS tape) and Brazil, Uruguay, and Peru 1982 (ECLA estimates).

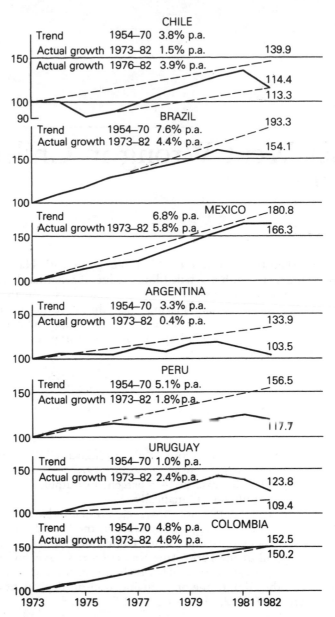

**FIGURE 8.1** Selected Latin American countries, growth performance, 1973–1982

A second, less well known feature of Latin American growth during the last decade is that all the major countries performed more poorly than they did in the 1954–70 period. This is shown in the figure by a comparison between the solid, actual growth path lines and the broken, historic trend lines. The latter represent the growth paths that would have been attained had the economies achieved their average 1954–70 growth rate since 1973.

In almost all cases the trend line is substantially above the actual performance line.

In particular, even at the peak of the 1973–82 cycle, neither Brazil nor Mexico, the two star performers in the Latin American growth circuit, were able to reach their historic growth path. Chile, like Mexico and Brazil, almost reached its historic growth path at its cycle's peak, but then fell far below the trend path in the 1982 decline. The percentage deviation from the historic growth path in 1982 for Chile was 18.2 percent, for Brazil 20.3 percent, and for Mexico 10 percent.

Among the other countries, the performance of Argentina and Peru was extremely poor. Average growth for the whole period was low, and even their highest points in the 1973–82 cycle fell substantially below the historic trend line, by 7.1 and 17.8 percent respectively.

In contrast to these countries, Colombia and Uruguay did well relative to their historic trends. Colombia remained fairly close to its historic trend for the whole 1973–82 period, while Uruguay actual outstripped its 1954–70 performance, even taking into account the 1982 downturn, estimated here at 10 percent. Colombia benefited from the coffee and drug booms and consciously avoided the other countries' dependence on foreign borrowing. Uruguay shows up well owing to the combination of (a) its 1954–70 stagnation; (b) its financial liberalization (without much trade liberalization); and (c) the benefits of maintaining an open capital market next door to Argentina. Uruguay's strong performance, especially in light of its 1974–5 IMF stabilization program, suggests that financial liberalization can bring significant benefits even in the absence of trade liberalization.

The comparative graphic approach also suggests that, in evaluating what happened in Chile during 1973–82, it is extremely important to consider the 1973–6 period. While a couple of the other Latin American countries also suffered slowdowns during these years, in Chile output fell more than 12 percent compared with the 1973 base. This drop resulted from a combination of the collapse of copper prices, which were still at this low level in 1982; the adjustments required following the Allende period; and the tough stabilization program begun in April 1975. It is important to note that trade liberalization probably played little or no role in this decline. The cuts in tariffs apparently did not begin to have serious effects until 1976, since imports, including petroleum, were only 17 percent of GDP in 1977, versus 15 percent in 1973 and 1971. Financial liberalization was also unimportant at this time, as I discuss below.

In sharp contrast, Chile's growth performance was spectacular between 1976 and 1981 (8 percent p.a.), especially considering that growth slowed in all the other countries (except Uruguay) during this period. In fact, Chile's performance since 1976 would put it on an historic growth path beginning in that year, even including the 1982 collapse. This is shown by the lower broken line in figure 8.1, top panel. (In none of the other countries would starting from 1976 make any significant difference in the proportionate 1982 deviation from the historic growth line.)

Thus, the treatment of the 1973–6 period is crucial in evaluating the Chilean experience since 1973. If one regards 1973–6 simply as a normal

cycle in the growth process, then the economy would be expected to return to its normal growth path, and the overall 1973–82 performance is poor.[3] On the other hand, if one regards the program as a necessary adjustment to the Allende regime and takes into account the semi-permanent collapse in the terms of trade, then Chile's 1976–82 growth performance, even including 1982, is above average for the region. What went wrong in Chile? Perhaps the question doesn't need an answer; perhaps 1982 is just a sharp downturn in a large business cycle.

## II   COULD THE 1982 CRASH HAVE BEEN AVOIDED?

Various causes have been cited for the 1982 Chilean crisis. To those opposed to the free market, the current problems lie in an excessive degree of liberalization, and an unwillingness to follow Keynesian precepts. In more sophisticated analyses these ideas are combined with the idea that excessive openness left the economy overly vulnerable to the external shocks of (a) the drop in copper prices, (b) the cut-off of foreign capital inflows to an economy overdosing on debt, and (c) the rise in real interest rates in international capital markets.[4]

Proponents of liberalization and market-oriented solutions instead blame errors in one economic policy or another, rather than the overall strategy. The more extreme argue that liberalization did not go far enough. The less extreme point to problems in policy implementation — an erroneous pegging of the exchange rate and an inflexible system of wage adjustment — combined with the aforementioned international shocks. Although I am in sympathy with the latter view, I do think there are two important points to be made here. First, the exchange rate policy contributed to the 1979–81 growth performance as well as the 1982 crash. Most estimates show a substantial decline in the real exchange rate between 1979 and 1981, which would have provided a cyclical boost to growth in the context of many theoretical models. Thus, a balanced judgment of exchange policy cannot treat policy in 1979–82 as an isolated incident but must consider the effects of the regime as a whole, as Robert Lucas's critique of economic policy making has pointed out so effectively.

Second, proponents of liberalization and market-oriented solutions who say better policy would have avoided the 1982 crash remind me of those proponents of planning and of Keynesian economics who admit that their policy requirements have experienced problems in practice but who interpret these as problems of poor implementation in a specific situation.

---

[3] In this regard it is worth noting that various indicators of industrial capacity utilization suggest that increase in capacity utilization after 1976 accounted for at most 1–2 percentage points of growth per annum and that the cyclical rebound was over by 1977.

[4] The rise in LIBOR rates was about 25 percent in 1981, amounting to an increase in debt service equivalent to about 1.5 percent of Chilean GDP.

If all policy regimes worked as well as claimed, then there would be little to choose between them. My own preference for a market-oriented approach is based on the probable performance of the different systems in practice, rather than on their theoretical properties. Moreover, it must be recognized that, if the implementation of a market system is dependent on orders from a central authority, then the same authority could easily be persuaded to adopt policies over which economists disagree, leading to disastrous results.

In sum, until a prettier model comes along, the proponents of liberalization must accept Chile, warts and all, as the principal example of how a free-market, developing economy operates and of the problems it can encounter. In the same way, proponents of centrally planned, developing economies must accept something like Cuba or Tanzania as the likely outcome of their recommendations until a better example comes along. Peter the Great said, "He who lives by the sword, dies by the sword." Perhaps those who need immoderate authority to introduce economic change should expect some of the changes to have immoderate effects.

## III  THE FINANCIAL CRISIS OF 1982 AND ITS RELATION TO THE LACK OF FINANCIAL LIBERALIZATION

A striking feature of the 1982 Chilean crisis is the high percentage of illiquid, if not insolvent, firms, and the corresponding illiquid state of the financial system. As I will argue below, this problem is related to the lack of financial liberalization between 1974 and 1978 and to government policies pursued since then. The resulting unsound condition of the financial system has created a situation which casts serious doubts on Chile's ability to continue its market-oriented approach to economic policy.

Financial sector liberalization proceeded much more slowly than goods market liberalization in Chile. On the international side, foreign capital inflows were severely restricted until late 1977. In particular, the ability of commercial banks to intermediate in foreign funds was restrained by tight limits on such borrowings relative to the banks' capital and reserves and by a minimum stay requirement. While domestic interest rates were liberalized in 1975, the need for a large inflation tax kept reserve requirements and spreads high for some time, resulting in a positive real deposit rate and average annual real lending rates of between 20 and 30 percent until 1979.

The high real loan rates and the recession of 1974–6, combined with the privatization of the banking system and the CORFO enterprises, made it possible to buy up financial and industrial companies at knockdown prices, albeit with high risks. This was particularly true for purchases made by those with access to borrowed foreign exchange — *ex post*, the rate of depreciation lagged inflation by 25 percent between 1975 and 1978. The result was a scramble for control of banks, with their access to cheap

credit, and a return of Chilean capital through non-bank channels, a return which was fairly large relative to the sale prices of the corporations.[5]

By 1978 this process produced a financial sector and an industrial sector which were controlled by a few groups that had been willing to take large risks and to use their financial power and access to foreign exchange to pyramid investments, unhindered by banking regulations on exposure. Moreover, government guarantees on deposits encouraged businessmen to sell out to those who were willing to leverage themselves highly and then deposit the proceeds — in effect, to lend for their own takeovers. In contrast, an earlier opening of financial markets, including easier entry into banking, would have lowered real interest rates and created more competition for industrial assets, thereby reducing the tendencies toward concentration in finance and industry. And better regulation would also have reduced over-leveraging.

Real interest rates did fall initially when the exchange rate was fixed at Ch$39/US$1 in 1979 and the capital market remained opened. However, in 1981 real rates in local currency returned to their previous levels, as real rates in world markets rose and as the growing peso overvaluation and the scramble for liquidity in the recession produced an increasing differential between peso and dollar loans. For a time the "groups" were able to use their financial power to roll over their growing interest charges, at a corresponding increase in their already dangerous debt–equity ratios. This process was helped by the government's implicit guarantee of bank deposits. Eventually, however, it became clear that the promised real interest rates could not be paid to depositors. To prevent a financial collapse, the government was forced to intervene in the banks and attempt to restructure the corporate debts. Further pressure was placed on the corporations by the devaluations, which sharply increased their debt burden in local currency.

The net result has been that a government nominally committed to market principles finds itself in the contradictary role of the country's principal guarantor and lender to, if not implicit owner of, enterprises. Moreover, the government now faces the difficult task of transferring some of the enormous corporate financial losses to the public, either through a direct bailout with further government participation, or through a write-down of deposits in the financial sector. Under these circumstances, it will be interesting to see if the government's market-oriented approach can survive. Perhaps it is already dead.

---

[5] Between 1974 and 1978 CORFO received about US$300 million for industrial enterprises and US$200 million for bank stock. During the same period the net inflow of foreign financial capital was US$2.3 billion. About 40 percent of the gross inflow came under the rubric "other."

# 9

# A Primer on the Chilean Economy, 1973–1983

*Arnold C. Harberger*

This chapter has the purpose of sketching, for interested parties, some key facts concerning the Chilean economy in the past decade. Emphasis has been placed on matters related to economic fluctuations, unemployment, monetary and exchange-rate policy, etc. The discussion tries to give the necessary background for understanding the interpreting the roots of Chile's serious economic crisis in 1982–3.

1. *The Chilean stabilization process that started in 1973–4 did not involve a major monetary shock.* The major monetary magnitudes were still expanding at over 200 percent per year in 1975 (two years after the military coup), at over 100 percent per year in 1977, and at over 50 percent per year in 1980. In 1981 the average excess of month-end money supply above that of the previous year was 25 percent for $M_1$ and 93 percent for $M_2$. And though $M_1$ dropped slightly in nominal terms in 1982 as against 1981, $M_2$ continued to grow at a 15 percent annual rate. Moreover the rate of price increase did not fall significantly below 30 percent until 1981. In fact, rates similar to those of the "world inflation" really were achieved only from about June 1980 to June 1982 for wholesale prices and from about January 1981 to June 1982 for consumer prices.

2. *There was great variation in real money balances.* The ratio of $M_2$ to GDP averaged about 10 percent in the 1960s. During the (mostly) repressed inflation of the Allende years it averaged about 12.5 percent (see table 9.1). When the repressed inflation became an open one (1974–6) real cash balances ($M_2$) plummeted to around 5.5 percent of GDP. From then on they made a dramatic recovery, moving up to over 25 percent of GDP in 1982. The major part of this increase in the $M_2$/GDP relationship took place under the fixed exchange rate of 39 pesos to the US dollar, initiated in July 1979 and abandoned in June 1982 (Banco Central de Chile, 1983a, p. 218).

3. *International reserves grew dramatically under Chile's fixed exchange rate.* Chile had $273 million of international reserves at the end of 1977, and $1,058 million at the end of 1978. By December 1979 these reserves had risen to $2,313 million, and by December 1980 to $4,074 million. Reserves

TABLE 9.1  Chilean inflation rates

| | Annual average rates | | | December to December | |
| | CPI | WPI | GDP deflator | CPI | WPI |
|---|---|---|---|---|---|
| 1980 | 35.1 | 39.6 | 29.3 | 31.2 | 28.1 |
| 1981 | 19.7 | 9.1 | 13.2 | 9.5 | −3.9 |
| 1982 | 9.9 | 7.2 | 11.3 | 20.7 | 39.6 |

*Source*: Banco Central de Chile (1983a, pp. 217, 121, 125).

were not much affected as the crisis began brewing in 1981 — falling only by some $300 million during that year. By the first devaluation (June 1982) they had dropped to $3,319 million, and by the second devaluation (August 1982) they were down to $2,947 — still amply above their 1978 or 1979 levels. The important message here is that, if Chile had pursued a floating rate policy starting sometime in 1978 or 1979, with other things remaining more or less the same, her exchange rate would probably have appreciated in nominal as well as real terms.

4. *Chile's real exchange rate appreciated dramatically under the fixed rate of 39 pesos to the dollar.* Calculating Chile's real exchange rate with the dollar as the nominal peso price of the dollar times the US GNP deflator divided by the Chilean GDP deflator, and setting the 1960 9 average real rate at 100, we find remarkable stability of the annual (average) real rates from 1960 to 1970. Only once did the average real rate exceed an index of 105 (it was 109 in 1963), and not until 1971 did it fall below an index of 94. But then in the Allende period it deteriorated rapidly, reaching an index level of 82 in 1972.

Negative international reserves plus great difficulties in obtaining foreign credits forced the new military government into a policy of explicitly stimulating exports. This brought the real exchange rate to an index of 158 in 1975, followed by 126 in 1976. From there on a steady deterioration occurred, with the index reaching 109 in 1978, 97 in 1979, 85 in 1980, and 83 in 1981 (Harberger, 1981).

The degree of appreciation is understated by the above figures in the sense that they deal with the relationship between the peso and the US dollar. Since from 1980 onwards the dollar appreciated dramatically against the other major currencies, the Chilean peso did so also, on top of its appreciation vis-à-vis the dollar that we have calculated above.

5. *The great appreciation of the peso was not so bad.* Non-mineral exports grew from around $100 million in 1972 to $477 million in 1975 (when the real exchange rate peaked). They continued to grow as the real exchange rate declined, reaching nearly $1 billion in 1978, $1.5 billion in 1979, and

$1.9 billion in 1980 before tailing off to $1.65 billion in 1981 and $1.55 billion in 1982.

Industrial production fell dramatically in 1975, but rose steadily thereafter, reaching its recent peaks in March (119.6) and July (121.2) 1981.

Unemployment at the national level declined from 14.1 percent in October–December 1978 to 10.4 percent in October–December 1980. In greater Santiago, the unemployment rate fell from 14.8 percent in the first quarter of 1979 (i.e., before the exchange rate was fixed) to an almost constant 8.3 percent during the first three quarters of 1981.

The key reason why things were so good in Chile in 1981 was an inflow of capital, equal (over the whole year) to about 15 percent of GDP. In short, spending exceeded production by about 15 percent. This extra force of demand helped support a good level of economic activity and a low level of unemployment, *despite* a highly appreciated exchange rate. Had this voluntary capital inflow continued at its 1981 pace, the Chilean economy probably would have stayed in pretty good shape during 1982 and 1983 (Banco Central de Chile, 1983a, pp. 75, 177, 201, 244).

6. *The proximate cause of Chile's current trouble was the sharp reduction in the rate of net capital inflow*, from about 15 percent of GDP in 1981 to about 5 percent of GDP in 1982 (see Banco Central de Chile, 1983a, p. 237). This dramatic shift created an imperative need for the real exchange rate to rise, especially in the light of the fact that the foreign credits received by Chile in recent years had been used mainly to purchase nontradable goods (especially to finance, directly or indirectly, a construction boom). In short, an exchange rate which appeared to be reasonably viable (in the presence of a very large capital inflow mainly directly toward domestic goods and services) was no longer viable when the external financing flow virtually dried up.

7. *Chile's labor law made the necessary adjustment of the real exchange rate impossible.* The real exchange rate has many guises — among them (a) the nominal exchange rate multiplied by a foreign price index and divided by a domestic one; (b) the internal (i.e. within-country) price level of tradable goods deflated by the internal price level of nontradables; and (c) the ratio of the nominal exchange rate to an index of wages. Definition (b) can be seen to revert to (a) if the foreign price index is the foreign price level of goods traded (with Chile) and the domestic price level is the price level of nontradables; (c) can be seen to approximate to (b) given that the nominal exchange rate is the predominant *local* variable in determining the internal prices of world-marketed goods, and the wage level is the principal input into services, which in turn make up the bulk of nontradables.

The adjustment that was called for by the shutting down of the capital inflow can thus be seen to entail either (a) a reduction in wages (assuming the nominal exchange rate remained fixed), or (b) a rise in the nominal exchange rate (assuming wages remained fixed).

Neither of the above two alternatives ensued up to June 1982. The result was that the pressure to raise the real exchange rate made itself felt in a dramatic increase in the rate of unemployment. Unemployment in greater

Santiago marched ineluctably upward, from 8.1 percent in the third quarter
of 1981 to 11 percent in the fourth; then from 15 percent in the first quarter
of 1982 to 19.1 percent in the second (Banco Central de Chile, 1983a,
p. 182).

It was, to my mind, the unconscionable rise in the unemployment rate,
rather than anything connected with the loss of foreign reserves, that
triggered the devaluation of June 1982. But the devaluation was impossible
until the labor law was changed. This law, written when the Chilean
economy was at the height of its late-1970s boom, mandated essentially
that every new labor contract must provide *at a minimum* a full cost-of-
living adjustment from the date of the previous contract. For practical
purposes, it made reductions in real wages *illegal* in any covered activity.

Nothing could be accomplished to bring about the required adjustment
while this labor law was in effect. Yet something obviously had to be
done. According to reliable reports, the preferred alternative of the economic team was a decreed reduction of 15–20 percent in all wages and
salaries (perhaps with some exceptions at the lowest levels), so as to be
able to maintain the exchange rate at 39 pesos to the US dollar. The reports
go on to say that this proposal was taken seriously, and discussed at the
highest levels of government. The final decision, however, was instead to
devalue the peso. Yet even for the devaluation to work, a modification of
the labor law was necessary. This modification was finally made; it provided that the real wages pacted in new labor contracts could fall below
their previous level, but not below a floor equal to their level at the
moment the labor law had taken effect. This left an ample margin for
downward real-wage adjustment, and indeed, Chile's experience since the
June 1982 devaluation attests that a serious modification (devaluation) of
the real exchange rate was indeed made possible.

8. *The monetary effects of the Chilean devaluations tended to frustrate their
purpose, at least for some time.* A devaluation was declared in June 1982,
from 39 to 46 pesos to the dollar. This devaluation was "calibrated" to
approximate what would have happened if Chile, rather than pegging to
the dollar in July 1979, had instead pegged the peso to a basket of major
currencies (roughly on a trade-weighted basis). Although I believe, in
retrospect, that the policy of pegging to a basket would have been better
for Chile than pegging to the dollar, and that with such a policy Chile
might have averted a major crisis, the failure of the attempt (*ex post*, in
June 1982) to replicate this scenario is quite clear. The new peg, which
was to follow local inflation in a crawling peg fashion, did not last more
than two months. It was replaced by a short period of a free float, in
which the upward pressure on the exchange rate proved severe, and finally
was followed by the reinstitution of serious exchange controls, with a
parallel market side by side with the official one.

From June 1982 to June 1983 the real exchange rate rose by some 50
percent, as the nominal official rate doubled (from 39 to 78 pesos to the
US dollar), while consumer prices rose by about a third (with US prices
increasing only modestly). The "objective" of an increased real exchange

rate (which in my view, given the circumstances of the capital market, was an absolute necessity) was thus achieved, but its intended purpose of reducing unemployment was substantially frustrated. In fact, post-devaluation unemployment exceeded the second-quarter level of 19.1 percent, and reached 23.9 percent in the third and 21.9 percent in the fourth quarter of 1982 and 21.8 percent and 19.6 percent in the first and second quarters of 1983.

9. *These monetary effects entailed a reduction in desired holdings of peso cash balances combined with a dramatic drain on dollar reserves.* The fall in real $M_2$ signified a reduction in the banking system's capacity to grant credits to domestic borrowers; the loss of reserves worked in the other direction. The net result was that real domestic credit fell only slightly during the period between the June devaluation and May 1983 (see table 9.2).

10. *On "good" and "bad" credits — the Achilles' heel of the Chilean economic experiment.* It is now becoming very clear that the condition of the Chilean banking system played a major role in determining the course of economic events in the period since 1974. Recall that, at the time of the military coup in September 1973, hundreds of Chilean corporations were in government hands, nearly all of them generating substantial losses. Those which had been simply "intervened" by the government (i.e., not expropriated) were returned to their owners, but those which had been officially expropriated were (with a few exceptions, like the major copper mines) sold at auction to the highest bidder.

Regardless of the category to which they belonged, the firms were in a weak financial position at the time they passed back from government to private hands. The deep recession of 1974–5 can only have made things worse. While I know of no study which explicitly traces the economic fate of the enterprises in question, there can be little doubt that a significant fraction of them must have reached the borderline of technical bankruptcy at some point during the 1975 recession.

It is probable that, starting at that relatively early point, the Chilean banks began to accumulate a stock of bad loans. Rather than write off

TABLE 9.2

| | Real money holdings ($M_2$) (billions 1978 pesos) | International reserves (millions US$) |
|---|---|---|
| June 1982 | 150.1 | 3319 |
| August 1982 | 147.9 | 2947 |
| December 1982 | 132.0 | 2577 |
| March 1983 | 116.0 | 1578 |
| May 1983 | 107.1 | 1518 |

*Source*: Banco Central de Chile (1983a, pp. 1323, 1378).

these loans as bad debts, the typical practice appears to have been to roll
them over, accumulating interest along the way. The apparent reason for
this practice was that, upon recognizing a bad loan as such, a bank would
have to reduce its capital and surplus so as to reflect the loss. This, in turn,
would reduce all sorts of legal limits – on lending, on deposits, on borrowing from abroad, etc. — all of which were typically expressed as
multiples of capital and surplus.

As time went on, it appears that the volume of bad loans held by the
banking system grew. The consequence was that the supply of credit
available for "genuine" loans was progressively squeezed. This super-
imposition of what in effect was a "false" demand for credit on top of a
true or good demand is probably the main reason why Chilean interest
rates remained so high throughout most of the 1975–82 period. The high
interest rates — which hovered most of the time around 3–4 percent per
month in real terms – were in turn partly responsible for putting in peril
the financial situation of yet other companies, which may have begun the
period in relatively healthy condition but simply could not withstand the
steady drain on their resources that the high interest rates entailed.

The beginning of the present banking crisis in Chile can probably be
dated around May 1981, with the failure of the major private sector sugar
company, CRAV. It was not the failure as such that caused the problem,
but rather the laxity of banking practices which was revealed as the evidence
unfolded. (Most banks had made their loans to CRAV essentially without
collateral, "on the signature only" of its distinguished director, Don Jorge
Ross.)                                        •

During July–September 1981 it appeared that the financial system was
surmounting the crisis. Interest rates, which had risen sharply in the wake
of the CRAV failure, began to drift downward, and calm seemed to
have been restored in the Chilean financial community. However, new
rumblings appeared in October, and by November 1981 eight financial
institutions were "intervened" by the central bank. These eight included
four banks (of which the largest was the Banco Español) and four *financieras*,
which together accounted for about half the assets of the entire financial
system.

The decision of the government was finally to "bail out" these institutions fully — in the sense of guaranteeing the payment of their obligations
both to their depositors and to their other creditors. In doing so, the
government followed a precedent set several years earlier when the Banco
Osorno had failed in an isolated occurrence. Most qualified observers feel
that it was a mistake to bail out failing institutions so fully — especially
since there is essentially a complete continuum of possibilities — bailout
of principal but no interest; bailouts of principal plus part of interest;
bailout of 90 percent of principal but no interest; etc.

It was the precedent set by these earlier bailout operations which served
as the ostensible motivation under which the international private banking
community virtually insisted on a comparable bailout of practically the
entire Chilean banking system when the crisis wave hit once again in
January 1983. The end result of a lengthy process of negotiations was that

the government effectively extended its own guarantee to all outstanding foreign debts of the Chilean banking system.

11. *The consequence of the progressive bailouts of Chile's banks is a wad of bad or dubious paper in the portfolio of the central bank.* This paper, as long as it is present, limits the capacity of the banking system to make loans to viable enterprises. To the extent that bank credit serves as a productive input (or lubricant) in the economic process, the constricted amount of resources available for credits to truly viable enterprises will limit the pace of Chile's recovery.

In effect, there is nothing plausible that the policy-makers can do to make real $M_2$ go up — indeed, the weakening of confidence over the past year has made it fall significantly. International reserves, on the other hand, have already fallen to only a little more than a third of the earlier peak levels. The policy-makers don't want to lose more, and have agreed not to do so, but what is more important is that, even if they were "used", the existing reserves are not big enough to finance a very big dose of stimulatory credit expansion. Thus we can pretty much rule out any major expansion of credit in real terms.

12. *Outlook.* The story of the Chilean economy in 1981–2 is grim, and the outlook for the future is somber. It will almost surely take at least two years for the 1981 level of real output to be regained, and for the unemployment rate in the greater Santiago labor market to drop back to the 10–12 percent range within which it oscillated during the late 1970s. There seems to be no policy capable of eliciting a quicker recovery; rather, the scenario of recovering to 1981 levels within two years is itself optimistic.

Key danger signals would be (a) further efforts on the part of the public to flee from the currency; and (b) further substantial reductions in real money holdings. Such reductions would have as their counterpart a further squeezing of the amount of "good" credit (in real terms) available to the system.

Hopeful signs are as follows:

(a) The unemployment rate, though high, is significantly below its earlier peak of 23.9 percent.
(b) Preliminary figures show quarterly GDP up by 4 percent in the second quarter of 1983 compared with the first. Industrial production is also up from its recent troughs.
(c) Up to August 1983, Chile has shown the policy restraint necessary to ensure that the nominal devaluation of the peso also entails a significant real devaluation. This has given a new stimulus to tradable goods production (particularly of non-mineral exports).
(d) Quotations in the parallel market, which earlier had reached levels in excess of 130 pesos per US dollar, have in recent months ranged between 85 and 95 pesos (compared with an official rate of around 78).
(e) In spite of a number of government retreats from the liberal, non-interventionist policy system that prevailed between, say, 1975 and

1982, the basic structure of economic policy in Chile is sounder than that in most other Latin American countries. Chile still has a basically uniform tariff (now at a 20 percent rate), a sound tax system, expenditure restraint on the part of government which has kept public sector deficits down to manageable (i.e., non inflationary) proportions, a reasonably "economic" pricing policy of public sector enterprises, etc. These attributes of the policy structure should give Chile a certain edge over other countries in the struggle (universal these days among the Latin American countries) for economic recovery.

REFERENCES

Banco Central de Chile (1983a), *Indicadores Economicos v Sociales, 1960–1982*. Santiago: Banco Central de Chile.
Banco Central de Chile (1983b), *Boletin Mensual*, June.
Harberger, Arnold C. (1981), "The Real Exchange Rate of Chile: A Preliminary Survey." Unpublished paper; undated using sources cited in original paper.

# 10

# Stabilization with Liberalization: An Evaluation of Ten Years of Chile's Experience with Free Market Policies, 1973–1983

*Sebastian Edwards*

## I INTRODUCTION

The recent (post-1973) economic experience in Chile has attracted considerable attention, both from professional economists and from the media.[1,2] Most observers have been particularly impressed by the sharp contrasts observed in Chile in such a short period of time. For example, while in 1973 Chile had one of the highest rates of inflation in the world (over 600 percent), in 1981 it experienced one of the lowest rates of inflation (9.5 percent). Also, while in 1975 real GNP *declined* by 12.9 percent during 1977–80 real GNP grew at an average rate of 8.5 percent per annum. In 1982, however, the country faced a new recession, with real GNP dropping by 14.5 percent, and in 1983 a further reduction of real GNP of around 3 percent was expected. The fact that these episodes developed while the military government was actively pursuing free-market-oriented policies,

[1] Reprinted with the permission of the *Journal of Economic Development and Cultural Change*, Vol. 33(2), Jan. 1985, pp. 223–54.
[2] For an analysis of the Chilean economy before 1970 see, for example, Behrman (1976, 1977), Corbo (1974), French-Davis (1973), Trivelli and Trivelli (1979), and Corbo and Meller (1982). For an analysis of the 1970s see Hachette (1978), Harberger (1982), Foxley (1982), Arellano et al. (1982), and Edwards (1985). Regarding media coverage, see for example, *Time* magazine, January 14, 1980; the *Wall Street Journal*, October 5, 1979 and January 18, 1980; and *The Economist*, February 2 1980; see also *New York Times*, December 8, 1982.

which greatly liberalized the economy, adds considerable interest to the Chilean case.[3]

The year 1973 marked an important turning point in Chile's economic and political history. In September the military took over the government from President Salvador Allende, and a period of dramatic economic changes began, with Chile being transformed from an economy isolated from the rest of the world, with strong government intervention, into a liberalized, world-integrated economy, where market forces were freely left to guide most of the economy's decisions. The 1973–81 period was characterized by important achievements: inflation was greatly reduced; the government deficit was virtually eliminated; the economy went through a dramatic liberalization of its foreign sector, with tariffs being reduced to a 10 percent uniform level; and price controls, including interest rates, were fully eliminated. Probably one of the most interesting aspects of the Chilean economy during this period is that major stabilization and liberalization attempts were undertaken simultaneously. Moreover, the Chilean economic authorities introduced a novel stabilization program based on the fact that the economy's links with the rest of the world had greatly increased as a result of the liberalization of trade. In this stabilization strategy the manipulation of the nominal exchange rate replaced monetary control as the central tool of the anti-inflationary effort.[4]

The free market policies implemented by the military regime since 1973 can be viewed as a reaction to a long tradition of government intervention and controls that had characterized the Chilean economy since the 1940s.[5] Between 1940 and 1970 Chile's growth record was modest: real GDP grew at an average rate of 3.7 percent per year, while real per capita GDP grew at 1.7 percent per year. During these 30 years Chile basically had followed an import substitution development strategy, which greatly closed the economy off from the rest of the world. In general, the empirical evidence available suggests that this inward-looking strategy had some negative effects on Chile's economic growth, by reducing domestic savings, introducing distortions and inefficiencies, and tending to increase capital–labor ratios. Also, this period was characterized by high government deficits and chronic inflation (see note 2).

From an economic growth perspective, 1973–83 was characterized by a highly variable record. During this period Chile experienced one of the

[3] The Chilean experience is particularly interesting since for many years economists have argued that developing countries should follow liberalization processes similar to the one that took place in Chile in the mid- and late 1970s. See, for example, Krueger (1978).

[4] For analytical discussions of the characteristics of this approach to stabilization, see the recent articles by Blejer and Mathieson (1981) and Djacij (1982).

[5] These free market policies were proposed and implemented by a group of economists popularly known as the "Chicago boys."

highest rates of growth in her history — 9.5 percent in 1977 — and also some of the highest *declines* in real GDP: −12.9 percent in 1975 and −14.5 percent in 1982. Table 10.1 presents data on real GDP and real per capita GDP between 1970 and 1983. As may be seen, the first two years of the military regime (1974–5) were characterized by a decline in real per capita GDP. This reduction in economic activity was specially dramatic in 1975 — GDP per capita declined by 14.4 percent — as a consequence of the stabilization program and the decline in the terms of trade. On the other hand, in the years 1977–80 extraordinarily high rates of growth of GDP, averaging 8.5 percent per year, were achieved. However, as may be seen from the table, real per capital GDP reached its 1971 level only in 1980. A crucial question, then, which will be discussed below, is to what extent these high growth rates were due only to a recovery process, starting from a very low initial level of GDP. Finally, starting in late 1981, Chile entered into a deep recession, with real GDP declining dramatically during 1982 and 1983.

The purpose of this chapter is to examine in some detail Chile's economic performance during the post-military coup period. The analysis provides an evaluation of ten years of military regime, placing emphasis on the stabilization and liberalization policies. Special attention is given to the

TABLE 10.1  Real gross domestic product and real gross domestic product per capita in Chile, 1970–1983

| Year | (1) Real GDP (billions 1977 US$) | (2) Rate of growth of real GDP (%) | (3) Per capita real GDP (1977 US$) | (4) Rate of growth of per capita real GDP (%) |
|---|---|---|---|---|
| 1970 | 13.1 | 2.1 | 1403 | 0.2 |
| 1971 | 14.3 | 9.0 | 1502 | 7.1 |
| 1972 | 14.1 | −1.2 | 1459 | −2.9 |
| 1973 | 13.4 | −5.6 | 1355 | −7.1 |
| 1974 | 13.5 | 1.0 | 1345 | −0.7 |
| 1975 | 11.7 | −12.9 | 1152 | −14.4 |
| 1976 | 12.2 | 3.5 | 1172 | 1.8 |
| 1977 | 13.4 | 9.9 | 1266 | 8.0 |
| 1978 | 14.5 | 8.2 | 1347 | 6.4 |
| 1979 | 15.7 | 8.3 | 1434 | 6.5 |
| 1980 | 16.8 | 7.5 | 1516 | 5.7 |
| 1981 | 17.7 | 5.3 | 1568 | 3.4 |
| 1982[a] | 15.1 | −14.5 | 1312 | −16.3 |
| 1983[b] | 14.7 | −2.6 | 1257 | −4.2 |

a Preliminary
[b] Estimated by Universidad de Chile.
*Source*: Banco Central de Chile.

more recent (1982–83) events which have led to one of the worst recessions in the country's history.

The chapter is organized in the following form. In section II the stabilization program and the employment problem are discussed, and the crucial role played by the exchange rate policy in the anti-inflationary program is emphasized. In section III the liberalization of international trade is discussed. Section IV, on the other hand, presents an analysis of the liberalization of the domestic financial markets and of the capital account of the balance of payments. In this section it is noted that the Chilean economy was characterized during this period by extremely high interest rates and low domestic saving ratios. Section V presents a brief discussion on the sources of growth between 1975 and 1980. Section VI focuses on the 1982–3 recession, including the January 1983 agreement with the IMF; it is argued that this recession was (partially) the result of policy inconsistencies. Finally, in section VII some concluding remarks are offered.

## II  THE STABILIZATION PROGRAM AND THE EMPLOYMENT PROBLEM

In October 1973 the military government announced that the reduction of inflation — which had exceeded 600 percent in the previous 12 months — was one of its main economic goals.[6] Other important short-run objectives were the reduction of government controls, the reduction of the fiscal deficit, the reorganization of the productive sector, and the avoidance of a major balance of payments crisis. While, during the first 18 months of the regime, some of these objectives were (partially) achieved — relative prices were realigned, a unified exchange rate was established, the balance of payments crisis was avoided, and government finances were somewhat straightened — inflation was still out of control, with the rate of growth of consumer prices reaching 370 percent in 1974.

Until April 1975 a gradualist anti-inflationary approach had been followed. At that time, however, this gradualist policy was abandoned, and an abrupt stabilization program was implemented. This was based on traditional views regarding economic stabilization in a closed economy, and called for a drastic reduction in inflation in one year. The main characteristics of the program were: (a) an across-the-board reduction in government expenditure (between 15 and 25 percent); (b) a 10 percent temporary hike in income taxes; (c) an acceleration of the program of reducing the size of the public sector, which had begun in 1974; and (d) a tight monetary policy (see Mendez, 1979).

Table 10.2 presents some information regarding inflation and stabilization during the 1970s and early 1980s. As may be seen from columns

[6] See speech by Minister Gotuzzo, reproduced in Mendez (1979).

TABLE 10.2  Inflation and stabilization, 1973–1982

| Year (Dec.–Dec.) | (1) Inflation rate % (Dec.–Dec.) | (5) Govt expend. (millions 1977 US$) | (6) Govt expend. % GDP | (7) Govt rev. (millions 1977 US$) | (8) Govt rev. % GDP | Fiscal deficit (millions US$) | Fiscal deficit % GDP | Rate of growth of $M_1$ (%) (Dec.–Dec.) | Proportion of total credit received by govt | Rate of devaluation of peso (%) (Dec.–Dec.) | Balance of payments (millions[a] US$) |
|---|---|---|---|---|---|---|---|---|---|---|---|
| 1970 | 34.9 | 3681 | 28.1 | 3301 | 25.2 | 380 | 2.9 | — | 0.56 | 20.0 | — |
| 1971 | 22.1 | 4633 | 32.4 | 2989 | 21.2 | 1644 | 11.2 | 110 | 0.69 | 33.3 | — |
| 1972 | 487.5 | 4540 | 32.2 | 2637 | 18.7 | 1903 | 13.5 | 157 | 0.77 | 56.3 | — |
| 1973 | 605.9 | 5990 | 44.7 | 2693 | 20.1 | 3297 | 24.6 | 317 | 0.88 | 1340.0 | −21 |
| 1974 | 369.2 | 4374 | 32.4 | 2957 | 21.9 | 1417 | 10.5 | 272 | 0.85 | 419.4 | −55 |
| 1975 | 343.2 | 3206 | 27.4 | 2902 | 24.8 | 304 | 2.6 | 258 | 0.85 | 354.5 | −344 |
| 1976 | 197.9 | 3148 | 25.8 | 2867 | 23.5 | 281 | 2.3 | 194 | 0.75 | 104.9 | 414 |
| 1977 | 84.2 | 3337 | 24.9 | 3095 | 23.1 | 242 | 1.9 | 108 | 0.59 | 60.5 | 113 |
| 1978 | 37.2 | 3451 | 23.8 | 3335 | 23.0 | 116 | 0.9 | 67 | 0.40 | 21.4 | 712 |
| 1979 | 38.0 | 3627 | 23.1 | 3878 | 24.7 | −251 | −1.7 | 65 | 0.29 | 14.9 | 1047 |
| 1980 | 31.2 | 4200 | 25.0 | 4284 | 25.5 | −84 | −0.6 | 57 | 0.10 | 0.0 | 1244 |
| 1981 | 9.5 | 4195 | 23.7 | 4726 | 26.7 | −531 | −3.0 | −60 | 0.02 | 0.0 | 70 |
| 1982 | 20.7 | 4379 | 29.0 | 4032 | 26.7 | 347 | −2.3 | 9 | 0.07 | 88.3 | −1165 |

[a] A minus sign means deficit. Data for 1970–2 are not available because in 1980 the central bank changed the way balance of payment statistics are recorded.

Sources: Column (1) is taken from INE for years 1970–2 and 1979–82, and from Cortazar and Marshall (1980) for 1973–8; columns (2)–(4) are taken from Exposicion de la Hacienda Publica, 1981; columns (5) and (6) are taken from International Financial Statistics; columns (7) and (8) are taken from Indicadores Economicos y Sociales 1960–1982.

(2), (3), and (4), the main feature of the 1975 stabilization package was a major fiscal shock which resulted in 80 percent real reduction of the fiscal deficit and, thus, in the reduction of one of the major sources of inflation. This decline in the level of the deficit in 1975 was accomplished mainly by the reduction in government sector expenditures, basically through the reduction of the number of civil servants. It has been estimated that the fiscal crunch resulted in a reduction in government employment of about 80,000 workers, or 2.4 percent of the labor force (Edwards, 1980).

As reflected in this table, government revenues as a percentage of GDP were also substantially increased in 1975. This was accomplished through a comprehensive tax reform that introduced a flat value-added tax; a full indexation of the tax system; an elimination of most exemptions and subsidies; a unification of the corporation and non-corporation income taxes into a flat-rate business tax, and an integration of personal and business income taxes.[7]

The stabilization effort of 1975 also relied on a tighter monetary policy. Even though Harberger (1982) has argued that it can hardly be said that there was a monetary crunch, during the initial phase of the stabilization program the control of monetary aggregates was a central aspect of the overall policy.[8]

The 1975 stabilization program promptly impacted on inflation, with the rate of growth of prices declining from 69 percent in the second quarter of 1975 to 26 percent in the fourth quarter of 1975. However, by early 1976 it seemed that, in spite of the virtual elimination of the major source of money creation — the fiscal deficit — the rate of growth of prices was regaining its old pace, with the rate of inflation climbing, in the first quarter of 1976, to 47 percent. At this time a major change in the stabilization strategy took place, with the emphasis moving away from the control of the quantity of money as the major anti-inflationary tool. The manipulation of the nominal exchange rate became the basic stabilization instrument. It was argued that, as a result of the opening of the economy to the rest of the world — tariffs had already been reduced from an average of 94 percent in 1973 to an average of 33 percent — a stabilization program designed for a closed economy was largely ineffective. It was further argued that, since in an open economy there is a close link between the

[7] In rigor the process of tax reform began in late 1974. However, only toward mid-1975 was its impact felt in the economy. For an exposition of the main aspects of the reform see Minister Cauas' speech, reproduced in Mendez (1979, p. 119).

[8] See also Harberger (1981b). Other experts — for example Alejandro Foxley — also agree that there wasn't a monetary crunch in Chile; see Cline and Weintraub (1981, p. 233). The main reason why in 1975 we oberved a reduction in the fiscal deficit, while credit creation by the central bank continued (see table 10.2), rests on the fact that government enterprises — which are not part of the fiscal sector — still ran huge deficits; see Harberger (1982) and Foxley (1981, discussion).

domestic rate of price changes and the rate of devaluation (plus the rate-of-world inflation), the domestic rate of inflation depended basically on the behavior of the exchange economy.[9] In June 1976 the government *revalued* the Chilean peso by 10 percent as a means of breaking inflationary expectations. In 1977 a new 10 percent appreciation was implemented; and in January 1978 a novel policy of preannouncing changes in the exchange rate (the so-called "exchange rate table") was introduced as a means of further reducing the domestic rate of inflation.

With the trade reform having reduced most import barriers, it was expected that this system of preannounced devaluations would tend to work in a way similar to a fixed exchange rate regime, with inflation tending to be, on average, equal to the world rate of inflation *plus* the rate of devaluation. Initially, however, the rate of inflation exceeded the sum of the devaluation and world inflation, resulting in a real appreciation of the Chilean peso.[10] In June 1979, and as a form to further reduce the domestic rate of inflation, the preannounced devaluation system was ended and a fixed exchange rate, with the peso pegged to the US dollar at a rate of 39 pesos per dollar, was adopted. During the next months the rate of inflation declined substantially, but still exceeded the world inflation, generating a further real appreciation of the Chilean peso. Finally, in 1981 the domestic rate of inflation converged to the world level, with the annual change of consumer prices being only 9.5 percent in that year.

On the production side, the immediate short-run effect of the stabilization program was to generate a large reduction in the level of economic activity in 1975. The fiscal shock plus the sharp decline in Chile's terms of trade resulted in a reduction of GDP in 1975 of 12.9 percent, and in a steep increase in the rate of unemployment to almost 20 percent in September of that year. Even though the economy rapidly began to recover after 1975, with real GDP reaching its 1974 level in 1977, unemployment remained at extraordinarily high levels throughout the period. Table 10.3 presents data on the labor force (column (1)), unemployment (columns (2) and (3)), and the so-called Minimum Employment Program — which consists of a low-wage public works program designed to cope with the unemployment problem — and real wages (columns (4)–(6)). As may be seen from this table, open unemployment (which excludes the Minimum Employment Program) never dropped below 10 percent, and experienced a dramatic jump in 1982. The high rate of unemployment during the late

[9] To a certain extent this policy was based on the analytical structure provided by the simple version of the monetary approach to the balance of payments. See the extensive discussion in Blejer and Landau (1984).

[10] As Diaz-Alejandro (1981) has pointed out, this inital discrepancy between domestic inflation and the sum of world inflation and the devaluation rate has been a common characteristic of the recent Southern Cone stabilization programs. For discussions on the preannounced devaluation system, which was also adopted by Argentina, see Calvo (1981), Blejer and Mathieson (1981), and Djajic (1982).

TABLE 10.3   Unemployment and wages in Chile, 1970–1982[a]

| | (1) | (2) | (3) | (4) | (5) | (6) |
| | | | | | Min. Employment | |
| | | Total | Open | Min. | Program as | |
| | Total labor | unemploy- | unemploy- | Employment | % of labor | Index of real |
| | force | ment | ment rate | Program | force | wages[b] |
| Year | ('000) | ('000) | (%) | ('000) | (%) | (1970=100) |
|------|---------|---------|------|--------|-----|--------|
| 1970 | 2909.4 | 100.5 | 3.5 | — | — | 100.0 |
| 1971 | 2967.4 | 96.6 | 3.3 | — | — | 129.0 |
| 1972 | 2979.9 | 97.6 | 3.3 | — | — | 114.5 |
| 1973 | n.a. | n.a. | n.a. | — | — | 64.4 |
| 1974 | n.a. | n.a. | n.a. | — | — | 60.0 |
| 1975 | 3114.7 | 464.6 | 14.9 | 118.7 | 3.8 | 63.9 |
| 1976 | 3182.3 | 405.0 | 12.7 | 209.3 | 6.6 | 76.5 |
| 1977 | 3199.0 | 378.5 | 11.8 | 179.6 | 5.6 | 81.3 |
| 1978 | 3476.6 | 485.3 | 14.1 | 124.2 | 3.6 | 82.9 |
| 1979 | 3477.5 | 474.2 | 13.6 | 152.2 | 4.4 | 83.7 |
| 1980 | 3635.5 | 378.4 | 10.4 | 207.2 | 5.7 | 96.2 |
| 1981 | 3688.0 | 417.0 | 11.3 | 171.3 | 4.6 | 109.5 |
| 1982 | 3503.6 | 679.1 | 19.4 | 322.7 | 9.2 | 107.9 |

[a] The labor force and unemployment figures (columns (1), (2), and (3)) refer to periods Sept.–Dec. for 1970 and Oct.–Dec. for the rest of the years. These are, however, the best data available at a national level. Quarterly data are available for the Greater Santiago area. The data on the Minimum Employment Program (column (4)) refer to the Oct.–Dec. average of each year.
[b] To construct the real wage index the GDP deflator was used. The reason for this is that the official price index has been manipulated, and understates inflation (see Cortazar and Marshall, 1980).
*Sources*: Banco Central de Chile and Instituto Nacional de Estadisticas.


1970s was due to a number of reasons, including the negative effect of the stabilization program on the demand for labor, the reduction of the public sector — which resulted in the elimination of approximately 100,000 jobs — and the liberalization of foreign trade, which generated a major readjustment in the manufacturing sector. In spite of the persistence of a high rate of unemployment, real wages and salaries slowly increased between 1976 and 1980, and in 1981 they finally surpassed their 1970 level.[11]

[11] Calvo (1982) has suggested that the Chilean unemployment might be of an equilibrium quasi-voluntary type. For an analysis of the recent unemployment problem in Chile see Edwards (1980). It is important to notice that the increase in

There are two important characteristics of the behaviour of the labor market during this period that deserve special attention. First, a minimum wage was in effect throughout the period. Between 1975 and 1979 the minimum wage increased in real terms by 20 percent. There is no doubt that the presence of this minimum wage law should be added to the list of explanations for the persistence of high rates of unemployment during the recovery process (Edwards, 1982b). Second, during this period a backward indexation system, where nominal wages were automatically adjusted by the inflation rate in the previous months, was in effect. This indexation procedure was implicitly established during the first year of the regime, and later was formally incorporated into the 1979 labor law. Of course, one of the main features of a backward indexation system is that, in a situation characterized by decreasing inflation, *real* wages will automatically increase as a result of the indexation mechanism. This was indeed the case in Chile, especially in 1980 and 1982 (see table 10.3).

There is no doubt that the stabilization policy was largely successful in the sense that it practically eliminated inflation in a fairly short period of time. However, an important question — not yet to be answered — is to what extent this stabilization program was unnecessarily harsh in terms of output reduction. Even though a definitive answer to this question would require additional research, there are some indications that the costs of reducing inflation might have been unnecessarily high. For example, as Diaz-Alejandro (1981) has argued, the reduction in public investment during this period added to the costs of the stabilization program. Additionally, the 1976 revaluation of the peso, by tending to raise the relative price of nontradable goods, made the adjustment in this sector more difficult. In effect, the revaluation of the peso tended to generate an excess supply in the nontradable goods sector at a time when it was required to *reduce* the excess supply already created by the decline in the rate of growth of domestic credit. Also, the subsequent use of the exchange rate as the major stabilization tool resulted in an important real appreciation of the peso and a significant loss in the degree of competitiveness of the domestic industries. As will be argued in section VI below, the adoption of a fixed exchange rate in June 1979 — as the final step of the stabilization process — with an inflexible real wage (by law) was a serious policy mistake, which precipitated the 1982–3 recession.

---

real wages reported in table 10.3 is lower than the official rate of growth of wages as reported, for example, by the Banco Central de Chile. The reason is that in table 10.3 the real wage index has been computed by using the GDP deflator as the relevant price index, instead of the CPI. It is generally accepted that the official CPI underestimates inflation: see Cortazar and Marshall (1980); Harberger (1982). On the evolution of income distribution during this period see, for example, Cortazar (1982).

## III   THE LIBERALIZATION OF INTERNATIONAL TRADE

The major objective of the military economic program was to transform Chile into a free-market-oriented economy. This was to be achieved through a number of measures, including the privatization of state-owned enterprises, the reduction of the size of the public sector, the liberalization of the foreign sector (both the current and capital accounts of the balance of payments), the liberalization of the domestic financial sector, and the freeing of other key markets. In this section the liberalization of foreign trade is discussed, while the next section is devoted to the analysis of the liberalization of the domestic financial market and of the current account of the balance of payments.

One of the most dramatic policy measures undertaken by the military regime was the opening of international trade. In a five-year period, all quantitative impediments to trade were eliminated and import tariffs were reduced from an average of 100 percent to a uniform 10 percent level. This tariff reduction process took place in two stages. The first was carried out within the framework of the Andean Common Market (Pacto Andino), and tariffs were reduced to a range between 10 and 55 percent. The second stage began with Chile's withdrawal from the Andean Pact. In early 1977 the Minister of Finance announced that the trade liberalization process was to be intensified, and that with a few exceptions — the most notable being automobiles — by the end of 1979 import tariffs on *all goods* were to be 10 percent.[12] Table 10.4 contains information on the evolution of nominal tariffs and effective rates of protection by sectors between 1975 and 1979. As may be seen, while in 1975 the dispersion of nominal sectoral tariffs was moderate — with the exception of Basic Metallic Industries, the average tariffs ranged from 58 percent to 74 percent — the dispersion of the effective rates of protection was extremely high. In fact, the standard deviation of nominal tariffs in 1975 was 13.4 percent, while for effective tariffs it was 51 percent.

During its early stages, the tariff reduction process was complemented by an exchange rate policy aimed at maintaining — or even increasing — the real exchange rate. The purpose of this policy was to compensate the loss of competitiveness in the import substitution sectors resulting from the tariff reductions.[13] However, as discussed in the previous section,

---

[12] Sjaastad (1982) has suggested that this second stage of the trade liberalization program — the reduction of tariffs to a uniform 10 percent — was the result of pressures by some groups in the private sector. For an analysis of the trade liberalization process see Sjaastad and Cortez (1981). See also Ffrench–Davis (1981) and Vergara (1981). However, in 1983, as a measure to fight the effects of the recession, tariffs were temporarily raised to 20 percent. There were, however, some exceptions, with higher tariffs applied to milk and other products.

[13] On the relation between exchange rates and a tariff reform see Balassa (1982).

TABLE 10.4  Effective and nominal rates of protection in some sectors, 1975 and 1979 (percentages)

| Sector | *(1)* *Effective tariff, 1975* | *(2)* *Nominal tariff, 1975* | *(3)* *Effective tariff, 1979* | *(4)* *Nominal tariff, 1979* |
|---|---|---|---|---|
| Agriculture, Forestry and Fishery | −36 | n.a. | 10 | 10 |
| Food, Beverages, Tobacco, Textiles, and Leather Products | 72 | 74 | 10 | 10 |
| Timber, Furniture, and Paper Products | 11 | 68 | 10 | 10 |
| Non-metallic Mineral Products | −38 | 62 | 10 | 10 |
| Basic Metallic Industries | 38 | 38 | 10 | 10 |
| Chemicals and Derivatives of Coal, Oil, and Rubber | 47 | 58 | 10 | 10 |
| Metallic and Metallurgical Industries[a] | 95 | 73 | 10 | 10 |

[a] Excludes the automobile sector.
*Source*: Column (1) from Edwards (1977a); columns (2), (3), and (4) from data presented in Pollack (1980).

toward mid-1976 the rate of change of the exchange rate became the major stabilization tool, with the rate of devaluation being deliberately kept below the ongoing domestic inflation. Between 1975 and 1976 the real exchange rate declined 20 percent and between 1976 and 1977 it declined a further 14 percent. This reduction of the real exchange rate was accentuated after June 1979, when the nominal exchange rate was fixed to the US dollar (see Harberger, 1981a).

The tariff reduction processes, and the accompanying exchange rate policy, greatly affected the structure of production and growth in Chile. Initially, the major beneficiaries of this process were non-traditional (or non-copper) exports, which experienced a sharp increase, growing from 11 percent of total exports in 1970 to 34 percent in 1980.[14]

[14] The increase in non-traditional exports during the initial stages of a liberalization has been observed in a number of countries; see, for example, Krueger (1978).

In table 10.5 the rate of growth of GDP at the sectoral level is presented. Surprisingly, the tariff reduction process did not have a very large impact on the manufacturing sector as a whole, whose share in GDP was reduced only from 24.3 percent in 1965–70 to 21.5 percent in 1980. However, the structure of production *within* the manufacturing sector was greatly affected. Those industries that traditionally had had a very high level of protection experienced large output losses, with many firms closing as a consequence of bankruptcy (see Ffrench-Davis, 1981; Vergara, 1981). Seven out of 20 manufacturing subsectors had a lower level of production in 1980 than in 1970 (see Edwards, 1983, for a more detailed discussion). Some of these sectors, especially textiles and leather goods, had traditionally had a high degree of protection. On the other hand, the industries that experienced an increase in production during the 1970s achieved this by greatly increasing the level of efficiency, introducing new technologies, and adopting modern management systems. Table 10.6 presents some data on employment and productivity, by sectors, in 1976 and 1980. As may be seen, the manufacturing sector as a whole experienced an important increase in productivity. Other sectors where efficiency was substantially increased were Commerce and Financial Services.

The trade liberalization process also had an important impact on agricultural production. The traditional negative effective protection that this sector enjoyed was eliminated, and the fairly high real exchange rate that prevailed during 1975–9 promoted a number of non-traditional agricultural exports. While the share of the agricultural sector in GDP remained basically constant (it was 6.5 percent in 1965–70 and 7.0 percent in 1978–81), there were major changes in the composition of production, with resources tending to move away from the so-called "traditional products" toward export-oriented crops. However, the lack of adequate data makes it particularly difficult to evaluate the overall performance of the agricultural sector during this period.

In general, the change in the structure of production between 1970 and 1980 was due largely to the process of tariff reduction.[15] However, other policy measures, such as the creation of the domestic capital market, also affected the composition of GDP. As is revealed in table 10.5, the sectors that on average grew fastest between 1976 and 1981 were Commerce and Financial Services. The fast growth of the first was due basically to the change in orientation of the economy toward an open, free market system. On the other hand, the Financial Services sector grew as a result of the financial reform that liberalized interest rates, reduced the regulations to the banking sector, and allowed the establishment of foreign banks.

A subject that has been extensively debated in Chile is the extent to which the process of tariff reductions "contributed" to the unemployment

---

[15] Notice, however, that theoretically (in a world with more than two goods) it is not possible to know if the increase of effective protection in a particular sector will result in an increase in production in that sector.

TABLE 10.5  Rate of growth of real GDP, by sectors, 1970–1982 (percentages)

| Sector | 1970 | 1975 | 1976 | 1977 | 1978 | 1979 | 1980 | 1981 | 1982[a] |
|---|---|---|---|---|---|---|---|---|---|
| Agriculture and Forestry | 3.6 | 4.8 | -2.9 | 10.4 | -4.9 | 5.6 | 1.8 | 2.2 | -3.3 |
| Fishery | -5.4 | -6.7 | 33.9 | 15.4 | 17.9 | 14.3 | 7.5 | 13.6 | 8.8 |
| Mining | -3.0 | -11.3 | 12.2 | 2.7 | 1.6 | 5.4 | 5.9 | 3.6 | 5.7 |
| Manufacturing | 2.0 | -25.5 | 6.0 | 8.5 | 9.3 | 7.9 | 6.2 | 2.6 | -21.6 |
| Electricity, Gas, and Water | 5.3 | -3.8 | 5.8 | 5.8 | 6.7 | 6.8 | 5.9 | 3.5 | -29.0 |
| Construction | 5.5 | -26.0 | -16.5 | -0.9 | 8.1 | 23.9 | 25.7 | 16.2 | -0.2 |
| Commerce | -1.5 | -17.1 | 2.5 | 24.8 | 20.0 | 11.0 | 10.8 | 5.7 | -17.8 |
| Transport and Communication | 4.7 | -7.7 | 4.7 | 10.8 | 8.4 | 9.0 | 11.1 | 5.4 | -9.9 |
| Financial Services | 15.4 | -4.2 | 9.3 | 14.5 | 20.2 | 28.0 | 22.1 | 8.5 | n.a. |
| Services of Dwellings | 3.7 | 1.8 | 0.7 | 0.6 | 0.9 | 0.5 | 1.0 | 1.7 | n.a. |
| Public Administration | 1.5 | 1.9 | 5.9 | 1.8 | -3.1 | -1.2 | -3.3 | -1.6 | n.a. |
| Education | 2.6 | 1.8 | -2.3 | 2.4 | 2.2 | 1.9 | -0.6 | n.a. | n.a. |
| Health | 3.1 | -1.7 | 4.2 | 2.7 | 3.2 | 5.7 | 3.1 | n.a. | n.a. |
| Other Services | 1.4 | -4.5 | 3.5 | 5.7 | 5.7 | 6.4 | 5.6 | n.a. | n.a. |
| GDP | 2.1 | -12.9 | 3.5 | 9.9 | 8.2 | 8.3 | 7.5 | 5.3 | -14.3 |

[a] Preliminary
Source: Banco Central de Chile.

TABLE 10.6    Employment and productivity, by economic sector, 1976 and
1980

| Sector | 1976 | | | 1980 | | |
|---|---|---|---|---|---|---|
| | Employ-ment ('000) | Employ-ment total (%) | Value added/1000 workers (millions 1977 US$) | Employ-ment ('000) | Employ-ment total (%) | Value added/1000 workers (millions 1977 US$) |
| Agriculture | 500.3 | 18.0 | 2.4 | 499.9 | 15.8 | 2.7 |
| Mining | 73.2 | 2.6 | 14.3 | 66.6 | 2.1 | 18.3 |
| Manufacturing | 467.7 | 16.8 | 5.7 | 511.5 | 16.1 | 7.1 |
| Public Utilities | 28.5 | 1.0 | 10.0 | 24.0 | 0.8 | 9.3 |
| Construction | 103.9 | 3.7 | 5.3 | 142.6 | 4.5 | 6.4 |
| Commerce | 439.9 | 15.8 | 3.8 | 580.0 | 18.3 | 5.3 |
| Transport | 172.2 | 6.2 | 3.7 | 199.6 | 6.3 | 4.7 |
| Financial Services | 63.6 | 2.3 | 11.6 | 98.2 | 3.1 | 16.1 |
| Communal Services | 921.2 | 33.1 | n.a. | 1040.8 | 32.8 | n.a. |
| Other Sources | 8.7 | 0.3 | n.a. | 6.3 | 0.2 | n.a. |
| Total | 2779.2 | 100.0 | n.a. | 3169.5 | 100.0 | n.a. |

*Sources:* Banco Central de Chile and Instituto Nacional de Estadisticas.

problem. Elsewhere (Edwards, 1982a) I have developed a model that
assumes short-run factor specificity and sticky real wages, in order to
analyze the short-run unemployment effects of the tariff reform. The
results from this study indicate that an upper bound for the unemployment
effect of this reform is 3.5 percentage points of the labor force, or 129,000
people, with the bulk of this unemployment located in the Food, Bever-
ages, Tobacco, Textiles, and Leather Products subsectors (57,000 people).
Even though this is not a negligible number, it does indicate that an
explanation for the bulk of the unemployment should be sought elsewhere.
    In summary, it is possible to state that the trade reform had a major
impact on the growth and structure of production in Chile. Resources
were reallocated toward competitive sectors and the level of efficiency in
the tradable goods sector was greatly improved. Even though this process
raised unemployment in the short run, in the medium run there was a
tendency for employment to increase in the expanding sectors (see Coeymans, 1978). In early 1983, however, as a means of combating the
recession, tariffs were increased to a uniform level of 20 percent. Even
though this represented a partial reversal of the liberalization policy, the

Chilean foreign sector was still significantly freer than most developing countries, and fairly close to what economists have generally advocated (see Krueger, 1978; McKinnon, 1982).

## IV. THE LIBERALIZATION OF THE DOMESTIC FINANCIAL SECTOR AND OF THE CAPITAL ACCOUNT OF THE BALANCE OF PAYMENTS

A major policy objective of the military regime was the liberalization and modernization of the financial sector. Until 1973 the domestic capital market had been highly repressed, with most banks being government-owned. Real interest rates were negative, and there were quantitative restrictions on credit. The liberalization process began slowly in early 1974, with the freeing of interest rates, the relaxation of some restrictions on the banking sector, and the creation of new financial institutions.[16] International capital movements, however, were strictly controlled until mid-1979. In June of that year the government decided to begin a process of liberalization of the capital account of the balance of payments, and some restrictions on medium- and long-run capital movements were lifted. The final steps in this process were taken in April 1980, when regulations regarding the maximum monthly inflow of foreign capital were lifted.[17] Short-term capital movements, however, were still forbidden. In spite of the fact that only medium- and long-term capital movements were allowed, the opening of the capital account resulted in a massive inflow of foreign capital. In 1980 capital inflows more than doubled with respect to 1979 — US\$ 2,499 million vs. US\$ 1,242 million — and in 1981 the level of capital inflows doubled again, to US\$ 4,507 million.[18]

One of the most important consequences of the opening of the capital account was that the resulting massive capital inflows generated a further real appreciation of the peso. To the extent that nontradable goods are normal, lifting existing restrictions on foreign borrowing will result in higher expenditures on these goods (as well as on tradables), and in a real appreciation. In the particular case of Chile, a high proportion of the funds obtained from abroad were used to finance nontradables — and especially in the construction sector (see table 10.5). The effect of capital inflows on the real exchange rate has been extensively discussed by a number of

[16] However, according to international standards, the banking sector was still highly repressed. By the end of 1974, for example, the effective rate of *required bank reserves* was 66 percent!

[17] For a detailed analysis of the institutional itinerary of the capital account liberalization, see Arellano (1982).

[18] These figures refer to funds allowed in accordance with Article 14 of the Exchange Law. Most private funds were imported this way.

authors, including McKinnon (1982), Diaz-Alejandro (1981), Munoz (1982), Corbo and Edwards (1981), and Edwards (1985). Harberger (1982), for example, has estimated that in the case of Chile the opening of the capital account can explain up to 25 points of the appreciation of the peso.

One of the most puzzling characteristics of the behavior of the Chilean financial sector between 1977 and 1982 has been the extremely high *real* interest rates that prevailed throughout most of the period. These real rates, which average above 30 percent per annum for long periods of time, remained high despite a major rise in total credit and the massive inflow of foreign capital in late 1980 and 1981. Table 10.7 presents some summary

TABLE 10.7　Interest rates, inflation, money and exchange rates in Chile, quarterly data, 1977–1981

| | (1)<br>Nominal<br>borrowing<br>interest annual<br>rate<br>(%) | (2)<br>Annualized<br>inflation<br>rate<br>(%) | (3)<br>LIBOR<br>interest rate<br>(%) | (4)<br>High-powered<br>money<br>(1978(1)=100) | (5)<br>Quantity of money<br>(M₃)(1978(1)=100) |
|---|---|---|---|---|---|
| 1977(1) | 124.6 | 100.0 | 5.6 | 46.9 | 47.5 |
| 1977(2) | 83.6 | 59.2 | 6.1 | 56.0 | 57.3 |
| 1977(3) | 70.8 | 54.3 | 7.2 | 71.7 | 66.7 |
| 1977(4) | 99.8 | 45.4 | 7.6 | 88.4 | 80.7 |
| 1978(1) | 70.7 | 32.7 | 7.7 | 100.0 | 100.0 |
| 1978(2) | 55.6 | 30.6 | 8.5 | 102.2 | 108.2 |
| 1978(3) | 55.5 | 38.2 | 9.3 | 106.5 | 113.2 |
| 1978(4) | 70.0 | 20.5 | 12.0 | 115.2 | 126.2 |
| 1979(1) | 47.3 | 30.2 | 10.7 | 116.4 | 147.0 |
| 1979(2) | 44.1 | 35.1 | 10.7 | 112.9 | 149.6 |
| 1979(3) | 42.7 | 62.0 | 12.0 | 109.5 | 152.8 |
| 1979(4) | 46.1 | 30.9 | 14.6 | 120.2 | 163.6 |
| 1980(1) | 52.0 | 31.4 | 17.0 | 107.6 | 187.6 |
| 1980(2) | 32.7 | 30.7 | 11.3 | 121.4 | 195.1 |
| 1980(3) | 31.8 | 28.6 | 12.2 | 122.2 | 208.4 |
| 1980(4) | 34.2 | 34.4 | 16.2 | 126.0 | 217.9 |
| 1981(1) | 45.0 | 11.5 | 16.5 | 111.0 | 249.4 |
| 1981(2) | 40.9 | 11.1 | 17.2 | 109.7 | 273.2 |
| 1981(3) | 38.8 | 11.6 | 18.5 | 105.4 | 297.9 |
| 1981(4) | 42.5 | 4.2 | 14.8 | 99.3 | 309.3 |
| 1982(1) | 48.2 | 7.0 | 15.6 | 117.8 | 367.7 |
| 1982(2) | 49.9 | 4.2 | 16.2 | 133.0 | 353.3 |
| 1982(3) | 66.5 | 11.3 | 12.1 | 140.8 | 360.4 |
| 1982(4) | 89.5 | 20.7 | 9.5 | 167.5 | 379.1 |

*Source*: Banco Central de Chile and IFS.

statistics of the behavior of the financial sector. As may be seen, with the exception of July–Sepember 1979 and August–November 1980, real rates of interest were extremely high. This table also shows the large differential between the domestic nominal interest rates (column (1)) and international nominal rate (column 4)). These differentials, however, can be partially explained by the existence of financial exchange rate and country risk premiums (see Edwards, 1982a).

What is most surprising, however, is that the liberalization of the domestic financial market, and the existence for the first time in a long time of positive real interest rates, did not result in an increase in domestic savings, as was widely expected by the economic authorities and other experts.[19] In fact, not only did domestic savings not increase, but they were at one of the lowest historical levels. Also, gross domestic investment was remarkably low during the period, with public sector investment being at one of its lowest levels. As may be seen in table 10.8, only in 1980 did gross domestic investment surpass 20 percent. Harberger (1982) has suggested that the low level of domestic savings can be explained by the behavior of asset prices during the period (see also Barandiaran et al.,

TABLE 10.8  Investment and savings in Chile, 1970–1982 (percentages)

| Year | (Gross dom. invest./GDP) | Gross cap. formation on fixed cap./GDP | Depreciation /GDP | (Net dom. savings/GDP) | (Gross dom. savings/ GDP) | Foreign savings/GDP |
|------|------|------|------|------|------|------|
| 1970 | 23.4 | 20.4 | 11.0 | 10.6 | 21.6 | 1.7 |
| 1971 | 20.8 | 18.3 | 11.9 | 6.0 | 17.8 | 2.9 |
| 1972 | 15.2 | 14.8 | 10.4 | (0.1) | 10.4 | 4.8 |
| 1973 | 14.3 | 14.7 | 19.2 | (9.7) | 9.5 | 4.8 |
| 1974 | 25.8 | 17.4 | 11.8 | 13.5 | 25.3 | 0.5 |
| 1975 | 14.0 | 15.4 | 15.7 | (7.2) | 8.5 | 5.6 |
| 1976 | 13.6 | 12.7 | 14.1 | 1.4 | 15.4 | (1.9) |
| 1977 | 14.4 | 13.3 | 11.7 | (1.0) | 10.7 | 3.7 |
| 1978 | 16.5 | 14.5 | 10.5 | 1.1 | 11.6 | 4.8 |
| 1979 | 19.6 | 15.6 | 11.0 | 2.7 | 13.7 | 5.9 |
| 1980 | 23.9 | 17.8 | 11.4 | 4.1 | 15.5 | 8.5 |
| 1981 | 22.0 | 18.5 | n.a. | n.a. | 7.5 | 14.5 |
| 1982[a] | 9.6 | 13.8 | n.a. | n.a. | n.a. | n.a. |

[a] Preliminary.
*Source*: Banco Central de Chile.

[19] These expectations were based on the analysis of financially repressed economies by McKinnon (1982) among others.

1982). Starting in 1976, asset prices increased dramatically, with the real index of stock prices, for example, rising by 323 percent between 1977 and 1980! To the extent that savings decisions depend, in a Metzlerian fashion, on the differential between actual and desired wealth, this dramatic increase in asset prices, and consequently in perceived wealth, could indeed provide an explanation of the poor savings effort during the period.

An alternative explanation for the low level of domestic savings is related to the privatization policy pursued by the government. In 1974, as a means of reducing the importance of the public sector, a process of privatization of government-owned firms was implemented, with firms being auctioned to private (domestic and foreign) bidders. In general, the government used the proceeds from these sales to finance current expenditure. Then, from a practical point of view, the private savings used to acquire these firms were matched by *negative* government savings.[20]

Since domestic savings were very low, gross capital formation was financed increasingly by foreign savings. In 1980 foreign savings reached 8.5 percent of GDP, while in 1981 they rose to 14.5 percent of GDP, representing 66 percent of total gross domestic investment. The current account deficits associated with these high levels of foreign savings began to generate a serious foreign indebtedness problem in 1981. In that year total foreign debt increased almost 50 percent — from US$ 10,987 million to US$ 15,546 million — reaching 50 percent of GDP (see Edwards, 1982b).

It was thought at the time by the economic authorities and other observers that, since most of the new debt had been contracted by the private sector (without any government guarantee), this increase in foreign indebtedness would not represent a threat for the country as a whole: if a domestic private borrower could not pay his foreign obligations, that was a *private* problem between him and the foreign creditor, which would be solved through a regular bankruptcy procedure.[21] As the facts showed later, this distinction between private and public debt was highly artificial, and the Chilean government ended up taking over all of the private sector foreign debt, independently of the fact that the original borrowers went bankrupt and there were no previous government guarantees on those loans (see Diaz-Alejandro, 1985).

As has been noted by a number of observers (Harberger, 1982; Sjaastad, 1982; Calvo, 1982), the behavior of interest rates constitutes one of the major puzzles of the recent Chilean experience. At present there does not appear to be an acceptable solution to this puzzle; however, any analysis that attempts to deal with the interest rate behavior during the Chilean experiment should at least recognize the following elements:

(a) There was an important increase in the *demand* for credit, triggered by an increase in perceived wealth and permanent income. This higher

---

[20] See several issues of *Exposicion de la Hacienda Publica* for the way in which the fiscal budget was financed.

[21] See, for example, *Exposicion de la Hacienda Publica*, 1980.

demand for credit was directed toward both investment projects and an increase in consumption. Toward the end of 1981 the demand for credit continued to grow; however, this time it was essentially a demand by firms that expected to avoid bankruptcy (see Barandiaran et al., 1982).

(b) There was a continuous increase in the expectation of devaluation, stemming from the decline in the real exchange rate after June 1976. The higher current account deficits of 1980 and 1981, the low rate of domestic savings, and the dramatic increase of foreign indebtedness also helped to increase these expectations.

(c) An increase in the world interest rate affected the effective cost at which Chile could borrow abroad. Between the first quarter of 1979 and the third quarter of 1981 the nominal LIBOR rate increased from 10.7 to 18.5 percent.

(d) Transaction costs posed obstacles to arbitrage. (This point has been stressed by Sjaastad, 1982.)

(e) There was an increase in the country risk premium attached by the international financial community to Chile. This was basically the result of the rapid growth of the foreign debt, and the extremely low level of investment. Also, the collapse of a major conglomerate (CRAV) and some banks during 1981 forced foreign banks to reassess their risk perception of Chilean borrowers.

In general, it appears that Chile's inability to increase domestic savings and gross domestic investment indicated, from the early years of the military regime, that the rate of growth of the economy could not be consistently high for a long period of time.

## V.   SAVINGS, INVESTMENT, AND THE SOURCES OF GROWTH

Although capital accumulation is hardly the only source of growth, the extremely modest level of investment in 1977–80 makes one wonder how Chile managed to grow so fast during this period. In this section this problem is investigated by presenting an analysis of the sources of growth in Chile during 1976–80.[22] Since a thorough study of the sources of growth in Chile during the military regime would require information that is not readily available, the results presented in this section should be considered as only preliminary estimates.

---

[22] There are a number of studies on the sources of growth in Chile before 1970. See, for example, Harberger and Selowsky (1966), Elias (1978), and Schmidt-Hebbel (1981). Most of these studies suggest that improvement in the quality of labor made important contributions to growth. This evidence is also supported by Selowsky and Taylor (1973). On the relationship between capital accumulation and other sources of growth in accounting type of models, see Edwards (1985).

Any accounting study of the sources of growth in Chile in the recent period faces two basic problems. First, it should incorporate the effects on growth of the efficiency gains associated with the resource reallocation process generated by the liberalization of the economy.[23] Second, it should take into account the changes in the degree of capital utilization observed throughout this period.

With respect to the resource reallocation effect, some studies have attempted to estimate the (static) welfare gains resulting from a reduction, or total elimination, of distortions in Chile. More than 25 years ago, Harberger (1959) estimated that the elimination of all distortions would result in a static increase in Chile's national welfare of about 15 percent of national income. He also indicated that this static effect would result in a higher rate of growth of 1–2 percentage points per year, for a limited period of time. Coeymans (1978) has recently estimated that the tariff liberalization process would result in a static improvement of Chile's welfare of around 3 percent of national income. Schmidt-Hebbel (1981), on the other hand, estimated that the recent liberalization policies (both trade and others) would result in a static increase in welfare of 10 percent income. He also suggested that this welfare improvement would be spread through ten years, contributing 1 percentage point per annum to the growth rate during this period. Although an exact computation of total welfare gains resulting from the liberalization of Chile's economy is beyond the scope of this chapter, it appears that the reallocation process had a fairly significant impact on growth between 1977 and 1980. Specifically, Schmidt-Hebbel's (1981) estimate can be considered as a lower bound for this static efficiency gain.

The second problem that has to be faced in the discussion of more recent sources of growth in Chile is the degree of capital utilization. Schmidt-Hebbel (1981) has estimated three alternative series of capital utilization for this period. All of them indicate a sharp decline in the rate of use of capital in 1975 — ranging from 6.7 to 13.4 percent — with a subsequent recuperation between 1976 and 1979. While two of his series indicate that in 1979 the degree of capital utilization was still below that of 1974, the third one suggests that the rate of use of the capital stock had reached its 1974 level as early as 1977. These estimates, then, tend to indicate that changes in the rate of capital utilization played an important role during the recent (1977–80) growth process. Furthermore, as will be argued below, this change in capacity utilization constitutes a crucial step in the understanding of Chile's extraordinarily high rates of growth in the late 1970s.

---

[23] Accounting studies of the sources of growth do not always incorporate this resource reallocation effect. Some exceptions are Robinson (1971) and Denison and Chung (1976). It is important to note that, from a theoretical point of view, in a second-best world the reduction (or even elimination) of some distortions only may result in welfare losses; see for example Bhagwati and Srinivasan (1980).

In order to obtain some orders of magnitude on the importance of some of the sources of growth during this period, I computed the contributions to growth of changes in the stock of physical capital and changes in employment. If it is true that changes in the degree of capital utilization and efficiency improvements made important contributions to growth during the period, we would expect that the residuals obtained from this exercise would be very large — that is, larger than the residuals obtained in this type of computation for Chile before 1970. Table 10.9 shows estimates of the stock of capital between 1970 and 1981. These figures were computed using the infinite inventory technique suggested by Harberger (1978b) and data from the new National Accounts. Table 10.10, on the other hand, shows the contribution to growth of changes in the quantities of capital and labor between 1975 and 1980 and of imputed contributions to growth of changes in capacity utilization and gains in efficiency generated by the liberalization program. In these computations labor was assigned a share of 52 percent of GDP, while capital was assigned a 48 percent share.[24] The data on changes in the stock of capital were taken from table 10.9, and the data on the evolution of employment were obtained from Edwards (1980).

Column (4) in table 10.10 shows the "grand residual" obtained after having taken into account the contributions of the quantities of capital and labor to growth. As expected, these residuals are very high — indeed,

TABLE 10.9 Stock of reproducible capital, 1970–1981 (Millions of 1977 US$)

| Year | Equipment and machinery | Building and construction | Inventories | Total |
|---|---|---|---|---|
| 1970 | 7551 | 25,797 | 1733 | 35,081 |
| 1971 | 7763 | 26,957 | 2885 | 37,608 |
| 1972 | 7769 | 27,750 | 2141 | 37,660 |
| 1973 | 7846 | 28,325 | 2088 | 38,259 |
| 1974 | 7863 | 29,316 | 3220 | 40,399 |
| 1975 | 7878 | 29,749 | 3057 | 40,684 |
| 1976 | 7830 | 29,966 | 3165 | 40,961 |
| 1977 | 7997 | 30,203 | 3312 | 41,512 |
| 1978 | 8327 | 30,568 | 3601 | 42,496 |
| 1979 | 8774 | 31,133 | 4231 | 44,138 |
| 1980 | 9422 | 31,993 | 5268 | 46,683 |

*Sources*: Constructed from National Accounts data obtained from Banco Central de Chile.

[24] Between 1970 and 1980 labor's share in GDP was 52.9 percent with capital having a 47.1 percent share.

TABLE 10.10 Sources of growth in Chile, 1975–1980

| Year | (1) Actual rate of growth of GDP | (2) Contributions of changes in physical capital | (3) Contributions of changes in quantity of labor | (4) "Grand Residual" ((1)−(2)−(3)) | (5) Contribution of efficiency gains | (6) Contribution of change in capacity utilization | (7) Residual ((1)−(2)−(3)−(5)−(6)) |
|---|---|---|---|---|---|---|---|
| 1975 | −12.9 | −3.7 | 0.3 | −9.5 | — | −5.4 | −4.1 |
| 1976 | 3.5 | 1.3 | 0.3 | 1.9 | — | 1.0 | 0.9 |
| 1977 | 9.9 | 3.8 | 0.6 | 5.5 | 1.5 | 1.6 | 2.4 |
| 1978 | 8.2 | 1.4 | 1.2 | 5.6 | 1.5 | 0.4 | 3.7 |
| 1979 | 8.3 | 1.1 | 1.9 | 5.3 | 1.5 | 0.7 | 3.1 |
| 1980 | 7.5 | 3.2 | 2.8 | 1.5 | 1.5 | — | 0.0 |

Sources: Column (1), Banco Central de Chile; column (2), taken from table 10.9; column (3), computed from Edwards (1980); column (5), estimated from Schmidt-Hebbel (1981); column (6), computed from data presented in Schmidt-Hebbel (1981).

much higher than those obtained in earlier accounting studies on the sources of growth in Chile — indicating that during the 1977–80 period factors other than changes in the quantities of capital and labor played an important role in growth. As I have argued, the most plausible variables are efficiency gains and changes in the degree of capital utilization. Indeed, if we asume that between 1977 and 1980 the resource reallocation process contributed 1.5 percentage points to annual growth, and if we use Schmidt-Hebbel's estimates of the degree of capital utilization, these residuals are significantly reduced.[25] This is shown in columns (5), (6), and (7) of table 10.10. However, these residuals are still fairly large — in fact, larger than what can be attributed to higher "quality" of labor and capital, and "technical progress" — suggesting that there are still some measurement problems, and that a full understanding of the growth process in Chile between 1977 and 1982 will require additional research.

## VI.  THE 1982–83 RECESSION

By late 1981 it became apparent that the high rates of growth experienced during the previous years were coming to an end. The fourth quarter of 1981 was characterized by extaordinarily high real interest rates, exceeding 40 percent; a huge current account deficit, amounting to almost 15 percent of GDP; rising unemployment; and a reduction in real GDP of 3.3 percent with respect to the fourth quarter of 1980. On the positive side, inflation was only 9 percent that year.

In 1982 the economic situation became almost chaotic. GDP declined by 14.3 percent; open unemployment (excluding the Minimum Employment Program) reached 23.7 percent in September of that year; the exchange rate was devalued by almost 100 percent; a major financial crisis developed; and there were serious problems in servicing the foreign debt. Table 10.11 presents the behavior of some of the most important macroeconomic variables between the first quarter of 1980 and the second quarter of 1983. As may be seen, the recession slowed up, quite abruptly, during the fourth quarter of 1981. In this section the causes of this extraordinary turn of events in late 1981 will be analyzed. Also, some important developments that took place during 1982–3 — like the agreement with the IMF, and the increase in the level of import tariffs — will be discussed.

The main thesis of this section is that the 1982–3 recession was, to a large extent, triggered by policy inconsistencies and mistakes. However, it is also recognized that the world economic situation had a negative impact on the Chilean economy. In that respect the decline in the terms of trade by almost 23 percent between 1980 and 1982, and the higher world interest rates, were particularly harmful. With respect to policy

---

[25] This assumed gain in efficiency is somewhat higher than that estimated by Schmidt-Hebbel (1981).

TABLE 10.11  Behavior of some key macroeconomic variables in Chile, 1980–1983

| | (1) Real GDP (millions 1977 pesos) | (2) Real GDP with respect to same qtr prev. yr (% change) | (3) Open rate of unemployment | (4) Min. Employment Program as % labor force | (5) Rate of inflation (yearly) (%) | (6) Exchange rate (pesos/dollar) | (7) Real borrowing interest rate (annualized) (%) | (8) Foreign savings (millions 1977 US$) |
|---|---|---|---|---|---|---|---|---|
| 1980(1) | 86,936 | n.a. | 12.0 | 4.7 | 38.7 | 39.0 | | 259 |
| (2) | 86,750 | n.a. | — | — | 32.9 | 39.0 | | 253 |
| (3) | 89,122 | n.a. | 12.3 | 5.6 | 31.3 | 39.0 | | 297 |
| (4) | 97,638 | n.a. | — | — | | 39.0 | 5.6 | 507 |
| 1981(1) | 94,274 | 8.4 | 11.0 | 4.7 | 28.4 | 39.0 | 36.5 | 602 |
| (2) | 96,233 | 7.2 | — | — | 22.8 | 39.0 | 35.6 | 593 |
| (3) | 99,317 | 11.4 | 12.4 | 4.6 | 18.0 | 39.0 | 35.2 | 973 |
| (4) | 94,408 | -3.3 | — | — | 11.4 | 39.0 | 47.8 | 780 |
| 1982(1) | 85,714 | -9.1 | 18.4 | 4.2 | 7.6 | 39.0 | 53.1 | 565 |
| (2) | 84,230 | -12.5 | — | — | 4.5 | 46.5 | 47.3 | 300 |
| (3) | 81,015 | -18.4 | 23.7 | 7.0 | 8.3 | 67.4 | 13.0 | 341 |
| (4) | 78,196 | -17.2 | — | — | 19.0 | 73.4 | 30.7 | 266 |
| 1983(1) | 77,611 | -9.5 | 22.0 | 9.6 | 23.0 | 73.4 | 29.5 | 82 |
| (2) | 80,489 | -4.4 | — | — | 30.8 | 77.7 | 13.5 | 81 |

Sources: Columns (3) and (4) from Universidad de Chile; columns (1), (2), (7), and (8) from Banco Central de Chile; columns (5) and (6) from IFS.

inconsistencies, the exchange rate policy, which in June 1979 had fixed the peso to the dollar, and the wage rate policy — which precluded by law any downward adjustment in real wages — became highly inconsistent in mid-1981.[26]

Between the second quarter of 1980 — when the last steps toward opening the capital account to medium- and long-term flows were taken — and the third quarter of 1981, Chile was flooded by foreign capital. In 1980 the capital inflows (i.e., the surplus of the capital account) amounted to US$ 3.2 billion, representing 11.5 percent of GDP. In 1981 this figure climbed to an extraordinary level of US$ 4.8 billion, or 14.4 percent of GDP. This increase in the level of capital inflows had a number of consequences. First, it allowed the financing of a major increase in expenditure, on both tradable and nontradable goods, including a large construction book (see table 10.5). Second, and as a result of the higher expenditure on nontradables, the real exchange rate appreciated significantly. This real appreciation — which amounted to 27 percent between the third quarter of 1979 and the first quarter of 1982 — significantly reduced the degree of competitiveness of Chile's export and import-competing industries, with exports being particularly harmed (see table 10.12). Third, the level of the foreign debt (especially private debt) increased dramatically, exceeding 50 percent of GDP in late 1981.

However, this level of capital inflows was not sustainable in the long run, and in the second half of 1981 the inflow of foreign funds started to decline. In the fourth quarter of that year, the capital account surplus dropped to US$ 800 million, from an average of over US$ 1.2 billion during the three previous quarters. In the first quarter of 1982 the capital account surplus was US$ 500 billion; in the second quarter it was US$ 295 million; and in the third quarter there was a capital account *deficit* of US$ 170 million.

In order for the economy to adjust to this lower inflow of foreign capital, and consequently of expenditure, a *real* devaluation of the peso was now required. Since the nominal exchange rate was fixed (at 39 pesos to the US dollar), this adjustment had to· take place through a decline in the nominal price of nontradable goods, and of real wages.[27] The problem, however, was that, according to the indexation mechanism incorporated into the labor law of 1979, real wages were virtually inflexible downward. At this point it became apparent to most observers that a fixed exchange rate and the existing real wage policy were highly inconsistent, and that

[26] For discussions on the 1982–3 recession in Chile see, for example, Corbo (1982) and Sjaastad (1982). With regard to fixing the peso, the choice of the dollar as the currency of reference was unfortunate. During most of the 1980–3 period the dollar appreciated against other major currencies, and this explains approximately 10 percentage points of the appreciation of the peso.

[27] Rigorously, a world inflation higher than the domestic inflation would also do it.

TABLE 10.12  Real Exchange Rate in Chile, quarterly data, 1979–1983
(1979(3) = 100)

| | *(1)*<br><br>*Index of basket*<br>*of nom. exch.*<br>*rates* | *(2)*<br><br><br><br>*Chile's CPI* | *(3)*<br>*Index of*<br>*consumer prices*<br>*for group of*<br>*industrial*<br>*countries*[a] | *(4)*<br><br>*Index of basket*<br>*real exch. rate*<br>*(1)×(3)/(2)* |
|---|---|---|---|---|
| 1979(1) | 95.1 | 83.7 | 99.1 | 112.7 |
| (2) | 99.4 | 90.2 | 105.2 | 116.0 |
| (3) | 100.0 | 100.0 | 100.0 | 100.0 |
| (4) | 98.8 | 109.1 | 110.5 | 100.0 |
| 1980(1) | 95.4 | 116.4 | 114.2 | 93.6 |
| (2) | 100.2 | 125.1 | 118.0 | 94.6 |
| (3) | 100.3 | 133.1 | 120.0 | 90.4 |
| (4) | 99.4 | 143.3 | 122.7 | 85.1 |
| 1981(1) | 95.0 | 149.4 | 125.3 | 79.7 |
| (2) | 92.9 | 153.7 | 128.2 | 77.5 |
| (3) | 92.7 | 157.0 | 130.9 | 77.3 |
| (4) | 93.9 | 159.6 | 133.1 | 78.3 |
| 1982(1) | 90.3 | 160.8 | 134.4 | 75.5 |
| (2) | 96.8 | 160.5 | 136.5 | 82.4 |
| (3) | 127.6 | 170.1 | 138.7 | 104.0 |
| (4) | 139.5 | 190.0 | 139.8 | 102.6 |
| 1983(1) | 138.3 | 198.3 | 140.3 | 97.8 |
| (2) | 143.8 | 209.8 | n.a. | n.a. |

[a] The industrialized countries considered (shares in parentheses) are: USA (55%),
Germany (12%), Italy (5%), France (7%), and Japan (21%).

their coexistence represented a policy mistake. As Corbo and Edwards
(1981), Sjaastad (1982), and Barandiaran et al. (1982) have indicated, these
policies amounted to improving two numeraires in the economy. As a
result of this inflexibility in real wages, relative prices did not adjust.
Quantities, however, did, with the resulting reduction in production and
employment.

One way — and a traditional one — to solve the crisis would have been
to devalue the peso. The purpose of this measure, of course, would have
been to generate a *real* devaluation, and an improvement in the degree of
competitiveness of the economy. However, and again owing to the wage

rate policy, it is not clear to what extent a nominal devaluation would have succeeded. If wages are 100 percent indexed, a devaluation will be fully translated into higher wages and prices, being to a large extent self-defeating.[28]

In spite of the crisis, between the second half of 1981 and the first half of 1982 the government followed a passive policy, arguing that the economy would automatically adjust to the new circumstances. In particular, the economic authorities strongly rejected the idea of intervening in the exchange rate market, and even stated that to devalue would be equivalent to committing economic suicide. Throughout the period, the government followed a passive monetary policy — the so-called "neutral" monetary policy — where all increases in high-powered money were the result of increases in the central bank's holdings of international reserves.

As the situation became more serious toward late 1981, the public rapidly began to lose confidence in the government's policies. In particular, the sustainability of the exchange rate was questioned, and in spite of several official statements a strong speculation against the peso developed, with economic agents readjusting their portfolios toward a higher proportion of foreign-exchange-denominated assets. Of course, the higher expectations of devaluation were translated into higher domestic interest rates, further hurting the overall picture. In June 1982 the government finally decided to abandon the "automatic adjustment" approach, and to pursue a more active policy. The peso was devalued by 18 percent, and the indexation clause of the labor law was amended.

This was too little, however, and too late. At this point the loss of credibility in the government's policies was almost complete, and the devaluation accelerated the speculation against the peso, with the resulting large loss of international reserves in the weeks that followed devaluation. Also, the international financial community did not react positively to these measures, and the flow of funds toward Chile was significantly reduced. The June devaluation was followed by a brief experiment with flexible rates, and by a dual rate system. In early 1983 the new minister of finance declared the peso inconvertible, imposed severe exchange controls, and implemented a temporary hike in import tariffs to a uniform 20 percent level. In 12 months — between June 1982 and June 1983 — the Chilean peso had been devalued by 99 percent. Since inflation during this period was only 32.7 percent, a real devaluation had taken place, helping some of the export sectors. There were some observers, however, who believed that the adjustment of the price level had not been completed in June 1983, and that a tight monetary policy would be required to assure the success of the devaluation policy (see Universidad de Chile, 1983). This also seems to be the view taken by the government.

Toward mid-1981, and as a result of the real appreciation of the peso and the adverse world economic environment, a number of industries in

---

[28] On wage indexation policies in open economies see, for example, paper by Aizenman and Frenkel (1983).

the tradable goods sector ran into serious financial trouble. Most of these firms responded by borrowing heavily from the capital market. This situation, however, was complicated by the fact that there were close ownership relations between borrowers — the troubled firms — and lenders — the domestic banks. In fact, during this period domestic banks made a number of large loans to related firms, generating what was later called the "related portfolio" (*centera relacionada*). The problem was that most of these were *bad loans*, which eventually could not be repaid.[29] This generated a serious financial crisis, where firms were unable to pay their debts to local banks and local banks were unable to pay their debt to international banks. In January 1973 the government decided to act, intervening in four banks and ordering the liquidation of four more. As a result, the Chilean government took over the control of 70 percent of the domestic banking sector (see Universidad de Chile, 1983).

In late 1982 the government approached the IMF in order to obtain financial assistance. Private banks were also approached, and a rescheduling of the foreign debt was proposed. A standby loan was signed on January 10, 1983, according to which Chile would receive US$ 875 million. Private creditors also agreed to renegotiate the debt subject to the fulfillment of the conditions imposed by the Fund. The stabilization program had the traditional IMF conditionality characteristics, and called for a limited increase in domestic credit during 1983, a fiscal deficit below 2.3 percent of GDP, and a loss of reserves not exceeding US$ 606 million for the year. In early 1983, and as a complement to the IMF agreement, the government implemented the so-called Emergency Program, whose main points included the provision of relief to domestic debtors, the promotion of the construction sector, and the development of some public works to reduce unemployment. By the end of the first quarter of 1983, however, the limit on credit experience imposed by IMF had been exceeded, and the Emergency Plan was replaced by the so-called Operative Program. The objective of this program was to bring the economy back into line with IMF conditions. This was achieved by September 1983.

[29] The financial situation became more difficult after June 1982 when the peso was devalued. Agents who had debt denominated to a foreign exchange suddenly saw their debt doubled.

REFERENCES

Arellano, Jose P. et al. (1982), *Modelo Económico Chileno: Trayectoria de una Crítica*. Santiago: Editorial Aconcagua.
Balassa, Bela (1982), *Development Strategies in Semi-industrial Economies*. Baltimore: Johns Hopkins University Press.
Barandiaran, Edgardo (1983), "La Gran Recesión de 1982." Unpublished paper.
Barandiaran, Edgardo, Montt, Filipe and Pollack, Molly (1982), *Noveno Informe de Coyuntura*. Santiago, Chile: Depto. Estudios BHC.

Behrman, Jere (1976), *Foreign Trade Regimes and Economic Development: Chile.* Washington, DC: National Bureau of Economic Research.
Behrman, Jere (1977), *Macroeconomic Policy in a Developing Country: The Chilean Experience.* Amsterdam: North Holland.
Bhagwati, Jagdish and Srinivasan, T. N. (1980), "Revenue Seeking: A Generalization of the Theory of Tariffs," *Journal of Political Economy.*
Blejer, M. and Landau, L. (1984), *Economic Liberalization and Stabilization in Argentina, Chile and Uruguay: The Monetary Approach to the Balance of Payments.* Washington: World Bank.
Blejer, Mario I., and Mathieson, Donald J. (1981), "Preannouncement of Exchange Rate Changes as a Stabilization Instrument," *IMF Staff Papers.*
Calvo, Guillermo (1981), "Devaluation: Levels vs. Rates," *Journal of International Economics.*
Calvo, Guillermo (1982), "The Chilean Economy in the 1970's," in K. Brunner and A. Meltzer (ed), *Economic Policy in a World of Change*, Carnegie–Rochester Conference Series, vol. 17. Amsterdam: North-Holland Co.
Cline, William and Weintraub, Sidney (eds) (1981), *Economic Stabilization in Developing Countries.* Washington, DC: Brookings Institution.
Coeymans, Juan E. (1978), "Liberalización del Comercio Exterior y Sus Efectos Sobre la Asignación de Recursos y Empleo," *Cuadernos de Economía.*
Corbo, Vittorio (1974), *Inflation in Developing Countries.* Amsterdam: North-Holland Publishing Co.
Corbo, Vittorio (1982), "Recent Developments of Chilean Economy." Unpublished paper, prepared for the conference on "National Economic Policies in Chile," November 1982.
Corbo, Vittorio and Edwards, Sebastian (1981), "El Rol de Una Devaluación en la Economía Chilena Actual." Unpublished paper.
Corbo, Vittorio and Meller, Patricio (1982), "Alternative Trade Strategies and Employment Implications: Chile," in A. Krueger (ed.), *Trade and Employment in Developing Countries.* Chicago: University of Chicago Press.
Corbo, Vittorio and Pollack, Molly (1982), "Fuentes del Cambio de la Estructura Económica Chilena," Document no. 227, Santiago, Chile: Depto. Estudios BHC.
Cortazar, Rene (1982), "Chile: Distributive Results 1973–1982." Unpublished paper, prepared for the conference on "National Economic Policies in Chile," November.
Cortazar, Rene and Marshall, Jorge (1980), "Indice de Precios al Consumidor en Chile 1970–1978." Unpublished paper.
Denison, Edward and Chung, William (1976), *How Japan's Economy Grew So Fast?* Washington, DC: Brookings Institution.
Diaz-Alejandro, Carlos F. (1981), "Southern Cone Stabilization Plans," in William R. Cline and Sidney Weintraub (eds), *Economic Stabilization in Developing Countries.* Washington, DC: Brookings Institution.
Diaz-Alejandro, Carlos (1985), "Goodbye Financial Repression, Hello Financial Crush," *Journal of Development Economics.*
Djajic, Slobodan (1982), "Balance of Payments Dynamics and Exchange-rate Management," *Journal of International Money and Finance.*
Edwards, Sebastian (1977a), "El Efecto de un Arancel Externo Comun en la Balanza de Pagos y El Tipo de Cambio," *El Trimestre Económico.*
Edwards, Sebastian (1977b), "Una Nota sobre el Ahorro, la Inversión y el Crecimiento Economico en Chile," Document no. 167, Dept. Estudios BHC.

Edwards, Sebastian (1980), "El Problema del Empleo en Chile: 1975–1980 — Un Análisis Preliminar." Unpublished paper, Depto. Estudios BHC.

Edwards, Sebastian (1982a), "Minimum Wages and Trade Liberalization: Some Reflections Based on the Chilean Experience." Working Paper no. 230, Dept. of Economics, University of California at Los Angeles.

Edwards, Sebastian (1982b), "Deuda Externa, Ahorro Domestico, y Crecimiento Economico en Chilè," *Estudios Internacionales*.

Edwards, Sebastian (1982c), "Diferenciales de Inflación y Diferenciales de Progreso Tecnológico: Un Comentario," *Cuadernos de Economía*.

Edwards, Sebastian (1982d), "Interest Rates and Money in a Semi-open Economy: Chile 1979–81." Unpublished paper, Department of Economics, University of California at Los Angeles.

Edwards, Sebastian (1983), "The Relationship Between Inflation and Growth in Latin America," *American Economic Review*.

Edwards, Sebastian (1985), "Economic Policy and The Record of Economic Growth in Chile: 1973–1982," in G. Walton (ed.), *National Economic Policies in Chile*. Greenwhich, Conn.: JAI Press.

Elias, Victor (1978), "The Sources of Growth in Latin America," *Review of Economics and Statistics*.

Ffrench-Davis, Ricardo (1973), *Políticas Económicas en Chile 1952–1970*. Santiago: Nueva Universidad.

Ffrench-Davis, Ricardo (1981), "Liberalizacion de Importaciones," *Estudios Cieplan*.

Ffrench-Davis, Ricardo and Arellano, Jose P. (1981), "Apertura Financiera Externa: La Experiencia Chilena en 1973–80." Unpublished paper, CIEPLAN.

Foxley, Alejandro (1981), "Stabilization Policies and Their Effects on Employment and Income Distribution: A Latin American Perspective," in William Cline and 3. Weintraub (eds), *Economic Stabilization in Developing Countries*, Washington DC: Brookings Institution.

Foxley, Alejandro (1982), "Towards a Market Economy: Chile 1974–1975," *Journal of Development Economics*.

Hachette, Dominique (1978), "Aspectos Macroeconomicos de la Economía Chilena 1973–1976," Documento de Trabajo, no. 55, I. Economía, Universidad Catolica, Santiago.

Harberger, Arnold C. (1959), "Using the Resources at Hand More Efficiently," *American Economic Review*.

Harberger, Arnold C. (1978a), "A Primer on Inflation," *Journal of Money, Credit and Banking*.

Harberger, Arnold C. (1978b), "Perspectives on Capital and Technology in LDCs." Unpublished paper.

Harberger, Arnold C. (1981a), "The Real Exchange Rate in Chile." Unpublished paper.

Harberger, Arnold C. (1981b), "Comment on Foxley," in William Cline and S. Weintraub (eds), *Economic Stabilization in Developing Countries*. Washington, DC: Brookings Institution.

Harberger, Arnold C. (1982), "The Chilean Economy in the 1970's: Crisis, Stabilization, Liberalization, Reform," in K. Brunner and A. Meltzer (eds), *Economic Policy in a World of Change*, Carnegie–Rochester Conference Series on Public Policy, vol. 17, Amsterdam: North-Holland Co.

Harberger, Arnold and Edwards, Sebastian (1982), "Lessons of Experience Under Fixed Exchange Rates," in Mark Gerowitz et al. (eds), *The Theory and Experience of Economic Development*. London: George Allen & Unwin.

Harberger, Arnold and Selowsky, Marcelo (1966), "Las Fuentes del Crecimiento en Chile: 1940–1962," *Cuadernos de Economía*.

Krueger, Anne (1974), "The Political Economy of the Rent-seeking Society," *American Economic Review*.

Leijonhufvud, Axel (1981), *Information and Coordination: Essays in Macroeconomic Theory*. Oxford: Oxford University Press.

McKinnon, Ronald J. (1982), "The Order of Economic Liberalization: Lessons from Chile and Argentina," in K. Brunner and A. Meltzer (eds), *Economic Policy in a World of Change*, Carnegie–Rochester Conference Series on Public Policy, vol. 17, Amsterdam: North-Holland.

Mendez, Juan Carlos (1979), *Economic Policy in Chile*. Santiago: Dirección de Presupuestos.

Munoz, Oscar (1982), "Crecimiento y Desequilibrios en Chile," *Estudios Ciéplan*.

Pollack, Molly (1980), "El Sector Industrial en el Periodo 1960–1979." Unpublished paper, BHC.

Robinson, Sherman (1971), "Sources of Growth in Less Developed Countries," *Quarterly Journal of Economics*.

Schmidt-Hebbel, Klaus (1981), "Análisis del Crecimiento Económico en Chile en al Periodo 1960–1979 y Proyecciones para 1980–2000." Document no. 140, Depto. Estudios BHC.

Selowsky, Marcelo (1969), "On the Measurement of Educational Contribution to Growth," *Quarterly Journal of Economics*.

Selowsky, Marcelo and Taylor, Lance (1973), "The Economics of Malnourished Children," *Economic Development and Cultural Change*.

Sjaastad, Larry (1982), "The Failure of Economic Liberalism in the Southern Core." Unpublished paper.

Sjaastad, Larry and Cortes, Hernan (eds) (1981), "La Reforma Comercial en Chile," *Cuadernos de Economía*.

Trivelli, Pablo and Trivelli, Hugo (1979), "El Crecimiento Económico en Chile," in *Treivtaycinco años de Descontinuidad Economica*.

Universidad de Chile (1983), *Revista de Economia*, Santiago, Chile.

Vergara, Pilar (1981), "Apertura Externa y Desarrollo Economico," *Estudios Ciéplan*.

# Comment

*Frank Veneroso*

To further explore the issues raised by James Hanson, I think it is worth looking at two issues: (a) the financial problem that Chile now faces; and (b) the real interest rate problem.

Arnold Harberger says that the problem of bad loans in Chile's banking system started in 1975, and that there was not a money crunch at that time. I do not think that is true at all. Chile's financial system in 1975 was a classic case of financial repression. There was very little debt against the capital stock; there was a very sharp and unexpected decline in the rate of monetary growth, from 20 to 6 percent per month between March and May; money was tight — firms were not very indebted, but they were illiquid.

Today there is a different problem, and it exists not only in Chile, but in several other important countries, such as Brazil. These are countries where there is too much debt; where the country has not only deepened financially but has deepened disastrously; where internal and external debt against the corporate capital stock become equal to that of capital stock; and where there is no equity left.

The problem with Chile today is that it has excessive indebtedness problems as well as perhaps a liquidity problem. The former is really an imbalance in the structure of the stock of financial claims on real wealth. There is nothing the matter with the real wealth. It is underemployed right now, but is no different than it was five years ago; it is just that the structure of financial claims is all wrong: it is all debts, and there is no equity left.

Is this important? I think it is, for it makes it very, very hard for an economy to recover. I remember an article by Irving Fisher, who made a tremendous amount of money in the stock market in the 1920s ($90 million in today's prices) but did not have a cent left by 1932. Not only was he a very great economist, but he was very well aware of what was happening in the Great Depression. He argued in that article that implicit high real interest rates caused real debt to grow, and that firms faced with high real interest rates and excessive debts tried to liquidate assets in order to repair their balance sheets. In other words, excessive indebtedness depresses investment, kills animal spirits, and results in a secular stagnation. We have to worry that something like this will happen in Chile.

How did Chile get to such a point? Well, they liberalized, and interest rates went wild. Something went wrong in a fairly unfettered market. We have to ask, what went wrong and why? Sebastian Edwards suggests two possible reasons. (a) He says there was an important increase in the demand for credit, and that this demand continued to grow. (b) However, in its later phase it was a demand for credit by firms that sought to avoid bankruptcy. I think that both of these things were at play; the second one was perhaps more important than the first, but nonetheless there was a complex interplay between the two.

In looking for an example of high interest rate pathology, I found it in a very peculiar place — Kuwait and the Persian Gulf. There we had the most extraordinary stock market bubble. You have to look to books like *Popular Delusions* and *The Madness of Crowds* to be able to find such cases in which an unfettered market absolutely explodes: three little countries (Kuwait, the United Arab Emirates (UAE), and Bahrain), with very little in the way of capital stock, with few firms, and with a stock market capitalization that eventually became third in the world next to the United States and Japan. Most interestingly, as this market capitalization grew, there was growth in a scaffold of debt at every step along the way. Interest rates on this debt approached 100 percent real at the market's peak.

Well, somewhere along the way, the dizzy spiral ended — these are all short-term call loans, and people *do* call those loans. Not only did prices drop; there simply was no trading anymore. There was an enormous financial collapse. In the end, debts far exceeded assets (if it is possible to put a price on them at all) when valued at their reproduction value.

It seems that every time there is a great economic success, we find something like this — for example, the Tulipomania of seventeenth-century Holland, the US stock market in 1929, and Kuwait and the Persian Gulf. There certainly was such a new era mentality, such euphoric expectations in Chile, in the late 1970s. If we look at what the groups did there, we see that they had a passion for borrowing to purchase assets which had gone to dizzying prices — ten times book value for a bank, or Japanese-style prices for real estate. There was a tremendous speculative demand for credit, a kind of free market excess a little like that of Kuwait.

That was not the problem. The most important problem came with the monetary squeeze in 1981. Chile was on the equivalent of a gold standard; there was a specie outflow, and interest rates rose. Rather than liquidate their assets in an attempt to repair their balance sheets, firms decided to capitalize those interest rates. They could do this because the people who owned the firms also owned the banks. The depositors did not put a brake on the banks because they had a government guarantee. There was a distress demand for credit that kept real rates very high. So at these very high interest rates, real debt was compounded. At 60 percent real, it does not take very long to get to a point where there is no equity left. I think that we now have that particular problem in Chile.

Regarding the first case, the speculative demand for credit, we say that when markets go wild we should move in and restrain them. When our

stock markets get too ebullient, we raise margin requirements or put limits on daily moves, or stop the trading in individual stocks. However, in this second case, the distress demand for credit, it seems as though the free market phenomena which caused these very high real interest rates resulted not from inadequate regulation (as some people think) but from a potential for government intervention which is going to be awfully hard to eradicate. The only reason why firms Ponzi-finance high real interest rates, bankers go along with it, and depositors do not care is that they believe that, somewhere along the line, the central bank will bail them out. It is a valid bet; after all, it happened in Argentina, and maybe the central bank or the government will rescue the Chilean firms again.

Some Wall Street analysts have talked a lot about credit crunches. I have often wondered what they mean by that term. You have to go back to the nineteenth century to understand it. In those days, there were no central banks and there was no deposit insurance. When there was a specie outflow and tight money, interest rates went up, but only for a very short time. The banks did not want bad loans; they were afraid of defaults and deposit outflows; no one protected depositors, and so they were very quick to withdraw their deposits and precipitate bank runs. When something went wrong, the banks did not price-ration questionable borrowers: they credit-rationed them. They did not allow high interest rates to persist: they called their questionable loans. Firms with deep equities and perfectly fine real assets found themselves illiquid. When their loans were called, their assets were sold under duress conditions at deep discounts, and imprudent entrepreneurs lost out. To avoid runs, banks faced with difficulties immediately stopped granting credit, and firms liquidated assets.

In today's world, people expect an intervention that will eventually deflate the real value of their debt and restore shareholders' equity. A monetary reform or confiscation, which has been suggested in Chile, does something of the same. As long as there are expectations of a government bailout when we liberalize interest rates under stabilization conditions, we will get perverse behavior and high real interest rates. Somehow, the only way to solve this problem is to rewrite the stock of financial claims on the real capital stock in a way that punishes those people who made imprudent bets and lost. In addition, the possibility of a government intervention or bailout must be eliminated, so that it is no longer a rational bet for firms and banks to Ponzi-finance these very high real interest rates.

# Index

renewed
in
person
5 May

due
12 May